Liberating Method
Feminism and Social Research

Liberating Method

*Feminism and
Social Research*

M A R J O R I E L . D E V A U L T

T E M P L E U N I V E R S I T Y P R E S S
Philadelphia

Temple University Press, Philadelphia 19122
Copyright © 1999 by Temple University
All rights reserved
Published 1999
Printed in the United States of America

♾ The paper used in this publication meets the requirements of American National
Standard for Information Sciences—Permanence of Paper for Printed Library Materials,
ANSI Z39.48–1984

Library of Congress Cataloging-in-Publication Data

DeVault, Marjorie L., 1950–
    Liberating method : feminism and social research / Marjorie L. DeVault.
       p.   cm.
    Includes bibliographic references and index.
    ISBN 1-56639-697-2 (cloth : alk. paper).— ISBN 1-56639-698-0 (pbk. : alk. paper)
     1. Feminism—Research—Methodology. 2. Social sciences—Research—
Methodology. 3. Feminist theory. 4. Interdisciplinary research.
I. Title.
HQ1180.D48   1999
305.4'01—dc21   98–31712
                                                               CIP

For my teachers:

Arlene, Howie, and Dorothy

Contents

Acknowledgments

THIS BOOK is dedicated to "my teachers," because I have felt their influence percolating throughout this text. I mean the formative teachers of my graduate-school years—Arlene Kaplan Daniels, Howard S. Becker, and Dorothy E. Smith. All three have been wonderfully nurturing mentors, and I am deeply grateful for their generosity. But of course, I've had many other teachers along the way. I have experienced feminist sociology as a collective phenomenon, and I owe a profound debt to the large network of colleagues who have been part of this activist movement in our discipline. Some are close friends and working colleagues; others— no less influential—I know primarily by reputation or through their activities at conferences and in feminist groups such as Sociologists for Women in Society and the Sex and Gender section of the American Sociological Association.

My students have also been important teachers. Many of the ideas I develop here became clearer to me as I worked at sharing them with graduate students, and I wish to honor their contributions to my thinking. I am continually challenged, surprised, inspired, and moved by their desire, intelligence, honesty, and hard work. The opportunity to co-teach a graduate seminar with my colleague Assata Zerai was a rare experience of extraordinary intellectual pleasure and productivity, and I continue to learn from her work with students as well. Chrys Ingraham, though officially a student when we met, has been a teacher since our first encounter. I thank her for much wit and wisdom, and also for her permission to include our jointly authored essay in this book.

The sociology department at Syracuse University has been a space of appreciation and relative freedom for me, and the Women's Studies program there has provided a richly challenging interdisciplinary context. I feel extremely fortunate to have landed in such a congenial working environment. My writing has been sustained in large part by the university's generous and flexible research-leave policy and by support from the Maxwell School of Citizenship and Public Affairs.

Two readers deserve special mention. As I completed this manuscript, my friend Julia Loughlin and my life partner Robert Chibka served as extremely intelligent and helpful critics; their wise counsel is much appreciated. And I wish to thank Michael Ames for enthusiastic editorial support.

Finally, some chapters are based on material first published elsewhere; I am grateful to the following for permission to use them in this volume:

Rutgers University Press, for permission to reprint as Chapter 1 "A Second-Generation Story," first published in *Feminist Sociology: Life Histories of a Movement,* ed. Barbara Laslett and Barrie Thorne, copyright © 1997 by Rutgers, The State University; and as Chapter 8 "Women Write Sociology," first published in *The Rhetoric of Social Research: Understood and Believed,* ed. Albert Hunter, copyright © 1990, by Rutgers, The State University. Reprinted by permission of Rutgers University Press.

Annual Reviews, for material for Chapter 2 from "Talking Back to Sociology: Distinctive Contributions of Feminist Methodology," with permission, from the *Annual Review of Sociology,* Volume 22, © 1996, by Annual Reviews.

The University of California Press, for "Talking and Listening from Women's Standpoint: Feminist Strategies for Interviewing and Analysis," as Chapter 4, © 1990 by The Society for the Study of Social Problems, which is reprinted from *Social Problems,* Vol. 37, No. 1, February 1990, pp. 96–116, by permission.

Sage Publications, for "Ethnicity and Expertise: Racial-Ethnic Knowledge in Sociological Research" as Chapter 5, Marjorie L. DeVault, *Gender & Society,* 9(5):612–631. Copyright © 1995 by Sociologists for Women in Society. Reprinted by permission of Sage Publications, Inc.

The University of Chicago Press, for "Novel Readings: The Social Organization of Interpretation," as Chapter 6, © 1990 by The University of Chicago. All rights reserved.

Routledge, for "Whose Science of Food and Health? Narratives of Profession and Activism from Public Health Nutrition" as Chapter 7. Copyright © 1998. From *Revisioning Women, Health and Healing* edited by Adele Clarke and Virginia Olesen. Reproduced by permission of Routledge, Inc.

Writing Sociology, for "Speaking Up, Carefully," as Chapter 10, which appeared in abbreviated form in the Fall 1994 issue of *Writing Sociology.*

Viking Penguin, for the use in Chapter 6 of excerpts from *The Late Bourgeois World* (pp. 17, 33, 86, 94, 95) by Nadine Gordimer. Copyright © 1966 (by Nadine Gordimer), renewed 1994 by Nadine Gordimer. Used by permission of Viking Penguin, a division of Penguin Putnam, Inc. Also reprinted by the permission of Russell & Volkening as agents for the author.

Liberating Method

Feminism and Social Research

I. INTRODUCTION

Who will make knowledge, and how? These questions animate the feminist and other liberatory projects that have profoundly changed scholarship over the last thirty years. Through these social protest movements, women and other "outsider" groups have challenged the right of the powerful to define realities for all of us. Their challenges have many sources, from global struggles against colonial rule to the intimate but no less political redefinitions of battered women who leave abusive relationships. Movements as diverse as the civil rights struggles of the 1960s, "women's liberation" in the 1970s, and queer theorizing in the 1990s have in common a determination to resist the authorized knowledge of their time and produce new understandings. Activists in these movements have understood that the right to establish "the facts" is central to the exercise of power; they have made that right central to resistance efforts as well.

While my title *Liberating Method* is meant to carry resonances with these multiple struggles against oppression, I use it to signify more specific and limited aims. I seek creative and durable revisions of research methods in the social sciences, strategies that will free activist researchers to resist routine practices upholding false and oppressive versions of scientific "truth." The essays in this book have grown from my participation in a feminist academic community. Members of this community have fought for access to the university—the dominant contemporary apparatus for knowledge production—with much success and many remaining challenges. Working now as scholars, we often worry that we will perpetuate the inequalities we intended to oppose, and we struggle to find the space and means to craft alternative practices. That struggle is conducted, in part, within the area labeled "feminist methodology" in the social sciences, which has become a lively arena for scholarly writing. This rich literature, the puzzles of my own scholarly practice, and the challenges of helping students undertake feminist research have led to my continuing reflections on how feminists might best use the tools of social scientific research.

I work as a sociologist located in what is often labeled the interpretive branch of that field; the label signifies an interest in the interactive processes through which people make meaning in social contexts. Interpretive sociologists are also committed to reflexive analysis of the knower as an element in the known. Not surprisingly, then, my approach to the puzzles of research practice rests in part on applying this sociological lens to research activities. I begin from the recognition that research, like any human activity, is socially organized and shaped by the institutional contexts in which it occurs. The task for feminist scholars, working within particular institutions, is to choose practical strategies responsive to the intersecting communities of discourse and politics that inspire us—the communities of scholarship and social movements. I often use the term "strategies," suggesting a middle ground between obeisance to established rules of scholarship and the kind of confrontational dismissal of those rules that can negate efforts to make change. I do not assume that feminist scholarship translates directly and easily into activism or that feminist scholars should necessarily lead social change. I believe that whatever transformation feminists can achieve through research activity requires participation in existing institutions of knowledge production, and that feminist researchers therefore ought to be committed to some form of participation.

I am also confident—despite the doubts of some—that feminism and empirical research are deeply compatible. I see feminism, at its core, as a practice of speaking truth. Its central ideas have arisen from systematic attention to previously unacknowledged experiences that women began to speak of together. Its character as a public movement depends on an insistence that women's talk is not mere gossip or folklore, but rather the basis for grounded knowledge of experiences obscured and distorted in the past; its aims include revealing and refining such knowledges. Feminism, then, is strengthened through various modes of truth-seeking, including empirical investigation. In addition, I am convinced that feminist insights can strengthen empirical investigation. The truths of feminism are smaller, more tailored, and more intensely pointed truths than the discredited "Truth" of grand theory and master narratives. They are truths that illuminate varied experiences rather than insist on one reality; they seem, to many of us, more sturdy and useful than abstract and ostensibly universal formulations.

As these comments suggest, I have tried to learn from scholarly movements arising from other struggles, and I hope that some of my reflections will be useful to them. My intent is to work toward feminist practices that challenge the many oppressions cross-cutting and complicating gender domination. Thus, I have tried to situate feminist methodological concerns so as to reveal their overlap with other liberatory strategies and also leave room for necessary specificities. In the most recent writing that appears at the end of this book, I have sometimes used the term "oppositional research" as a label that might refer to both feminist research committed to challenging many oppressions and also research with other kinds of liberatory foundations and aims.

The earliest of these essays were written around 1985, shortly after I completed my graduate education; others developed as I began to teach research methods and undertake my next research projects. They do not provide a comprehensive survey of feminist methodological thought, but rather chart my own route through this terrain. In compiling essays for this collection, I have emphasized those issues that have proven most compelling for me, and I have organized the essays around several key concerns for oppositional researchers. In keeping with the feminist idea that knowing a speaker will deepen one's understanding of her speech, the book opens with an explicitly autobiographical essay, intended as a gesture of disclosure.

Given their ambitious goals, feminist researchers must accept that their efforts will always be only partially successful. Further, the importance of seeking truths more humbly should certainly be one lesson of the liberation movements. Therefore, I mean to offer these essays in an open, invitational spirit, as part of a tradition I would like to honor and also nurture toward an increasingly thoughtful, searching, and expansive future.

1 Becoming a Feminist Scholar: A Second-Generation Story

I AM not a feminist pioneer. My intention in beginning this way is not to indulge in self-deprecatory apology but to provide a statement of historical context. As an early "daughter" of second-wave feminist scholars, my work and career have developed within a fragile, uneven, but steadily strengthening feminist community in the academy. In many ways, I have worked with a kind of comfort that I recognize as part of the privilege of coming later: I have been helped by feminist scholars before me, socialized into the profession by powerful mentors who are also feminists, and supported (for the most part) in my attempts to resist disciplinary tyranny. I have also learned to accommodate to the demands of the profession, and my adjustments to an academic career often sit uneasily beside my feminism. The community that supports my work often seems dangerously fragile. Finding a place in the discipline felt like a risky bet until quite recently; the fact that I have entered the field successfully is a source of pride and also cause for reflection on why I have been sorted in rather than out. I try to tell a story here that examines my historically situated self and that displays some of the conditions of my entry into both feminism and sociology.

GROWING UP: CULTURAL CONTRADICTIONS

I was born in 1950 to white middle-class parents who had constructed a traditional family of the era.[1] My parents, raised in mostly rural midwestern environments, valued education. My father, who went to college to become a music teacher, was encouraged to continue with graduate work and soon became a college teacher specializing in mathematics education. My mother, whose college work in art had been interrupted by their marriage, took up the work of a faculty wife (enthusiastically at first, I think, and then with increasing ambivalence). I was their first child, obedient, smart, and shy. I was much loved and, for better and worse, shaped by the values of the prevailing culture of my era and class. A kindergarten evaluation (preserved in my mother's lovingly detailed record of my development) encapsulates the contradictions of middle-class girlhood in that time: "Marjorie is extremely well-adjusted. I have never seen her cry or get upset, though she sometimes sucks on her skirt."

I was encouraged to apply myself academically, to think of myself as "special," and to make my own decisions. But it was never very clear where that decision-making might lead. For a while (during the Kennedy era), I remember that I aspired to what seemed a very influential post: politician's wife. I was a responsible, intelligent, and conscientious student, drifting toward a promising, if hazy, future. Gender patterns in this sort of middle-class family were just beginning to fracture: I remember, in my early teens, overhearing adult voices in heated discussion of *The Feminine Mystique*. Soon, a wave of painful divorces would begin in such families.

Politically, I grew up alongside the 1960s, just a bit too young (and too timid) to participate fully in the movements of the time. Off to college in 1968, I watched the activism of the period mostly from the sidelines, drawn away from classes and out to the streets only at moments of crisis—spring 1970, for instance, when U.S. troops invaded yet another Southeast Asian country and students like me were killed by soldiers on their campus.

I remember—just barely—that during those years "women's liberation" came to our campus one day: a group of slightly older activists from somewhere in the East, traveling through the country with a workshop for women. I remember, dimly, that I attended, with my roommates, that we sat on the floor and talked. And I remember that the discussion continued back in the dorm well into the night.[2] This early appearance of feminism was anomalous in my life, however. I was about to slide into marriage to my high school sweetheart, too early and far too blithely. It didn't take long to discover that this marriage would not work. I struggled with various accommodations: I became domestic, tried to suppress my ambition. And I wish I could say that I rebelled and left, but in fact it was his unhappiness that finally moved me along. I hadn't yet learned to be angry in any effective way.

DISCOVERIES

In my first year of college—1968—I discovered social science in an introductory psychology course taught by a very young woman faculty member. (I remember this young woman very vividly and sympathetically: in the image I retain, she sometimes trembled while lecturing. She was one of the four faculty women who taught me in that college, each of whom I can visualize now in precise detail. Significantly, I remember in this vivid way hardly any of the faculty who were men.) We were to write term papers, and after choosing the topic "subliminal perception," I went to look for the material referenced in our textbook, articles in a journal so esoteric sounding that I was sure the school library wouldn't have it: the *Journal of Abnormal and Social Psychology*. Of course, I found it, on the fourth floor, in a little garret at the top of what seemed a very musty branch of the old library.

My discovery in that garret was what captured me for social science and, eventually, sociology. I discovered that scholars argued back and forth about topics such as subliminal perception and that psychologists engaged in the most interesting exercise: they designed experiments to convince each other of their views. I spent many hours working on my paper, poring over dirty old journals, tracing debates back and forth. It was a time of private, intense emotion, an awakening to the excitement and creativity of scholarly work. I sensed then that scholarship could be a kind of conversation, and I wanted to be part of it. The tone of slightly illicit pleasure in this account captures the edge of ambivalence I felt in this discovery. I was still caught in the dilemmas of my socialization, unwilling to fully acknowledge my ambitions but equally unwilling to put them aside.

A few years later, around the time I was divorced, I discovered feminism. I did not join a consciousness-raising group or engage in political action. Instead, I encountered the women's movement in its academic context. I was then pursuing a master's degree in curriculum and instruction, with the idea of becoming an elementary school teacher (one of the failed strategies for accommodation to my marriage), and faculty members at my institution, the University of Wisconsin at Madison, were just beginning to bring feminist content to the teacher training program. I read about gender stereotyping in children's readers, began to think about my own life, and experienced that profound feminist "click" of awakened consciousness. I began to get angry, and—more importantly—I had a theory to explain why. I learned, for example, that women were socialized into a double bind: that being a "normal woman" was incompatible with being a "normal adult." And that men expected—and would demand— that women serve as audience for men's actions rather than become actors themselves. I remember long, solitary walks during that time, when I tasted these new insights and emotions and considered what they meant. And I remember discovering feminist writings that spoke directly to these feelings: Judy Chicago, Doris Lessing, Marge Piercy, the alternative journal *Country Women,* and others. I began to work on becoming a conscious, independent woman, and I found this project tremendously energizing.

With other women in the Department of Curriculum and Instruction, I began to explore what feminist scholarship might be. In the early 1970s, I was a member of that department's first graduate course in women's studies, "Issues in Sex-related Differences in Curriculum and Instruction," a seminar offered by Elizabeth Fennema, who had already begun to challenge the prevailing wisdom about girls' mathematics performance.[3] We had a wonderful time, but there were lurking anxieties; it seemed odd and a bit risky, then, to give serious attention to women and girls. Several times, I heard Liz, in the course of telling about the seminar, offer a laughing apology. "Well," she would say, "these students have to take the blame for all this." Smiling, we would correct her: credit, not blame! But I was struck by the sense of vulnerability that produced this kind of nervous joke.

Abandoning my plans for elementary teaching, I wrote a master's thesis that analyzed students' experiences in the university's two-year-old introductory women's studies course.[4] And then I left school, uncertain what would come next. By that time—the late 1970s—feminism had touched everyone in my family of origin. My parents were divorced, and my mother was establishing herself as a painter. She and I were especially close during this time; we encountered feminism together and shared books, friends, and ideas about our work and our fledgling careers. My sister Ileen was also becoming a feminist scholar: she was one of the first women's studies majors at the University of California, Berkeley, and she is now a feminist labor historian (DeVault 1990). We developed these common interests in different ways and times: she was radical while I was married, then moved toward labor studies when I was discovering feminism. But we finished our graduate work at nearly the same moment, found jobs at roughly the same time, and published books in successive years. Now we live in the same region and share professional networks, as well as the puzzles and frustrations of writing, teaching, and institutional politics. I suspect that my siblings and I were all looking for some integration of the implicit gender split we observed in the family: while Ileen and I followed our father into academic work, our brother became a musician and is active in the feminist men's movement.

Learning a discipline (and resisting it)

My feminism, then, was in place before I became a sociologist. In fact, I chose sociology rather casually—it was one among several possible fields—and in 1978, with little knowledge of what it would mean, I entered the Ph.D. program at Northwestern University. I knew only that I would do feminist scholarship, that the "sociological imagination" seemed relevant (I'd read C. Wright Mills [1959]), and that the department seemed hospitable. I met briefly with Arlene Kaplan Daniels, who would later become my thesis adviser, and she extended an enthusiastic invitation. We talked about her research on women as volunteer workers and an ongoing study of returning women students. "I'm just having a great time," I remember her saying, "and you're welcome to run alongside and join the fun!"

This sense of joining a collective project captures my experience of feminism in sociology during those years. Some might assume that, coming in a second generation, I had "training" to be a feminist sociologist, but it didn't feel that way. When I think of my development as a feminist scholar, I do not think primarily of coursework and mentoring relationships (these seem much more crucial for my development as a sociologist). Instead, the story I construct from those years is one of lessons learned from the "hidden curriculum" of my graduate program and of a collective intellectual project of resistance to the discipline in its traditional construction. This project was supported by an emerging feminist community, but it often felt like a private struggle.

In many ways, Northwestern provided a most congenial environment. I remember, with gratitude, that faculty gave us lots of freedom, took student work seriously, and insisted that we take it seriously, too. I saw the faculty as engaged and productive scholars who paid attention to each other's work. There were classroom experiences that are still vivid for me, as well as the extended student discussions over coffee that are so central to most graduate study. It was a program that left room for challenge to the disciplinary canon, and I found among the faculty and my graduate student colleagues a willingness to listen sympathetically to my questions about how women might be made more visible in sociological work.

I can also easily recall becoming aware of a pervasive and frightening atmosphere of sexism. I watched as two outstanding junior faculty women, Janet Lever and Naomi Aronson, were denied tenure, and I noticed that the two senior women were curiously distant from the centers of the graduate curriculum and departmental decision-making. Slowly, I began to see the institutional pressures that excluded women and the questions I wanted to ask. I was cheered and inspired by the presence of women faculty: I watched Arlene at work and learned from her example, and I was moved by Janet Abu-Lughod's (1981) elegant and forceful address to the Northwestern faculty, "Engendering Knowledge: Women and the University."[5] But as I came to know women faculty, I shared not only ideas but also their experiences of discomfort and marginalization as sociologists. The lives of junior faculty women were especially frightening; I wondered, often, if I could survive in the profession and if survival would be worth the pain that seemed inevitable.

During my time at Northwestern, the formative collective experiences for graduate students were Arnold (Ackie) Feldman's classical theory course and Howard Becker's fieldwork seminar. In the theory course we read Karl Marx, Max Weber, and Antonio Gramsci. I entered the program with virtually no sociology and began to read the first volume of *Capital*. I remember the sense of wonder that Ackie's close readings of this text could produce and my pleasure in discovering that sociology could dissect inequality with such precision. In the fieldwork seminar, we simply began to work. "Go out there and start writing fieldnotes," Howie told us. "Just write down everything you see." So we went out, wrote voluminous notes, and then came back to class to work on making sense of them.

These were very different classroom experiences. I remember Feldman pacing in front of the class, delivering extremely dense lectures that we tried to transcribe as completely as possible. It was difficult for most of us to formulate questions; usually one or two students (often marxists from other countries) were prepared to grasp the point quickly enough to discuss it, and the rest of us struggled just to keep up. We were taught to read Marx and Weber as complementary, completing each other's analyses so as to encompass both class and status inequalities. We did not hear much about gender (though we could ask or write about it, and some of us did). And theory appeared to be men's territory. It was almost always men who participated in the extra reading groups and who went on to work with Feldman. Nevertheless, the two courses I took with him were important for me. I was challenged to produce a rigorous kind of analysis that really explained something, showing how it happened. And I was given a set of theoretical tools. For several years I started every project with a ritual rereading of the several hundred pages of notes I had produced in these classes.

Becker's fieldwork seminar met in a special classroom furnished with dilapidated easy chairs. He began each class as if he had no plan at all: "So what's been happening?" he might ask. And from whatever we had to say, he would make a lesson in fieldwork. Some people were frustrated by this style of pedagogy, feeling that nothing much was happening, but I found these sessions utterly enchanting. As the weeks went by, we could see projects developing, analyses arising from our confusions in the field. Howie pushed us; there were simply no excuses for not getting started. He conveyed a tremendous respect for the work we were doing, finding the seeds of significance in our beginners' attempts at observation. He insisted that it was all very simple: we could just figure it out and write it down. And he pointed out that no project was really complete until it had been written up for publication. Here, too, gender did not appear unless we asked. Howie was impatient with the idea that one might come to a project with a feminist agenda; he didn't believe in agendas and didn't want to talk about them.

Some students veered toward one or the other of these approaches; many of us yearned to "have it all." Given this foundation (and this desire), I was more than ready for Dorothy Smith's visit to Northwestern in winter 1983 as guest lecturer for a quarter. Several of us had been reading her work with great interest, and women faculty in the department had arranged a visiting lectureship. We organized a seminar and Dorothy taught her own work, week by week, laying out for us the development of her thought about sociology, its problems, and the promise for women of a revised and stronger form of sociological analysis (Smith 1987, 1990a). With several friends, I studied this material in a nearly fanatical way. We met early to prepare for each class and again later to discuss what had happened in each session. Laboring over Dorothy's dense prose, I copied long excerpts into my notebook and composed lists of questions to ask in class. Whenever Dorothy spoke, I was there.

During Smith's visit, I began to envision a sociology that was more satisfying than any I'd known: it would build on materialist principles, retain a commitment to the world as people lived it, and insist that women's varied situations be kept in view. Dorothy's approach, more than any other, seemed to offer possibilities for moving beyond feminist critiques of established sociology and beginning to build something new. There were lessons in the hidden curriculum as well. For example, one of the startling revelations of the seminar lay in discovering its meaning for Dorothy: that this was her first opportunity to present her work so thoroughly as a unified body of thought and that she needed our response as much as we wanted to hear her words. The experience also supported my sense of feminist scholarship as collective project. One day in class, when I'd asked another earnest and anxious question about how to do this kind of sociology, Dorothy just smiled for a moment. "Well, Marj," she finally said, "I don't have all the answers. You'll have to figure some of this out for yourself."

My research topic, the invisible work of "feeding a family," arose from the feminist theoretical agenda I'd brought with me to sociology, as well as from questions about my own gendered experience. I'd been fascinated by the feminist idea that women's absence from most scholarly writing had shaped the assumptions and concepts of every discipline. I wanted to study aspects of life that "belonged" to women and to consider what it would mean to take those activities and concerns as seriously as we take the perspectives that arise from men's experiences; for this reason, I began to think about housework. There were, at that time, several sociological studies that took housework seriously, applying the perspectives that sociologists of work applied to paid jobs.[6] I was enormously grateful for these early studies, but I also tested them against my own experience—a fundamental feminist move—and felt that something was missing.

I was living at that time in a stormy, exciting, and ultimately disastrous relationship with a man who had become quite incapacitated by chronic depression. During the years we spent together, he became increasingly helpless; I was terribly ambivalent about the partnership but strongly committed to caring for this person I had loved so intensely. Life felt very difficult during those years; I brooded a lot about how to respond to his troubles, and I remember in one moment of reflection thinking that the womanly experience I wanted to capture in my work was this incredibly delicate craft of caring for others.

I did not go directly to my typewriter. Instead, I muddled along wondering if I would ever develop an acceptable thesis topic, experiencing a prolonged period of depression myself, and slowly beginning to write about women and food. I couldn't say what I was up to: I wrote about supermarkets, the health food movement, dietitians, food stamps, and food journalists. And I kept coming back to the household work of providing food. Stubbornly, I held onto my own experience and my intuitive sense of topic, which didn't seem to fit with the topics available in the discipline. My first clear statement of my topic came from my reading outside sociology, when I was able to point to Virginia Woolf's novel *To the Lighthouse* and say: "It's what Mrs. Ramsay does at her dinner party! Of course there isn't a name for it—that's the whole point." I wrote an essay about Mrs. Ramsay, and finally I was able to begin an ethnography of the unpaid work of "feeding a family" with some confidence that I might capture what made it so compelling for women.[7]

I wanted a feminist as my thesis adviser, and I chose to work with Arlene Kaplan Daniels. We shared a central concern for excavating those womanly activities rendered invisible or trivialized by social theory derived from the concerns of privileged men. Arlene's own work at that time was concerned with the "invisible careers" of women volunteers who became civic leaders (Daniels 1988). This study was leading her toward a more general analysis of varieties of "invisible work," which she presented as her presidential address to the Society for the Study of Social Problems in 1987 (Daniels 1987). In that piece, she synthesized writings by feminists (and others) about a wide range of nonmarket activities, arguing for an expansion of the concept of work as a crucial step in the project of including women's contributions more fully in sociological analyses of work and the social order.

Arlene's writing on invisible work displays the kind of strategically doubled vision that I absorbed from working with her and that I now see as crucial to my development. As a feminist, Arlene saw the promise of rethinking the grounding concepts of the discipline; as a sociologist, she conceptualized the innovative work that feminists were developing in terms that located it in relation to core questions of the discipline. Perhaps because she had long been a student of the professions, Arlene insisted on the importance of placing oneself firmly and clearly inside the discipline; she insisted that I write a dissertation that was not only innovative but also acceptable in the terms of the discipline.[8] These lessons were sometimes uncomfortable: I confess that I was often impatient when she counseled me cheerfully to become an "occupations and professions man"; I understood, but could not quite accept, the conditions that produced this advice (see her account, Daniels 1994). But I do believe that to steer the tricky course between innovation and acceptance is the most essential task for a feminist scholar: even though our aims may be transformative, innovative writing is recognized and appreciated only if it can be located successfully, somewhere, in relation to existing work.

My account of Arlene's mentorship would not be complete without some mention of the personal texture of our relationship—the complex and lively breadth of our interaction. One of my vivid memories: each time I put a chapter in Arlene's mailbox, I would soon afterward hear her extravagant voice booming down the hall as she skipped toward my office. "Marj, my dear Marj!" she would shout. "You finished another chapter! You deserve a reward; what would you like? A box of chocolates? Or shall I take you for sushi lunch tomorrow?" Sushi lunch was my favorite, so we would stroll down the street together, and I would have my reward. It felt wonderful. To emphasize this kind of help is not to trivialize Arlene's intellectual contribution to my work; rather, I mean to emphasize her recognition that intellectual work is best sustained through attention to emotional, as well as intellectual, needs. While I was her student, I ate and shopped with Arlene, as well as joining her at feminist lectures and meetings. She introduced me to her colleagues and "talked up" my work. I watched and learned as she helped to build a feminist world within the discipline and pulled me into that world.

COLLECTIVE WORK

My scholarship has always depended on the support of women colleagues and could not have developed as it has, I believe, without my relationships with other women. Twice, I've enjoyed long periods of intensive "partnered" reading and thinking. In graduate school, I worked with Sandra Schroeder and for several years after graduation with the late Marianne (Tracy) Paget. In neither case did we work collaboratively on joint projects or even on the same topics. But in both cases we shared feminist commitments, interests in experimentation and resistance, and some affinity in our styles of thought. In both cases, we paid loving attention to each other's work, read and talked about everything we wrote, and tried to hear and coax out for each other what we meant to do in our work.

Sandy and I scheduled weekly meetings throughout our dissertation work (a practice that amused us since we were housemates most of that time and shared an office as well); we considered each other essential, though unofficial, members of our dissertation committees. Tracy and I began our work together by reading all the work of Dorothy Smith that we could find, and we agreed that it made a difference to study her writing as a coherent, extended body of thought (the way students are routinely taught to understand canonical male theorists). We talked about reading other women sociologists in this way (inspired in part by the work that Shulamit Reinharz was doing to reclaim women sociologists of the past), but that project was precluded by Tracy's untimely death in 1989.[9]

These intense working relationships seem a bit like falling in love, at least in the sense that they don't come along very often and cannot be produced at will. But I have shared feminist ideas, reading, projects, and debates with many other groups and individual colleagues over the years. These relationships have been important because they have felt quite different from more conventional academic spaces. Within them, some understandings can be taken for granted, and one doesn't need to defend and legitimate feminist principles and assumptions. We can and do question our core ideas, as critics might, but this activity feels quite different when undertaken with sympathetic colleagues. Within such groups, we give lots of encouragement, we deal with emotional issues alongside intellectual ones, and we find nothing strange or suspect in that agenda. Finally, we have energy, fun, and, usually, a lot of laughter. Sometimes I feel that male colleagues are a bit jealous of these relationships (those male colleagues who know about them, at least), and I can see why they might feel that way: feminism has enlivened academic life for many of us. I am also conscious of a kind of separatism in these practices that feels not only pleasurable, but vital and nurturant. It is the kind of separatism that lesbian writer Marilyn Frye (1983) identifies as a useful sometime strategy for all women—a strategy that insists on women's own value, apart from men, and our value for each other (see also Krieger 1996).

GETTING IN

I chose to study sociology during a period of contracting opportunities for academic work; we were warned, on that hopeful first day of graduate school, that many of us would have difficulty finding jobs. Thus, for nine years—from 1978, when I entered graduate school, until 1987, when I was hired as an assistant professor at Syracuse University—I had a keen sense of the possibility that I would never find stable employment as a sociologist. After completing my degree in 1984, I searched for a permanent job for three years, scrambling to find work and moving every year. During one difficult year in Boston, I supported myself with part-time teaching: a more than full-time schedule for less than half-time pay. I was quietly enraged for much of that year; the most difficult job was managing those emotions and considering how long I could persist in such a life. It was then that I met Tracy Paget, who never held a permanent teaching post. During much of our time together, she supported her scholarly work as many artists support their creative projects: by enduring periods of temporary clerical work so that she could also have periods of uninterrupted writing. She didn't often tell about this strategy while she was alive; it didn't sound very "professional." But I think she wouldn't mind that I divulge the secret here. I think she would agree that it is important to speak about such women and their work. Challenging disciplinary tradition leaves many innovative scholars outside the institutions of scholarship and personally vulnerable. I believe that the discipline is impoverished by their absence.

One of the things that feminism has provided for me is an analysis of the evaluative and gatekeeping processes that structure these experiences. It has given me a way to think about some of the difficult moments in my professional life. I have learned to think long and hard about audiences for my writing, and I have learned to evaluate the gatekeepers: when my work is judged, I ask who is judging it and on what terms. When I hear, "But that's not sociology," I have learned to say (or at least think), "Maybe not yet."

During 1982–83, I began to work, with Patty Passuth, Lisa Jones, and other graduate students at Northwestern, on something we called "the gender project": a survey of graduate student experiences in our department, which we hoped would help us to understand the frustrations so many of us were feeling. We gathered data on attrition from the graduate program, interviewed all of the students in residence, and wrote an article-sized report for distribution to the department. Although the attrition data were incomplete, it seemed that during the decade we had studied, women had been more likely than men to drop out of the program, especially at the dissertation stage. Introducing the document, we wrote:

> In a survey of all students, we found subtle differences in the ways that male and female students described their interactions with faculty members. Relative to men, women tended to feel more marginal to the department, and believed they were taken less seriously. They reported receiving less help and encouragement than men, were more pessimistic about their chances for employment, and their expectations were more likely than men's to

have dropped since entering the program. A substantial number of women blamed themselves for the situations they described, reporting that their own work was marginal to the field, or that their experience in the program was "unusual" in some respect. (DeVault, Jones, and Passuth 1983:1)

In fine multimethod fashion, we presented tables and quotations from respondents to illustrate a pattern of "benign neglect" of women students. Although unwilling to "point with certainty" to causes, we suggested several factors that might explain these problems: the structural reality of a predominantly male faculty, documented differences in the interactional styles of men and women and the differential responses these styles elicit from others, and the incomplete acceptance of women's concerns within the discipline. Echoing "The Missing Feminist Revolution" (Stacey and Thorne 1985)—which must have been circulating at the time, though I don't think we had read it—we concluded:

> Another possible cause for the differential experience of men and women students is that by following their own concerns—an approach to research encouraged by this department—female students are more likely than men to be working on non-traditional topics or approaching traditional topics in original ways. Thus, they may have more difficulty formulating their ideas, and faculty may have a harder time understanding them or seeing the significance of their work.
>
> The research literature which incorporates women's perspectives into sociology—developed over the past 20 years—has been integrated into "mainstream" courses only to a limited extent. Researchers have found that after taking women's studies courses, female students report feeling more included in academic disciplines, more serious about themselves as scholars and more assertive about their studies. Thus, more active efforts to incorporate new knowledge especially relevant to women may help to combat female students' feelings of marginality. (DeVault, Jones, and Passuth 1983:33)

I have quoted at some length from this document because it illustrates my use of feminist analysis at that time to construct and sustain a sense of opposition to business as usual in graduate training. It also displays the construction of our activism within the boundaries of the institution and shows how the goal of "getting in" to the profession shaped the substance and form of our resistance. As I look back at this document, I am struck by its heartfelt but measured concern and by our earnestly "professional" tone. Our confidence in the effectiveness of "the facts," presented well, suggests a considerable measure of political naïveté, as well as the kind of comfort we felt within the program in spite of our complaints. And the carefully suppressed anger in the document points to the extent to which we had already accepted a powerful professional discipline.

I learned from my involvement in this project that researching injustice carries the seeds of cooptation: though it provoked much discussion, our report resulted mostly in calls for further research. I also learned, however, that speaking out about these problems could bring women together. We were surprised when women faculty in the department expressed gratitude that we had raised these issues. And the intense work of writing the report together was a powerful and energizing experience of collective analysis. For a while at least, our report constructed a lively solidarity among women in the department. Finally, I learned that my personal skills could be used to stir up some trouble within an institution and that stirring up trouble felt like a very good thing to do.

I have suggested that feminism was for me a theory that made immediate and personal sense. I do not mean to suggest that the kind of analysis just described exhausts the meanings of feminism or provides a full account; any adequate feminism must also fit for other women, most of whom are in situations quite different from those of sociology graduate students. In addition, my location as a woman intersects with other privileges and oppressions shaping my experience. It is for this reason that I have tried to display my middle-class, academic background in my telling of this story. I have wanted to give a sense for the particular kind of gendered life I have led and how it has shaped both my feminism and my career. (I learned several kinds of lessons, for example, from observation of my father's work life, including the following: that academic work could be profoundly satisfying; that an academic can chart her own course in many ways; that institutional politics requires particular kinds of entrepreneurship; and, perhaps most importantly, that the academy is no paradise [cf. Ryan and Shackrey 1984]. I also learned a style of demeanor and discourse, so that the kinds of talk required in institutional settings feel relatively familiar. I wanted to resist adopting wholesale my father's consuming absorption in work, which sometimes felt distancing to me as a child—I remember the often closed and inviolable door to his study—but that has been more difficult than I expected.)

My feminism has provided a perspective that sustains a useful, restrained resistance to some aspects of business as usual, while continuing other aspects of this "business" with a vengeance. It seems important to acknowledge these limits, but I want to resist the view that this version of feminism can serve only to support the advancement of privileged middle-class academics. As I analyzed my own marginality, I could readily see that there were similar obstacles for other underrepresented groups and that I would need to use my theory reflexively to analyze my own blindnesses and exclusions. My personal sense of oppression has, I think, helped me not only to hear but also to feel, with some urgency, the complaints of those excluded on bases other than gender. When students complain about my courses, I do not want to reply that I hadn't thought about lesbians (for example), that I couldn't find any material on women of color (for example), or that surely one class on women with disabilities (for example) is enough. These lame excuses sound far too familiar. And I am convinced—because I have worked so hard to convince those who resisted my feminist complaints—that really working to change the way I think will enliven my work and move us all forward.

And now . . .

Through the early years of my career, I've been motivated and sustained by a sense of resistance to disciplinary traditions that has bordered on hostility. Feminism has provided pathways (or lifelines) out of the discipline. I have read feminist works outside of sociology, and I often find that they are more productive of the insights I need than the writings of other sociologists. I do not mean that I ignore or dismiss feminist work in sociology but that I have been interested in the challenge of getting out of the discipline, and then back in, exiting and reentering with transformative ideas.

Now that I feel reasonably well established in the discipline, I find, tellingly, that I am more interested in sociology. I want to know more about the history of the discipline, and I feel more interested (in both senses) in its future. One can certainly read this shift as a simple economic response to a change in my situation; I would not discount this reading entirely. But I think this reaction to acceptance also signals the implicit messages about "ownership" of the discipline that are sent when some groups are virtually excluded from participation and hints at the costs to the profession of these kinds of exclusions.

Feminism has led me to questions about the disciplinary context within which I struggle to construct meaningful work. In the process of "becoming a sociologist," I have come to feel that I need to understand how sociology works, as a discipline, to include and exclude topics and perspectives, to advance and coopt projects of inquiry, to resist and tame transformative agendas. I want to understand what it means to adopt a "discipline": how a discipline produces a discourse that enables some projects and rules others out of bounds. One aspect of a recent project (on the work of dietitians and nutritionists) involves an exploration of the force of "disciplinarity" (see DeVault 1995 and chaps. 5 and 7 of this book). In pursuing this research, I have been interviewing professional women who are in positions similar to mine and whose career stories and concerns with work often mirror mine. We work inside the structures of institutional power but not at their centers, and this kind of position, as "marginal insider," gives rise to characteristic troubles and ambivalences. My aim is to make visible the sticky web of disciplinarity and professionalism within which they (and I) work. These interests arise, in part, from my own puzzles. They are also a product of new intellectual currents, including postmodern meditations on knowledge production and questions about the place of feminism within, among, and across disciplines. Thus, I still struggle with questions about locating myself as a feminist scholar.

In 1992, poised on the brink of tenure, I met the fifteen women and one man who had enrolled in my graduate seminar in feminist research. For the first class, I had chosen as our texts two poems: Kate Rushin's "The Bridge Poem" (1981) and Marge Piercy's "Unlearning to Not Speak" (1973). I had planned to read the poems aloud, and I had resolved to read with feeling. I was nervous, a bit hesitant, but the words carried me along, and my voice broke with feeling as I read. We all noticed, and that moment of emotion became a topic for discussion: why do we feel this way, and what does it mean? By the end of class, one student was ready to admit that she'd been dismayed at first to find poetry in a sociology classroom—so "soft" and womanish! Starting outside of the discipline, I think, had the effect I'd intended: we began to construct space for experimentation. About halfway through the semester, I noticed with surprise and some embarrassment that I was listening to students' presentations and worrying, "But is it sociology?" My feminism kept me quiet for the moment and gave them license to proceed. Near the end of the course, however, I began to feel an urgent need to lecture and warn them, to point out the necessity of living within, as well as between, disciplines. "I want you to be bold, take risks, and make trouble," I told them. "But I also want you to be here, to *survive* in this institutional space. For that, you have to accept a discipline."

In spite of the comforts of the second generation, survival hasn't felt easy. Some days, it seems that the feminist revolution is still missing: my feminist courses attract mostly women students, and I often feel that I live my professional life in a parallel female world apart from the "main business" of my institution and profession. Some days, I notice how many of us are now at work, and I think the revolution may be sneaking up on us, arriving while we're busy with office hours, so that we hardly have time to notice. As I write this last sentence, I am conscious of my easy use of the word "us," and I worry—about my sense that I might be turning into one of "them" and my desire to construct a "we" that continues to press at the boundaries of disciplinary traditions. Almost all the time, I'm interested to see what will come next.

II. WHAT IS FEMINIST METHODOLOGY?

SOCIAL MOVEMENT activists call attention to problems and attempt to forward their agendas through a discursive process that social analysts call "claims-making" (Spector and Kitsuse 1987). When feminist researchers began to use the term "feminist methodology," they staked a claim in the contentious territory of social science. Since then many interested observers have asked, "What is feminist methodology?"; and skeptics have often followed with, "What's so special about that?" The disciplinary controversy surrounding these questions provides an interesting (and typical) case study in the politics of knowledge. Insiders know feminist methodology from experience: we recognize a community of scholars working on common questions with common commitments, learning from one another, developing and extending practices that further feminist goals. Outsiders see these activities through a different lens and often assert that they represent "nothing new."

Most social scientists recognize, in principle, that "methods" should not be conceived as neutral "tools" to be picked up and put down at will, but rather as practices that imply distinctive ways of understanding the world. Still, the notion of "feminist method" suggests to many a kind of "how-to" manual with prescriptions for action, rather than broader commitments guiding research practice. Feminist methodologists have generally resisted this "cookbook" or "how-to" conception of their writing, claiming that what we have produced is a "perspective" that informs our use of a range of standard research tools (Reinharz 1992); Sandra Harding (1987) points to this kind of distinction with her argument that it is not feminists' methods but their methodology, or thinking about method, that is distinctive. These kinds of answers seem to me correct. Critics often hear them as weak answers to the question "Is there a distinctive feminist methodology?" since they seem to rely on tautology ("It's what feminists do") or on the relatively technical distinction between method and methodology. I believe, however, that they are strong answers, and that their strength becomes more apparent when we consider the context in which these questions are asked and answered.

Often, queries of feminist methodology carry contradictory demands: skeptics ask feminists to define their methodology so as to fit with the terms of conventional research paradigms, and also to make sharp, non-overlapping distinctions between feminist and mainstream methodologies. Deborah Gordon (1988) discusses this kind of response to feminist writing in some detail with respect to James Clifford's excuse for the absence of feminist scholars and texts in *Writing Culture*, the influential collection of essays on ethnographic innovation he edited with George Marcus (Clifford and Marcus 1986). Feminist scholarship is innovative, he argues, but not in the particular ways that he and other contributors find interesting (i.e., it's not the same as what they do). On the other hand, he claims, feminist work need not be discussed because it is not really so different from other innovative work (so it is the same, then?). Gordon suggests that we understand Clifford's view of feminist research as a consequence of a particular institutional and historical location—a position of male privilege, but privilege in question—privilege, perhaps, that sees its challengers and even applauds their presence, but prefers not to encounter them too directly. The blindnesses of privilege in this circumstance are not necessarily conspiratorial, but rather are part of a systemic institutional "management" of feminism that recognizes its contemporary force and simultaneously places it in a "strained position of servitude" (Gordon 1988:8).

Insistently skeptical questions can often be understood as an aspect of this sort of management of feminist scholarship. To focus prematurely on the question of whether feminist methodology "exists" or is "really different," before making a serious attempt to study the field, seems at heart an insistence on constructing questions about feminist method that define it out of existence. When I am pushed to define feminist methodology simply and completely in the terms of mainstream social science, I risk distorting what feminist methodologists do. Instead of rushing to answer, it may be more useful to notice that the question comes from a discourse that is not eager to make room for us. Feminist scholars insist that the answers to questions should fit with the contours of women's lives, including our own. Thus, the researchers doing feminist work, and using feminist methods, are the starting point and the anchor for my answer, rather than some established notion of what a "methodology" should look like. The apparently tautological answer ("It's what we do") asserts that feminist researchers should not be expected to explain their methodology fully and definitively in "twenty-five words or less" or in the token article or talk. It puts forward the strong claim that a body of diverse work exists and deserves attention on its own terms.

To resist the questions usually asked—to see that they may define us out of existence—is a fundamental feminist move and therefore itself an illustration of a method or strategy that feminist researchers share. The inspiration for my approach to this question, for example, is an essay by a feminist philosopher, Marilyn Frye (1983), who demonstrates that our conceptual system provides no room for lesbians and uses that demonstration as well to suggest that there is quite limited space even for women attached to men. Acknowledging Frye's discussion is another important part of my answer, because it illustrates how feminists learn from each other and use each other's insights to understand our varied situations.

The first essay in this section, "Talking Back to Sociology," was my attempt to speak, as forcefully as I could, to mainstream scholars who might be skeptical about the very existence of feminist methodology. It is also, more than most of the essays in this collection, an overview of a wide range of feminist methodological discussions. The second essay, "Institutional Ethnography," is narrower in focus in that it discusses one particular approach to feminist inquiry. There too, however, I am concerned with locating this strategy in relation to traditions and procedures of the disciplines—partly to make a place for this approach in existing discourses, and partly to identify and insist on its distinctiveness.

2 Talking Back to Sociology

Distinctive Contributions of Feminist Methodology

NEARLY EVERY writer on the topic agrees that there is no single feminist method, yet there is a substantial literature on "feminist methodology" representing a diverse community of sociologists in lively and sometimes contentious dialogue. In surveying this field of inquiry, I am conscious of writing for at least three audiences: those who have observed the growth of "feminist methodology" from the outside, and wish mostly to know more clearly "what it is"; those who have encountered the discourse of feminist methods as relative newcomers, perhaps ready to enter these dialogues and seeking places to begin; and those who have participated in the development of feminist methodology, who would use such a survey not only for definition and codification but as a site for discussion of the perplexing questions we now confront. For each of these audiences, it seems useful to begin with some reflection on sources.

ORIGIN STORIES

In 1995, feminist sociologists in the United States celebrated the twenty-fifth anniversary of Sociologists for Women in Society, an organization founded in the moment of social change and professional activism that brought women and sociologists of color more fully into the discipline. Feminist authors have recently produced several collections of autobiographies by women who have contributed to feminist sociology (Goetting and Fenstermaker 1995, Orlans and Wallace 1994, Thorne and Laslett 1997); histories of the "insurgent" organizations of the early seventies (Roby 1992; see also Wilkinson 1992); and an analysis of the caucus that supported gay and lesbian sociologists living increasingly open lives within the profession (Taylor and Raeburn 1995). This heightened interest in the history of scholarly activism is perhaps a sign of maturation, with connotations of both the wisdom and the limits that age can bring. The stories we tell now mark a consolidation of sorts by a generation of established scholars and bring questions about what a new generation will experience and contribute.

These histories locate feminist sociology as a product of the "second-wave"[1] feminism that developed, initially, in Europe and North America. That movement grew out of small beginnings in the 1960s, gathered momentum in the early 1970s, and has differentiated in the years since through specialization, conflict, and cooptation (see Freeman 1975, Evans 1979, Echols 1989; and on feminist organizations, Ferree and Martin 1995). Historians of the movement in the United States agree that it had several sources: chief among them were women's increasing labor force participation, "women's status" projects begun in political arenas in the early 1960s, and gender conflicts that arose in the civil rights and antiwar movements of the late 1960s and early 1970s (Freeman 1975, Evans 1979).

Many would agree that a method, consciousness raising, was at the heart of this women's movement. In various settings, small groups of women began to talk together, analyze, and act. The method of consciousness raising was fundamentally empirical; it provided a systematic mode of inquiry that challenged received knowledge and allowed women to learn from one another (Allen 1973, Combahee River Collective 1982). Whether caucusing within established organizations or building new connections, women who became feminists began to see an alternative basis for knowledge and authority in a newly discovered community of women and "women's experience." Subsequent developments would reveal the complex fragilities and resiliencies of this construction, which Donna Haraway characterizes as "a fiction and fact of the most crucial, political kind" (1985:65).

Though the women's movement began outside the university, feminists in nearly every discipline soon began to apply its methods to their context and work, embarking on a collective project of critique and transformation. They pointed to the omission and distortion of women's experiences in mainstream social science, the tendency to universalize the experience of men (and relatively privileged women), and the use of science to control women, whether through medicine and psychiatry, or through social scientific theories of family, work, sexuality, and deviance (Glazer-Malbin and Waehrer 1971, Millman and Kanter 1975). Scholars of African descent produced a complementary literature on racist and gender bias in scholarship during this period (Ladner 1971, Jackson 1973)—stimulated in part by "expert" opinion that blamed women for the ostensible deficiencies of African American families.

Feminist sociologists sought support from one another, from feminists in other disciplines and in women's and ethnic studies as these emerged, and, when possible, from allies situated more firmly in "mainstream" sociology.[2] White women entered academic work during these years in larger numbers than women of color, and more easily, and the women of color who worked in sociology during this period faced problems of divided interests and competing demands. Lesbian sociologists participated actively but often had to be closeted, even within the movement. Class backgrounds were relatively invisible, as in the discipline more generally. In addition, feminists came to academic work with varying histories of activism outside the university and found employment in institutions that made different demands and offered various possibilities. These patterns have shaped feminist research and continue to haunt our discussions of methodology.

Over the last twenty-five years, the academy has provided a relatively protected space for the development of feminist thought, but academic feminists have struggled with the tensions of working oppositionally from within powerful institutions of social control. They have created new cross-disciplinary audiences for work based on these feminist critiques as well as new curricula, journals, conferences, and organizations to support and disseminate the work (Kramarae and Spender 1992, McDermott 1994). Referring to this history is the beginning of my answer to questions about the distinctiveness of feminist writings on research methodology. I mean to suggest that learning the history of feminist scholarship—and recognizing its roots in the women's movement—are key to understanding it.

Feminist sociologists are committed to both feminism and social science, and they use the tools of the discipline to "talk back" to sociology in a spirited critique aimed at improving the ways we know society. In the discussion that follows, I characterize feminist methodology as a field of inquiry united by membership in these overlapping research communities—bound together not by agreement about answers but by shared commitments to questions. Then I examine recent work and questions currently on the agenda for feminist methodologists. I focus on sociological work, but I also draw from other disciplines where these have been especially influential in sociology.

FEMINISM, FEMINIST RESEARCH, AND FEMINIST METHODOLOGY

"Feminism" is a movement, and a set of beliefs, that problematize gender inequality. Feminists believe that women have been subordinated through men's greater power, variously expressed in different arenas. They value women's lives and concerns, and work to improve women's status. While this kind of definition is broadly inclusive, it is also misleadingly simple. There are many feminisms, with different emphases and aims. Jane Mansbridge (1995) suggests that despite this variation, feminists are united by a sense of accountability to a movement that is best conceived as a changing and contested discourse. In any occupation or organization, feminists make decisions about how to respond to institutional contexts that sometimes welcome and sometimes resist feminist insights; they consider how to use their resources (both material and intellectual) to further their feminist goals, and which demands of their institution should be resisted in the name of feminism. Thus, feminist methodology will not be found in some stable orthodoxy but in an evolving dialogue.

I wish to draw a distinction in this essay between "feminist research" and "feminist methodology." I understand "feminist research" as a broader category including any empirical study that incorporates or develops the insights of feminism. Feminist studies may use standard research methods, or they may involve explicit attention to methodological critique and innovation. I would like to reserve the term "feminist methodology" for explicitly methodological discussion that emerges from the feminist critique. I follow philosopher Sandra Harding's (1987) suggestion that we distinguish between "methods" (i.e., particular tools for research), "methodology" (theorizing about research practice), and "epistemology" (the study of how and what we can know). For the most part, feminist researchers have modified, rather than invented, research methods; however, feminist researchers have produced a distinctive body of writing about research practice and epistemology, and that is where I locate "feminist methodology."

SECOND-WAVE WRITING ON METHODOLOGY

Feminist sociologists of the second wave began immediately to think skeptically about existing research methods (see Reinharz 1985 on "feminist distrust") and to search for alternatives. By 1983, there was a substantial body of literature (Reinharz, Bombyk, and Wright 1983). The focus on methodology gained momentum during that decade, and when philosopher Sandra Harding edited an interdisciplinary anthology (1987) that illustrated feminist methods with exemplary work, sociologists were well represented; as authors of four of ten substantive chapters, they included Marcia Millman and Rosabeth Moss Kanter, Joyce Ladner, Dorothy E. Smith, and Bonnie Thornton Dill.

Two overviews of feminist research methods that have been especially influential in sociology (Cook and Fonow 1986, Reinharz 1992) also adopted the strategy of collecting exemplars of feminist research and looking for common features. These writers drew on the work of scholars who had been developing particular feminist approaches in some detail.

These included adaptations of survey and experimental methods (Eichler 1988), interview research (Oakley 1981), inductive fieldwork (Reinharz 1983), marxist and ethnomethodological approaches (Smith 1987, Stanley and Wise 1983/93), phenomenology (Leveque-Lopman 1988), action/ participatory research (Mies 1983, Maguire 1987), oral history (Personal Narratives Group 1989, Gluck and Patai 1991), and others. More recent additions to the list include feminist versions of experimental ethnography (*Inscriptions* 1988), and methods based on poststructuralist insights (Lather 1991, Game 1991, Ingraham 1994).

The range of approaches mentioned here reflects the fact that feminist researchers are located throughout the discipline. Shulamit Reinharz (1992) holds that feminists have used (and modified) every available research method; and her comprehensive review includes studies across the full range. The pluralism in this kind of definition is attractive to many feminists for several reasons, not least of which is a well-developed sense of the dangers of "ranking," whether of oppressions or methods. By insisting on diversity, this approach avoids needless division and leaves open the future strategies that feminist researchers might want to adopt. But the continuing proliferation of writing on feminist methodology suggests a strongly felt sense of difference from standard practice, however elusive that difference may seem to outsiders.

This reference to "outsiders" raises questions about membership in this research community. Some discussions of feminist methodology proceed without explicit reference to women as its main practitioners (though they may assume as much), perhaps out of a desire to emphasize the relevance of feminist research throughout the field. But it seems to me important to recognize the people at work in the construction of feminist methodology, and those people have been mostly women (though most writers agree that this association is contingent rather than essential). I would suggest as a model for making this connection Patricia Hill Collins's (1990) thoughtful consideration of the field of "Black feminist thought." She contends that a useful definition of this field must negotiate the tension between identity-based definitions, which would find Black feminist thought in the work of any African American woman, and excessively idealist definitions, which would rely solely on ideological criteria, without requiring any link between cultural identity and the development of Black feminist thought. Collins suggests that Black feminist thought is an intellectual tradition, tied to, but not isomorphic with, the everyday experiences of African American women. African American women are most likely and best prepared to develop theories out of that experience; though others may also contribute to such theorizing, they would need considerable knowledge of the traditions and experiences associated with the group. Echoing the importance of such ties, Belinda Kremer (1990) argues that women should "keep feminist research for ourselves." Harding (1991) allows that men can work inside feminist circles (and whites in antiracist projects), but emphasizes that doing so successfully requires learning enough to see and understand the consequences of varying social locations, including one's own. These kinds of considerations underlie my choice to devote so many introductory words to pointing toward a history of feminism in sociology, and women scholars' experience of that movement: understanding that history is key to understanding feminist methodology.

WHAT IS FEMINIST METHODOLOGY?

The heart of feminist methodology is a critique that views the apparatus of knowledge production as one site that has constructed and sustained women's oppression. This critical understanding provides, by implication, criteria for a different research practice:

1. Feminists seek a methodology that will do the work of "excavation," shifting the focus of standard practice from men's concerns in order to reveal the locations and perspectives of (all) women. The aim of much feminist research has been to "bring women in," that is, to find what has been ignored, censored, and suppressed, and to reveal both the diversity of actual women's lives and the ideological mechanisms that have made so many of those lives invisible. A key method for doing so—drawn in part from the legacy of consciousness raising—has involved work with the personal testimony of individual women, especially through methods such as ethnography, qualitative interviewing, life history, and narrative analysis (Anderson et al. 1990). However, it would be misleading to equate feminist responses to this methodological demand with qualitative methods, for two reasons. First, some feminists argue that quantitative techniques can also perform the work of "making visible" and are sometimes necessary or more compelling than personal testimony (Sprague and Zimmerman 1993). In addition, qualitative methods practiced in nonfeminist ways can easily reproduce the mainstream failure to notice women and their concerns. What makes a qualitative or a quantitative approach feminist is a commitment to finding women and their concerns. The point is not only to know about women, but to provide a fuller and more accurate account of society by including them (Nielsen 1990).

Often, feminist researchers use this strategy to find "voices" for themselves, or for women who share experiences that have been meaningful for them (Stanley and Wise 1979). But the commitment to excavation and inclusion makes feminist researchers accountable for considering women whose experiences are different as well. Negotiating the tension between investigating experiences with intense personal meaning and casting wider nets has been a continuing challenge. Western, Euro-American feminists have been roundly criticized (rightly, I believe) for too often presenting investigations of particular groups of women's lives in terms that are falsely universalized (Dill 1979, Baca Zinn et al. 1986). But the call for excavation makes feminist researchers accountable to recognize and correct such mistakes, and one strand in feminist methodological work involves sustained attempts to move beyond these incomplete and limiting analyses.

2. Feminists seek a science that minimizes harm and control in the research process. In response to the observation that researchers have often exploited or harmed women participants, and that scientific knowledge has sustained systematic oppressions of women, feminist methodologists have searched for practices that will minimize harm to women and limit negative consequences (Nebraska Feminist Collective 1983, 1988). Such concerns enter nonfeminist research discussions as well. What marks the feminist discourse is not only a particular concern for women's welfare, but particular sources for research strategies. Feminist researchers have drawn, more or less consciously, on the work of grass-roots and professional women's organizations to develop inclusive procedures and less hierarchical structures (Freeman 1973, Leidner 1991, Strobel 1995). Feminists have written of many experiments in leveling hierarchies of power and control in research relations, and they continue to debate whether and when such leveling is possible and how much should be demanded of feminist researchers.

3. Feminists seek a methodology that will support research of value to women, leading to social change or action beneficial to women. This criterion for feminist research is mentioned in virtually every discussion; by implication, authors point to many kinds of change that could satisfy this call, from changing theory or bringing new topics into the discipline, to consciousness raising or decolonization (for the researcher, the reader, or participants in the research), to producing data that will stimulate or support political action or policy decisions. The concern with change, like the call for research that does no harm, is shared by researchers working in other critical traditions. What makes practice distinctively feminist is its relevance to change in women's lives or in the systems of social organization that control women. Reviewing accounts of change accomplished through participatory research studies, Patricia Maguire (1987) notes that inequities in the benefits of projects are often obscured by gender-neutral language. Researchers had reported, for example, that "villagers" had increased access to resources when closer inspection revealed that male villagers had been the primary beneficiaries and the women left out.

Accomplishing change through feminist research and assessing whether it has occurred are, of course, quite difficult, and relatively little writing addresses these problems. (For some notable exceptions, however, see accounts of feminist participatory research in Maguire 1987 and Mies 1983, 1991; of policy-oriented work in Spalter-Roth and Hartmann 1991; and of activist work in Gordon 1993.) Too often, I believe, the call for change functions as a slogan in writing on feminist methodology, and authors make assumptions about change without sufficient examination of their own implicit theories of social change.

Together, these criteria for feminist methodology provide the outline for a possible alternative to the distanced, distorting, and dispassionately objective procedures of much social research. Whether the goals implied in these criteria are fully achievable is debatable (Acker, Barry, and Esseveld 1983) but probably less important than whether they are useful in redirecting research practice to produce better knowledge. My intention in this section has been to claim a distinctiveness for feminist methodology without giving it a fixed definition: I mean to suggest that it must always have an open and "provisional" character (Mohanty 1991a:15), but that it is nonetheless a "strikingly cumulative" (Reinharz 1992:246) discourse, held together by core commitments to addressing particular problems in the standard practice of social research and by a common history of learning through activism that provides much of its energy and insight.

RECENT EMPHASES IN FEMINIST METHODOLOGY

The 1990s have been a period of energy and growth in feminist methodology. Discussions have ranged through technical, ethical, and representational issues to the fundamental questions of how and what researchers claim to know.

The Great Divide: Qualitative and Quantitative Approaches

Like outsiders to this body of writing, feminist methodologists themselves often rely on competing or simply unarticulated assumptions about what does (or should) hold this body of work together, and those working to develop feminist methodology sometimes seem to write at cross-purposes. This seems especially true in writing on feminist uses of "qualitative" and "quantitative" methods (see, for example, Cancian 1992, 1993; Risman, Sprague, and Howard 1993). Like scholars in the discipline at large, feminist methodologists sometimes have difficulty communicating across this rather artificial distinction.

Many feminist researchers suggest that qualitative methods fit especially well with feminist goals. They "give voice" to women respondents, allowing them to participate in determining the direction and focus of research. They also emphasize particularity over generalization, which seems likely to aid in correcting the ungrounded and undifferentiated "view from nowhere" fostered by many positivist approaches. Indeed, some feminist researchers who work with qualitative methods seem to claim that these methods are more feminist than others (Mies 1991, Cancian 1993, and Kasper 1994 are possible examples), and some autobiographical accounts (longer ones such as Reinharz 1979 as well as brief asides, as in Stacey 1988 or Gorelick 1989) fuel this notion by recounting frustrations with training in dominant methods and subsequent uses of qualitative approaches.

However, Joey Sprague and Mary Zimmerman (1993) suggest that feminists have made major contributions by finding concepts and practices that resist "dualisms," and they urge resistance to the qualitative-quantitative division. Similarly, Mary Maynard and June Purvis, editors of a recent British anthology (1994), decry the tendency to associate feminist research so strongly with qualitative tools. Implicitly invoking the importance of uncovering hidden experiences, Liz Kelly, Sheila Burton, and Linda Regan (1994) question the presumption that women who participate in research will be more likely to share sensitive material in face-to-face interviews than via less personal survey techniques. Lynn Weber Cannon, Elizabeth Higginbotham, and Marianne L. A. Leung (1988) point out that small-scale qualitative projects may be more likely than quantitative studies to reproduce race and class biases of the discipline by including only participants who are relatively available to researchers. Others emphasize the consequences of research in urging that feminists not give up quantitative methods and their positivist foundations. Those focusing on policy issues point out that "hard" data are often most convincing outside the university (Spalter-Roth and Hartmann 1991). And Uma Narayan (1989) points out, from the perspective of a nonwestern feminist, that positivism is not always a problem, and certainly not the only one, in research in nonwestern nations. Religion and cultural tradition often contribute to women's oppression, and positivist science can be a force for liberation (and this seems true for Western societies as well).

Still, research methods seem to be labeled feminist more often by researchers working in interpretive traditions of sociology, and it seems safe to say that there is relatively little writing about quantitative *method* (despite much quantitative research) that announces itself as feminist (Greenhalgh and Jiali Li [1995:602] note, for instance, that "the term *feminist demographer* remains an oxymoron"). Those working with survey techniques or doing secondary analysis of large data sets, though they may label their projects feminist, are more likely to stress that their methods are those of a rigorous and mostly conventional social science. Explicit discussion of how feminism might modify quantitative practice seems relatively difficult to find.

One common approach to feminist quantitative work, which might be characterized as a feminist empiricism (Harding 1986), involves correcting gender and other cultural biases in standard procedure. Christine Oppong's (1982) work on household studies in nonwestern societies and Margrit Eichler's handbook *Nonsexist Research Methods* (1988) serve as relatively early examples. Both authors point to the many ways that standard survey techniques build in unnoticed assumptions about gender and culture. Those working with survey data have begun to alter survey design and analytic procedures to lessen or eliminate these sources of bias. However, attention to sexism in research procedure probably often depends on the presence of feminists within research teams, where they are usually more likely than others to call attention to these biases. In addition, these refinements are typically discussed as technical responses to social changes, so that connections to feminist theorizing and activism are obscured. One recent exception is Michael D. Smith's (1994) discussion of feminist strategies for improving survey data on violence against women. Drawing from previous feminist studies of rape and violence (including, for example, Russell 1982, Hanmer and Saunders 1984, Radford 1987, Gordon and Riger 1989, Sessar 1990, Stanko 1990), Smith identifies six strategic modifications of standard survey techniques: these include broadly rather than narrowly defining violence, assessing lifetime prevalence rather than annual rates of violence, using multiple measures in order to increase the probability that women will report violence they have experienced, composing open rather than closed questions so respondents can report experiences in their own terms, conceptualizing violence as a complex and multidimensional phenomenon and analyzing it as such, and devoting the resources necessary to train effective interviewers. He notes that while these kinds of improvements have begun to appear in mainstream research on violence, they originated and have been most consistently implemented in feminist studies. Further, one can see that these strategic decisions about the conduct of research are driven by the call to assess women's experiences more accurately, as well as by a feminist perspective on possible barriers to that project.

Of course, quantitative research always involves interpretation, and many researchers bring feminist theoretical insights to bear on quantitative research design and findings (Risman 1993). Some have begun to write more explicitly about how they have used feminist interpretive frameworks. Roberta Spalter-Roth and Heidi I. Hartmann (1991), for example, argue that effective feminist policy research requires a feminist standpoint as well as conventional tools such as cost-benefit analysis. They reject "hegemonic views that see *only one* public interest" (p. 44, emphasis in original), and they adapt the tools of policy research to evaluate the costs and benefits of various policies for women. (See also Steinberg, as cited in Reinharz 1992:91–92.)

Many feminists advocate combining quantitative and qualitative tools, often through collaboration with other researchers. Several European scholars have written about feminist cross-national studies: Jan Windebank (1992) suggests combining qualitative case studies with data from national employment surveys, and Cynthia Cockburn (1992) reports on a coordinated series of studies on technological change and gender relations undertaken by feminists in ten European countries, which required that the participants take account of varying national histories of social research and different perspectives on the value of qualitative and quantitative approaches. Similarly, Jane Millar (1992) examines the advantages of working collaboratively on a European Commission-funded project on "solo women" and discusses how national cultures impeded efforts to standardize definitions and concerns.

Susan Greenhalgh and Jiali Li (1995) argue for combining demography with ethnography. In an examination of imbalanced sex ratios that point to generations of "missing girls" in several Chinese villages, they interpret demographic data through feminist analyses of reproductive politics, considering how the data reflect changing interpretations of official state policies as they were implemented in local settings. The authors leave "the critique of demographic methods and underlying epistemologies for the future" (p. 605); still, their work represents a powerful call to keep that critique on the agenda for feminist scholars. Greenhalgh and Jiali Li are reluctant to assign a cause for feminist "detachment" from demography, mentioning as possible reasons such benign possibilities as "distaste . . . distrust . . . or simply lack of relevant expertise and research experience" (pp. 601–602). But they also point out that the kind of critique so central to feminist method may have negative consequences for demographers, who need continuing access to large data sets controlled by nations and organizations that often seek to deflect criticism. These authors advocate collaboration on political as well as intellectual grounds; they suggest that feminists working in other traditions have much to contribute theoretically and often have "more political space" (p. 605) in which to offer critical interpretations of demographic findings.

One further possible bridge between the qualitative and quantitative "branches" of feminist methodology may lie in analyses of statistics as they are constructed and used in particular organizational settings.

Dorothy Smith (1990a) suggests examining statistics as textual parts of a "ruling apparatus" that coordinates social relations. She examines data on gender and mental illness, for example, not as evidence of "real" differences, but as pointers toward the management of gendered responses to stress through different social services (see also Waring 1988, Dixon-Mueller 1991, and Hill 1993 on statistical accounts of women's work). Several chapters in Liz Stanley's collection of research conducted at Manchester University (1990a) provide suggestive examples of work based on a similar strategy (Farran 1990, Pugh 1990, Stanley 1990b).

Pursuing these kinds of analyses in more systematic ways would require that feminists trained in either method let go of some prejudice and ignorance: qualitative researchers would need to develop more familiarity with survey and other kinds of quantitative data and greater expertise in reading them, and quantitative analysts would need to be willing to operate with greater skepticism toward data and an epistemology that would keep the construction of statistical data more firmly and consistently in view. While quantitative researchers are surely aware of these underpinnings of their data, the technical practices of that research community require at some point a suspension of discussion of these issues. Analyses that hold them in view offer possibilities for bringing feminist issues more fully into the quantitative traditions of the discipline.

Research Relations: Possibilities and Problems

Feminists have been attracted to interview and ethnographic research partly because these methods offer possibilities for direct interaction with participants. Because these methods have been so widely used, there is now a great deal of feminist writing that documents in increasing detail the various ways that women (and less frequently, men—see Stanko 1994) interact in field research situations. Much of the earlier writing was based on the idea that women's shared interests and concerns would provide resources for dismantling the hierarchies, fictions, and avoidances of research based on positivist frameworks; the argument was that women could talk together more freely and reciprocally, using shared experience as a resource for interpretation (e.g., Oakley 1981, DeVault 1990). More recent writing has provided correctives to early statements that may have mistakenly portrayed feminist research as "rather comfortable and cosy" (Maynard and Purvis 1994). Some researchers have critiqued the notion that women enjoy the advantages of "insiders" when they study other women: Catherine Kohler Riessman (1987) argues that "gender is not enough" to produce easy rapport, and Josephine Beoku-Betts (1994) shows that "Black is not enough" in a discussion of fieldwork among

Gullah women in the Sea Islands of the southeastern United States (see also Zavella 1993 on "insider dilemmas" in research with Chicana informants, Phoenix 1994, DeVault 1995). Diane Reay (1995) discusses "the fallacy of easy access," and Pamela Cotterill (1992) complains that the feminist literature celebrating woman-to-woman interviewing did not prepare her for difficult questions regarding the boundaries between research and friendship relations.

Writing on interview research and ethnography has also focused on ethical issues and the potential for misrepresentation. The close relations that are possible seem to pose heightened dangers of exploitation, which led Judith Stacey to ask, "Can there be a feminist ethnography?" (1988), and much writing has been focused on the "dilemmas" of feminist fieldwork (Wolf 1996). Reay and Cotterill both question the ethics of aggressively pursuing participation in interview research, and ethnographers are much concerned with "imbalances of power" (Scanlon 1993). Cotterill also discusses interviews conducted under very adverse conditions with respondents usually considered especially vulnerable (poor, single mothers), who seemed willing to participate, but lived in conditions of such difficulty that unusual persistence was required to complete interviews. She notes that one option would be to curtail these interviews, or eliminate women in such situations from the sample; her persistence in working with them reflects the feminist strategy of seeking out those who might otherwise be ignored.

These writings have certainly put to rest the myth of "hygienic research" (Stanley and Wise 1983/93:114–115) by discussing in some detail the complexity of face-to-face research encounters. Strategies for confronting these dilemmas have been developed at several levels, through revisions of practice, choices based on ethical considerations, and experiments with representation. At the level of fieldwork practice, for example, Rosalind Edwards (1990) argues for acknowledging racial differences quite explicitly in order to facilitate more honest disclosure, and others have advocated methods for reviewing data with informants in order to resolve—or highlight—disagreements and contradictions (Billson 1991, Personal Narratives Group 1989, Gluck and Patai 1991, Bauer 1993, Skeggs 1994). Some writers, emphasizing the moral dilemmas of the fieldworker's relative freedom and control, have suggested that feminist fieldwork should include special efforts to give something back to participants (Scanlon 1993), or strategies for working with local groups to make change (Park 1992, Gordon 1993). A. Lynn Bolles (1993) suggests that one valuable role for Western feminists working in other parts of the world is to support indigenous research. Some feminist researchers argue that representational questions pose fundamental moral/ethical dilemmas; they seek solutions in writing strategies (Opie 1992; Rofel 1993; Wheatley 1994a,b, and response by Stacey 1994).

Feminists have written extensively on these dilemmas as they arise in face-to-face research methods, but of course concerns about exploitation and misrepresentation come into play whenever data come from human informants, no matter how distant the process of collection may be from analysis. Some wonder if feminists have overemphasized potential problems of power, producing "excessive demands" (Reinharz 1993) on feminist researchers. The focus on problems of exploitation has produced an association of qualitative feminist methodology with special ethical demands that sometimes seems to obscure other aspects of its distinctiveness. Although these discussions have been lively and productive, one risk is that they may require a moral purity in feminist (or perhaps in women's) qualitative research that is simply unattainable, while leaving similar questions relatively unnoticed in discussions of other research traditions.

Knowledge Claims: Feminist Epistemology

Although the initial feminist critique focused primarily on bias in the application of dominant methods, philosopher Sandra Harding (1986) contends that even this "empiricist" critique tends to subvert the notion of objectivity, since it points to knowledge as social product, and to influences of the knower on what is produced. Moving beyond this kind of critique has brought new questions. If the ground for feminist work is not the distance and dispassion of "objectivity," what will be the basis for legitimate authority? Part of the answer has been to embrace the apparent opposite, subjectivity, and to center inquiry around women's experiences and feelings (Jaggar 1989). However, the turn to subjectivity has been only part of the answer feminists have begun to develop (though it is sometimes mistakenly taken as the defining characteristic of feminist method). As Loraine Gelsthorpe (1992) points out, feminist methodologists have refused to choose between subjectivity and analytic rigor; they seek methods that can incorporate, or at least do not deny, subjectivity. Thus, for those working on feminist methodologies, theorizing links between experience and knowledge has been a central concern.

Many sociologists have taken up some version of what have come to be called "standpoint" approaches (e.g., Reinharz 1983, Stanley and Wise 1983/93, Smith 1987, Collins 1990). Dorothy Smith's is probably the most widely known and fully developed version of this project within sociology. Her writings over two decades (collected in Smith 1987, 1990a,b) record a long struggle to change a positivist sociology that is organized not only by men's concerns but by the demands of "ruling." (Ramazanoglu 1989 recounts a similar struggle.) Smith's aim is not merely to uncover or give testimony about experience but to make a place for it in analysis that will be focused differently and serve different interests. The feminist sociologist, in her formulation, must refuse to put aside her experience and, indeed, must make her bodily existence and activity a "starting point" for inquiry. From this beginning, the inquiry points toward an analysis of the social context for experience, the relations of ruling that organize daily life and connect all members of a society in systematic interactions.

Smith developed the approach primarily through examples from her life as a single mother, showing how she moved between the grounded activities of raising children and the abstractions of her academic work. She suggests that most women live some version of this movement between particularity and the extra-local projects of management and administration, whether through work as caregivers or in other subordinate positions in the social division of labor. Further, she argues that these positions—where social life is being "put together" from actual, embodied activity—provide a point of entry to investigation that is superior to the starting points derived from abstract theorizing. The argument is not that women know better by virtue of occupying these positions, but that the work accomplished there must be part of any adequate account of social organization.

Many others have taken up the notion of attention to women's experience (though not all have followed Smith's call to look beyond experience in the analysis), and this work has stimulated much discussion of the concepts of "standpoint" and "experience." The notion that some positions provide a "better view" of social organization or a preferred site from which to "start thought" (Harding 1991) seems to accord some knowers an "epistemic privilege" associated with their identities. However, critics point out that identity is not automatically associated with superior insight, and the sociological literature on insider-outsider dynamics certainly calls into question any easy assumption about the consequences for research of particular identities, which are always relative, crosscut by other differences, and often situational and contingent. Another view emphasizes how taking a standpoint invokes the particular experiences associated with some location in society; critics suggest that the idea of "women's standpoint" puts in place an account of experience that fits for only some women. They argue that analyses like Smith's risk emphasizing concerns of white (Collins 1992) or heterosexual women (Ingraham 1994). Smith responds (1992) that theorizing standpoint in either of these ways misses her intention: Rather than calling up a particular identity or set of experiences, the injunction to start inquiry from women's experience is a way of pointing the feminist researcher to material sites where people live their lives, so that "anyone's experience, however various, could become a beginning-place [for] inquiry" (90).

The notion of "women's experience" has been productive for feminist scholars, but it has also become a richly contested concept. Some critics of the emphasis on experience—often those feminists working in quantitative or marxist traditions—point out that individual views are always partial and often distorted by ideology, so that a woman's own testimony may simply reflect the biases of the larger society (Gorelick 1991, Risman 1993). Those influenced by poststructuralist theory argue further that experience always arises in language and discourse (Scott 1991), and that women's testimony will always be marked by language and desire (Clough 1993a; see also reply by Smith 1993 and Clough's 1993b response).

Those working empirically with approaches that make room for experience address these points in several different ways. Smith contends that women's "bifurcated" consciousness encompasses both the knowledge required to participate in social relations, organized largely through ideological processes, and the often incompletely articulated knowledge that comes from activity. She calls for explicit analysis of how women's activities are connected to the interests of "ruling" (especially Smith 1990a), and how the ideological processes of ruling shape, without fully determining, women's accounts of their experience; studies following Smith in this line of work are collected in Campbell and Manicom (1995). Frigga Haug and her colleagues (1987) use "memory-work"—the collective, critical analysis of written memories—to investigate the social and ideological underpinnings of subjectivity in a somewhat different way, more focused on the societal construction of gendered selves. Patricia Hill Collins (1990) develops an epistemology that builds on processes of knowledge creation in African American communities, where dialogue, caring, and personal accountability are central. She emphasizes that perspectives are always located and claims only a "partial truth" for the knowledge produced from a particular standpoint; she points out that knowledge that is admittedly partial is more trustworthy than partial knowledge presented as generally true. Liz Stanley and Sue Wise (1983/93) also suggest that different standpoints will produce different knowledges, and they accept as a consequence that knowledge claims will be based on a "fractured foundationalism."

These different stances among researchers working in different ways with women's perspectives point to varying epistemological ambitions across the range of feminist methodology. Like other scholars, feminists are considering the consequences for empirical work of the postmodern challenge to objectivity and a science based on a single narrative. Some have embraced a postmodern position that welcomes multiple versions of truth, and these have begun to write about alternative bases for assessing knowledge claims (Richardson 1993, Lather 1993). Others hold that empirical investigation should provide accurate accounts of a social world that can be known in common and should be assessed on that basis. (These include feminist empiricists like Risman 1993; those following Smith 1992, whose investigations focus on "actual" social practices; and some who seek an intermediate position.)

Kum-Kum Bhavnani (1993) suggests that researchers can strive for what she calls "feminist objectivity." She draws on the writings of feminist philosophers of science who propose replacing traditional constructions of objectivity with more durable claims to "situated knowledge" (Haraway 1988) or a "strong" (Harding 1992) or "dynamic" (Keller 1985) objectivity. Moving the suggestions of these writers to the terrain of empirical work, Bhavnani proposes that the process of producing knowledge should always be visible; the feminist researcher should find ways of recognizing and revealing to audiences the micropolitics of the research situation and should take responsibility for representing those who participate in ways that do not reproduce harmful stereotypes. In addition, researchers claiming feminist objectivity must be attentive to differences and to the limits of their knowledge claims. Echoing some of these themes, Collins (1990) proposes that a feminist Afro-centric epistemology would measure knowledge against concrete experience, test it through dialogue, and judge it in relation to an ethic of personal accountability.

Such emerging feminist formulations repudiate the traditional version of objectivity that requires a separation of knower and known. Out of skepticism for accounts that seem to have no grounded basis (but turn out to be anchored to dominant interests), feminists suggest making the researcher visible in any product of research. This call for visibility involves viewing the self, in Susan Krieger's (1991) terms, as resource rather than contaminant. Precisely how to use and locate the self most effectively remains unresolved. However, the demand for accountability can be seen as the rationale for experiments with autobiographical and dialogic modes of presenting research (e.g., Orr 1990, Kondo 1990, Ellis 1993, Linden 1993) as well as a thread that connects them to projects that are more traditional in format. (Even the feminist practice of identifying authors by their full names can be understood as a technical modification that helps to make particular researchers more "visible" in feminist texts.)

Another theme emerging in feminist epistemology involves shifting focus from individual knowers to the perspectives of groups or communities. This shift in focus should perhaps represent a reminder rather than a new idea, since the "experience" so valued in early feminist consciousness raising was in fact a collective construction. The reminder has come from feminists too often ignored in the feminisms that are most visible; this work is discussed below.

Shifting the Center (Again)

It is ironic (and costly; see Baca Zinn et al. 1986) that writing on feminist methodology has so rarely incorporated the perspectives of women from underrepresented groups and nations (and their male allies), even as these writers have become more central to feminist theory. Though attention to racial/ethnic differences and joint strategies for combating racism have had a continuing presence in second-wave activism and writing (Moraga and Anzaldúa 1981; Bulkin, Pratt, and Smith 1984), these efforts have typically been contentious and difficult, and contributions of women from underrepresented groups have too often been ignored or appropriated. Women from these groups continue to mount pointed challenges to emerging orthodoxies that ignore their perspectives.

From the beginning of the women's studies movement, African American feminist scholars have had a keen sense of the need to establish an autonomous presence. A landmark anthology (Hull, Bell Scott, and Smith 1982) stressed the precarious position of Black women in society and higher education, the knowledge gaps that result from their absence, and the importance of knowledge creation in Black women's communities; these themes continue to be central to "women of color" or "third world" feminism. The editors predicted that Black women's studies would "come into its own" in the 1980s but noted that this movement was only beginning. They saw "far too few courses and far too few Black women employed in institutions" (pp. xxvii–xxviii) and commented that "the majority of white women teachers and administrators have barely begun the process of self-examination which must precede productive action to change this situation" (p. xxviii).

The 1980s were indeed a time of putting these issues on the agenda. White feminists like Elizabeth Spelman (1988) wrote compellingly on the problems of false universalization; theorists began re-envisioning the concepts and strategies of their feminisms (e.g., Harding 1991); and feminists writing on research relations became more attentive to ethnic and cultural differences (as discussed above). More importantly, new writing from third world feminism combined work by social scientists and creative writers to offer new conceptualizations of identity, building more fundamental critiques of the disciplines and modeling evocative writing strategies (Anzaldúa 1990a; Mohanty, Russo, and Torres 1991). Social scientists began to consider strategies for empirical investigation that could be aligned with these perspectives.

Patricia Hill Collins's *Black Feminist Thought* (1990), while usually considered a work of theory, also treats methodological issues; the book concludes with an extended discussion of epistemology, and the entire text illustrates an approach to knowledge production that draws from and builds upon the "subjugated knowledge" shared within communities of African American women. Chela Sandoval (1991) also draws lessons from the strategies of particular communities—the activist communities of what she calls "U.S. third world feminism"—and finds in the everyday resistances of women of color a "method" (applicable beyond formal research, but certainly relevant there) of differential, oppositional consciousness. Arguing that dominant feminisms have been incapable of incorporating the lessons of U.S. third world feminism, she advocates a "self-conscious mobility" that would allow feminists to enact opposition more fluidly, "between and among" possible identities and tactics (p. 14). While adopting some strategies like those of Collins, Sandoval also emphasizes multiple identities and coalition across cultural communities.

Himani Bannerji (1995) extends marxist and feminist "standpoint" methods, arguing that gender, race/ethnicity, and nationality are always part of the organization of social activity, so that any adequate feminism (or marxism or antiracism) must take account of the simultaneity of social relations that more traditional accounts have tried to separate analytically. Without naturalizing ethnic differences, she attends to embodiedness, whether writing about her own experience of teaching in Canadian universities or about the sexual harassment of a Black woman working in a Canadian factory, analyzed as the product of a pervasive "racist sexism" woven into economic relations.

Chandra Talpede Mohanty (1991a,b), drawing on the study of colonialism and its legacy, seeks a social science that will contribute to the worldwide project of decolonization. She emphasizes multiple levels of work: consciousness raising (of both researcher and others), a reformulation of disciplines that have supported the colonial enterprise, and empirical investigations that reconstruct understandings of women's histories and contexts. Like Bannerji, she envisions a social science that encompasses the daily activities of third world women as well as the ruling relations that construct their oppression, and like Bannerji, she draws on the work of Dorothy Smith, suggesting that Smith's attention to "relations of ruling" may be especially useful in the investigation of colonial and postcolonial social organization.

Mohanty also begins to rework issues of consciousness, identity, and writing, noting that "the very practice of remembering and rewriting leads to the formation of politicized consciousness" (p. 34). Though she links this statement to the legacy of feminist consciousness raising, she also suggests that the texts of third world women challenge the "individualist subject" of much feminist writing. She argues that the feminism of women of color calls for rethinking the idea that "the personal is political," not because starting from experience is wrong, but because of the richness of collective rather than individual stories of agency and resistance. Drawing from Gloria Anzaldúa (1990b) and echoing Sandoval's notion of differential consciousness, she points to the strategic value of a multiple or "mestiza" consciousness, attentive to borders and negotiations through multiple locations.

This kind of methodological innovation is related to philosopher Maria Lugones's (1987) use of the term " 'world'-travelling" to refer to the ability to move across social boundaries that seems so central to the experiences of Black and third world women (and so foreign to the overprivileged). Lugones inspired political scientist Christine Sylvester's (1995) discussion of Western encounters with African feminisms. However, these provocative discussions of fluid and shifting identities sit somewhat uneasily alongside the analyses of Collins and Bannerji, whose methods emphasize the obduracy of social categories associated with ethnicity and their significance for people's recruitment into social relations.

These writers are rarely included in discussions of "feminist methodology," but I believe they point to the next stages in the project of building more adequate research practices. Their writings, and the roots of these writings in communities of resistance, lend some credence to notions of epistemic privilege—the idea that people in subordinated locations have access to perspectives that others miss. On the other hand, these writings begin to "open up" the histories, experiences, and self-representations of such communities, so that it seems more possible, and urgent, for all knowers to attend to the perspectives of others. These writers challenge scholars to think more carefully about what is at stake in how one gains such knowledge, and how it is used.

It may be useful, especially for academic feminists, to consider how much useful writing on "difference" has emerged from a lesbian-feminist women's community, and to recover these texts as part of our canon (e.g., Moraga and Anzaldúa 1981; Reagon 1983; Bulkin, Pratt, and Smith 1984; Lorde 1981). Lesbian activists, with a history of building community in a hostile context, have been pushed in immediate and concrete ways to confront culture- and class-based obstacles to sisterhood. Thus, writings that emerge from these contexts often have the grounded clarity that can come only from actual face-to-face struggle considered too important to abandon—struggle upon which survival depends.

Finally, it may be worth noting that the gender-related isolation and stress of doing research have been discussed in the writing of some non-European feminists (Hull, Bell Scott, and Smith 1982; Ramazanoglu 1989). Annecka Marshall (1994) writes poignantly of the pain and isolation she felt as a student and scholar in sexist-racist institutional contexts, giving an account of serious health problems that she tried to ignore but ultimately had to resolve before continuing her work. I do not mean to suggest that these kinds of problems are suffered only by third world feminists, but to highlight the fact that institutional settings which may have become increasingly comfortable for white feminist academics continue to be painfully alienating for others, and to suggest that these different positionings continue to shape the work produced by feminist scholars.

CONCLUSION: FEMINISM AND SOCIOLOGY

I close, in keeping with the sociology of knowledge approach I have adopted throughout this chapter, with a brief discussion of the connections through which feminist sociologists construct and sustain a discourse on feminist methodology. Strategizing about research practice has been strongly connected to feminist theory and necessarily so: Feminist understandings drive methodological innovation. Still, theory does not translate unproblematically to the questions of empirical investigation, and those working on methodology must shape the insights of theorists to their own needs. Feminist sociologists also value connections to feminists in other disciplines, whose related projects can often provide models for experimentation. Working across disciplines also helps to reveal disciplinary power and thus aids in strategizing about how to use it well and avoid its pitfalls. Feminist scholars are always more or less directly linked to activism, by virtue of their origins, but maintaining such connections requires continuing attention; sustaining connections to policymakers who might use feminist research requires another kind of attention.

Connections to our own disciplines are among the most vexed questions that occupy feminist scholars. Some argue convincingly for a strategic "disloyalty to the disciplines" (Stacey 1995), while others advocate strategic uses of disciplinary authority and legitimacy (Risman 1993). My approach in this essay relies on (and attempts to contribute to) a sense of distinctiveness in feminist sociological practice, and a commitment to articulating the value of disciplinary traditions. Paradoxically, but not for the first time, sociological approaches have provided tools for unmasking their own coercive power. Though feminists are in struggle with the discipline, it is the struggle of committed participants.

3 Institutional Ethnography

A Strategy for Feminist Inquiry

I had yet to understand the extent to which I identified with men, used their eyes.
I was really sliced in two.

Sheila Rowbotham (cited in Smith 1987:52)

What does it mean when the tools of a racist patriarchy are used to examine that
same patriarchy? It means that only the most narrow perimeters of change are
possible.

Audre Lorde (1981:98)

FEMINIST SCHOLARS weave together feminist ideas and existing
traditions of inquiry, using theories and methods with histories outside of
feminist thought. These traditions provide resources for feminist work,
but they require modification: they might be thought of as tools we grab
hold of, wrestle into more congenial forms, and use in ways that are often
anticonventional. Observing and learning from this kind of improvisa-
tion, examining and articulating our sometimes initially fumbling strategic choices and their consequences, we build new modes of investigation
more suited to our purposes.

Within sociology, one line of theorizing and methodological improvi-
sation has produced an approach labeled "institutional ethnography" (for
other accounts of the approach, see Campbell 1998, Grahame 1998). This
research approach has grown from the theoretical work and teaching of
Dorothy E. Smith, an influential second-wave feminist scholar who developed a strong critique of the ideological character of standard practice in
sociological research. Smith's critique, laid out in a series of theoretical
articles (collected in D. Smith 1987, 1990a, 1998), focuses on the peculiar process of objectification built into the standard practice of social research. She came to this critique through reflection on her training as a
sociologist: by noticing the peculiar feeling produced by going "out" to
the field and bringing "back" data—a strange separation between "where
I am" and "what I will examine." This outward gaze fosters the kind of
objectification that early feminists were also noticing in considering how

women learn to see from outside themselves (Rowbotham 1973). As a critique of sociology, the important point is not objectification in itself, but the relation it assumes and promotes between sociological research and ruling processes. Standard practice in sociology makes knowledge *of*, knowledge that fixes and pacifies its objects in order to bring them into the purview of ruling regimes. Smith wanted a practice of sociology that would produce knowledge *for* women (or people; Smith 1998)—knowledge that helps its producer understand her social world from her own location (D. Smith 1987, 1994).

Smith's critique is especially powerful, I believe, because it is deeply grounded in the intellectual traditions of sociology; it is the "intimate" critique of one who has learned these lessons well, lived them, puzzled over their contradictions for years, and eventually (with the emergence of the women's movement), found a language in which to articulate both problems and possibilities. The alternative strategy she offers is also tied to sociological traditions—in one sense, the question she asks in all of her writing is how the powerful tools of sociological analysis might be used effectively by "outsiders," for our own purposes rather than those of a governing regime.

SITUATING INSTITUTIONAL ETHNOGRAPHY

As a form of ethnographic inquiry, institutional ethnography is tied to a fieldwork tradition in social science. Fieldwork relies on several core commitments: to spend time in the field, to look closely and relatively unobtrusively, and to develop analyses that aim for faithfulness to what is actually happening in particular local settings. Fieldworkers have specialized in groups on the margins, "outsiders" whose views might not otherwise appear in the discourses of social scientists, and their sympathetic "insider" portraits of these groups have provided audiences in more normative locations with deeper understandings of experiences foreign to them. To the extent that such portraits make "sense" of these communities, they challenge prevailing ideologies and illuminate the contexts for marginal lives.

The rhetoric of the classical fieldwork tradition is straightforward: Just go, look, and write it all down; if findings emerge from the data, they will be properly "grounded." However, the feminist critique of the fieldwork tradition ("Where are the women?")—as well as critique from other groups ("What about race?")—insists that "looking" is not so straightforward after all. Feminists working within the fieldwork tradition have pointed out that the corpus of fieldwork studies produced before women entered the field in large numbers focused on men's lives and contexts. Men in the field, "just looking," had mostly managed not to see women;

white researchers who found themselves in predominantly white settings too often easily assumed that race was irrelevant.

The ostensibly straightforward "looking" of the fieldwork tradition poses another problem as well, which Smith identified as a problem of direction and purpose. The notion of "going out" into the field—so central to fieldwork rhetoric—captures this difficulty. The sociologist is to seek out "others," package their realities as "data," and bring those data "back" to a location where knowledge is mobilized in projects of administration and ruling. (The quintessential examples are the early ethnographies tied to colonial projects and, "at home," to urban poverty; see Wax 1971 for a useful history.) Knowledge produced in such fieldwork projects is useful, from the point of view of the powerful, because it provides a window into the margins. Smith's critique envisions another kind of analysis, an investigation in which the direction of looking is reversed. The institutional ethnographer takes up a point of view in a marginal location; she "looks" carefully and relatively unobtrusively, like any fieldworker, but she looks from the margins inward—toward centers of power and administration—searching to explicate the contingencies of ruling that shape local contexts. Through this conscious reorientation, she aims to produce knowledge for, rather than about, those in some particular location. Her analysis is an "insider's critique" (Smith 1990a : 204), rooted in but extending beyond a local setting.

The aim of institutional ethnography is to discover the social relations that organize a particular setting; in order to accomplish this goal, institutional ethnographers draw on theoretical tools from several sociological traditions. Institutional ethnographers attend to the details of interaction, borrowing from ethnomethodologists a precise and often microscopic analysis of how interactions are coordinated among members of a setting (Garfinkel 1967, Zimmerman 1974). Ethnomethodological approaches are useful for seeing and understanding, within a particular complex of relations, how social activity is produced from the "artful" moment-to-moment moves through which people sustain and coordinate collective activity.

The institutional ethnographic analysis of a social setting is also informed by marxist tools of analysis—not an abstract neomarxism, but the fundamental tool of Marx's method, historical materialism (Smith 1977, 1987). The analyst considers how the settings of interest have emerged from a specific history—how it has happened that things are organized this way rather than some other. This commitment does not necessarily mean that there is history written explicitly into an institutional ethnography. It means that, in this approach, settings cannot be treated as just "there." Rather, the social relations we find in a particular place represent moments that are created through the unfolding of social relations in time.

In addition, institutional ethnography can be situated as one tributary in the flood of poststructuralist scholarship that has developed since the 1970s (Smith 1997). There are important connections to Foucault in Smith's claim that a central feature of ruling in our society is its reliance on objectified forms of knowledge, organized in assemblages of texts. But in distinction to many Foucauldian theorists of ideology, institutional ethnographers are always interested in texts in use (Smith 1992). They examine processes of ruling in the production of texts in specific workplaces (such as schools, health care and criminal justice settings, government agencies, newsrooms, professional offices, and so on) and in the uses of texts (such as official records and reports) that organize people's activities in various settings (Smith 1996, Campbell and Manicom 1995).

These powerful tools for analysis—ethnomethodology, marxism, and a poststructuralist attention to textual process—are ingredients of institutional ethnography. But they are combined in distinctive ways.

AIMS AND UNDERPINNINGS

In teaching about institutional ethnography, Smith often speaks of her approach as a project of determining "how it's put together," a colloquial phrase that refers to the extralocal organization of everyday experience. The question is, "What's actually happening?" in a material, socially organized world—the world that all human actors inhabit together. These phrases provide a shorthand for a kind of analysis that links a local view of "how it works" to the coordinative processes that make it so. Institutional ethnography is always concerned with institutional connections, with relations across and among various sites of activity, and with the coordination of these sites via ruling regimes and their texts. For example, the traditional view in sociology sees the family household as a private, interior kind of place—a place of individual intention and activity. By contrast, an institutional ethnographic view proposes that household life is connected to multiple institutions outside—to institutions that organize paid work, education, health care, leisure activity, and the production and distribution of commodities. The point is not that these institutions determine what happens in family settings, in some heavy-handed and unitary way. Rather, these institutional sites (and the discourses organizing them) are treated as the terrain on which members of family groups must operate outside their homes. Thus, members of family groups organize home life (or don't) in relation to these other institutions, and the ways that their activities fit with those sites (or don't) have consequences for their family lives (DeVault 1991, Griffith 1995).

The emphasis on connectedness is key to understanding the institutional ethnographic ontology and epistemology, which combines a materialist foundation with a recognition of multiple views (Smith 1992, 1997). Unlike some postmodern formulations that locate the social entirely in discourse, institutional ethnographic analysis assumes an actual, material world. It also refuses any single view or narrative; the world "out there" looks quite different from different locations. Multiple views can be connected because of the places and interactions that bring people together from their different locations. Here, I do not mean "bring together" in a feeling sense, but very literally—as when a social worker travels to her job at a Headstart program in a poor neighborhood, when a waitress serves a business lunch in a downtown restaurant, or when a middle-aged male employee comes into my university office to empty the trash. The concreteness of these examples—the particularity they suggest—is meant to work as a kind of touchstone: this specificity is essential to the analysis and must remain in view in the institutional ethnographer's account.

One of Smith's metaphors for this kind of connection points to a distinction between "flat" theoretical models and the dimensional depth of the cube. If the sociologist's observations are visualized as points on the page, they could be organized in flat, two-dimensional groupings, or connected so as to define a single, three-dimensional object. One model produces a set of categories, useful for sorting and labeling people and groups (as, for example, middle-class, working-class, etc.). The other produces, suddenly, the coherence of the cube: a view of a system. Such an analysis makes visible an ensemble of related activities that produce the different experiences of various locations (see Figure 1, adapted from Smith 1987: 130–135). The metaphor of the cube is useful, but it can be misleading if it gives the impression of a static, unchanging social world—always, the same cube. In fact, the social relations structuring the "actual world" of interest to institutional ethnographers are constantly changing; as a result, analyses can never be settled or finished, but instead are thought of as "open at the edges"—always leading to new questions and projects.

Some feminists have been developing the idea of a "feminist"—or in Sandra Harding's terms, "strong"—version of objectivity (Keller 1985, Harding 1992, Bhavnani 1993), and the "cube" idea provides a basis for this sort of claim. When analysts encounter varying perspectives, or different views, they can recognize that these are still different views of a single, organized whole. The multiple narratives arising from different locations are important and interesting. And the idea that one can produce "objective" knowledge does not mean trying to resolve those differences, but looking for the connections that hold the thing together. In pursuing this kind of claim to objectivity, it is essential to remember that the researcher

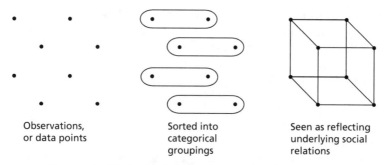

| Observations, or data points | Sorted into categorical groupings | Seen as reflecting underlying social relations |

FIGURE 1: Methods of connecting empirical observations
(Adapted from Smith 1987, Figs. 3.2–3.4)

can never operate from outside the "cube," viewing it from a distance. The analyst is connected as well, and sustaining any kind of knowledge claim should involve naming her place in these social relations.

INSTITUTIONAL ETHNOGRAPHY AND SOCIAL CHANGE

Research in the classic fieldwork tradition, like institutional ethnography, is concerned with a material world and committed to faithful attention to the activities of that world. Those commitments have allowed many qualitative researchers to make contributions to a critical sociology. However, ethnographic work in sociology has also been absorbed by a discipline that manages it in very powerful ways. Many of the powerful works of this tradition have political sources outside the discipline. But when ethnographic work is driven by the discipline, it tends to fragment the social world, serving up data in conceptual packages that too often lose their critical edge. People's lives are processed into instances of "mental illness" or "social support," for example, in ways that too often obscure the social relations of these activities. By contrast, institutional ethnography insists on a firm ground in a practical world as the source and motive for investigation. Questions are taken not from the categories and conventions of a disciplinary discourse, as in some other critical approaches,[1] but from the everyday puzzles of particular people living their work and household lives.

Such investigations are meant to point toward social transformation, but not through analysis alone. The account produced is not a proclamation of injustice or a call to arms; instead, it is organized to serve as a useful resource for groups engaged in efforts at change. In the institutional ethnographic formulation, "how it works" is a technical matter; thus, the often apparently mundane details of social organization are of interest. Explication is not a matter of exposing a grand structure of oppression, but of making visible the dailiness of practice within that structure, and people's various attempts to navigate through regimes of control.

The notion of "ruling regimes" conveys, in a general way, the expectation that institutional practices will be shaped by the logics of capitalist patriarchy. But one also expects contradictions, slippages, openings, and windows of possibility as regimes transform over time and accommodate new forms of accumulation and resistance. What the institutional ethnographer has to contribute, in this continually transforming terrain, is something like a map—not a definitive account, but the best available map at the moment. Such an account is meant to chart the specific practices that "operate" systems of oppression, and thus ought to be useful for activist groups deciding on strategies for change.

Two exemplary research efforts help to illustrate these dynamics. George Smith (1990) conducted two institutional ethnographic inquiries while working as a gay rights activist in Toronto. Both studies were motivated by relatively immediate political problems: one by a police crackdown on gay men's gathering places and the other by gaps in access to services for people living with AIDS. In both cases, some activists attributed these problems to a generalized homophobia; such an analysis suggests primarily educational strategies. Smith's investigations of both cases pointed toward more technical levers for change. He argued that changing provincial law would have more reliable effects on police behavior than diversity training, and that increasing access to AIDS services would require revisions in provincial systems for service delivery. His analyses were not intended to provide a complete picture of some general phenomenon—"attitudes toward homosexuality in Ontario," for instance. Instead, he investigated narrower questions of more immediate import for the activist work of which he was a part.

Marie Campbell's (1998) investigations of nursing administration in Victoria, Canada, illustrate how an institutional ethnographer who is not situated within an activist movement might still operate as a resource for groups facing these kinds of practical puzzles. Her investigations explore the effects of managerial regimes on the working lives of front-line nursing staff. Like George Smith's, her analyses examine in fine-grained detail how particular systems of record-keeping and administration shape the experiences of those they manage. Considering how various actors within the nursing home—managers, accountants, supervisors, and front-line staff—are connected, Campbell examines the effects of a new "total quality" management regime. By following a single decision—to substitute disposable for cloth incontinence diapers—she shows how nursing assistants are brought to substitute fiscal considerations for their everyday working knowledge. And by tracing the consequences of these changes—diapers that need changing more frequently, and administrative complaints about using too many of these supplies—she explains why nurses are busier and overstressed, and residents seem less happy with the care they receive. Such analyses might help nurses address these kinds of concerns, either in management meetings or more generally through labor organization and negotiation.

The institutional ethnographic approach to social change assumes a division of labor between scholars and activists—or at least a distinction between moments of inquiry and activism. Dorothy Smith suggests that researchers need relatively specialized skills and must devote more sustained attention to any investigation than is usually practical for front-line activists. Conversely, using research results effectively to promote change requires the pragmatic evaluative and strategic skills of activism, honed through more daily participation in front-line work than most researchers can manage. While some individuals, like George Smith, find ways to combine these roles, the idea is to make room for various kinds of partnerships. These comments point to a final element of institutional ethnographic investigation: to be fully realized, such inquiries should be conducted with an eye to their use by specific groups.

CODA

My epigraph recalls the words of Audre Lorde—from a moment in October 1979—that continue to warn feminists to be conscious of the tools we wield in attempts to make change. Speaking at an academic conference—as the token Black lesbian panelist—Lorde pointed to absences in the conference. The absence of lesbian consciousness, of Black women's knowledge, of the concerns of poor and third world women, she pointed out, made it impossible for women to work together, creatively, toward "new ways to actively 'be' in the world" (Lorde 1981:99). Explaining her point, Lorde called on the words of a white European feminist predecessor, Simone DeBeauvoir: "It is in the knowledge of the genuine conditions of our lives that we must draw our strength to live and our reasons for acting." But she quickly added: "Racism and homophobia are real conditions of all of our lives" (p. 101).

The dynamic of borrowing and extending—picking up tools and reshaping them, testing their malleability and observing their performance, noting their problems and making corrections—is the essential dynamic of research as resistance. I mean to suggest (following Dorothy Smith's own insistence on the point) that institutional ethnography is a research tool in the making. It is a tool built from critique and one that aims to make knowledge from "the genuine conditions of our lives." It is also a tool to try out and extend, revising as we explore in fuller detail the cross-cutting oppressions of multiple and shifting relations of power.

III. EXCAVATION

FEMINIST SCHOLARSHIP has emphasized the recovery of unrecognized, distorted, and suppressed aspects of women's work and experience. It has often dealt with emergent topics—housework, sexual harassment, reproductive politics—that required "excavation" and elaboration before analysis could even begin. Thus, as feminist research has accumulated, feminist scholars have developed a repertoire of strategies for attending to neglected experiences and dimensions of social life. My aim in this section is to articulate one such approach. While the idea of focusing on absences and gaps may sound somewhat mystical—like a kind of "intuition"—it is actually founded on collective understandings and habits of thought that feminists have developed through discussion and analysis.

The rebirth of feminism in the 1960s was a process founded on this kind of discovery. Betty Friedan's book about middle-class housewives, *The Feminine Mystique* (1963), for example, identified and explored a "problem with no name." Radical women gathered in consciousness-raising groups; as they told stories of subordination in left-wing activities, they began to see a web of social control defining and limiting their roles and called it "sexism." As these ideas and activities coalesced into an organized social movement, feminists began to question the absence of women in historical records. Searching for predecessors, they discovered generations of "forgotten" women, and they began to see how easily women and their achievements could disappear from view. All of these activities led women to reevaluate their relationships as well, and the new lenses through which feminists saw one another sometimes brought previously hidden lesbian lives into view.

The term "excavation"—used to point to a research goal—is meant to capture this process of uncovering and articulating what has been hidden or unacknowledged and the sense of discovery that accompanies that process. It refers to a kind of investigation that begins with what can be seen and heard but holds in mind a sense that there is more to find—like the archeologist's knowledge that any bone or fragment of pottery, for instance, points toward a complete organism or object. Investigation of this sort is a matter of uncovering evidentiary artifacts, studying them with respect, and working to understand how they illuminate and extend what is already known.

The essays in this section treat women's talk as artifactual and develop strategies for analyzing interview data so as to reveal meanings that may not be readily apparent. This method of working with interview data has sprung from two sources. I have relied in part on the understandings of talk developed by ethnomethodological sociologists (Garfinkel 1967, Psathas 1995). These analysts emphasize the exquisitely organized character of talk: the delicate coordination of sound, movement, and timing that allows conversation to go forward. Speakers take turns, for example; they nod recognition and understanding; listeners "fill in" the unspoken "et cetera" needed to make sense of any utterance. Conversation is structured through shared practices that are "seen but unnoticed," known and continually in use even though they are unarticulated. (Indeed, the attempt to watch oneself using these practices often causes conversation to break down.) This view of talk allows the analyst to see the details of interview data as artifacts offering clues toward analyses of experience and interaction.

The second source for this work has been my feminist-inspired conviction that women's talk holds meanings worth discovering, and my awareness of how easily those meanings could be missed. The various discoveries of feminism—of powerful but unnamed social processes, of predecessors in every field, and of an earlier women's movement that faded from view—combine to point to a world only partially visible in the more familiar accounts of powerful men. As feminists share these discoveries, we become familiar with the social processes of exclusion and marginalization that can obscure women's experiences, and we gain confidence that there is more to be seen. As I worked with women's talk, I became increasingly reluctant to dismiss any utterance as trivial or, in the classically sexist formulation, as "chitchat" or "gossip." I had learned from other feminist scholars to recognize such judgments and labels as mechanisms of controlling women and their contributions to public discourse. This view also suggests that speakers with limited power and access to public discourse will use other spaces for expression and that they might share unspoken understandings that rarely find clear and explicit expression. These feminist awarenesses motivated my analyses of interview talk.

The sense of possibility carried in the term "excavation" is only a beginning. The word serves as a stimulus and reminder, guiding the detailed analytic work that follows. The approach is effective because it relies on a coherent view of the social world; that is, it arises from an analysis of oppression, operating through social processes that connect those marginalized in various ways to those with the power to exclude and ignore them. Though my excavational work has involved interview data, the idea characterizes other feminist research approaches as well. Feminist survey researchers seek to include more women respondents and to develop better ways of asking about sensitive topics; feminist ethnographers seek out those excluded from the classic style of "street ethnography"; feminist policy researchers consider the interests of those otherwise ignored in conventional formulations; and so on.

I have found the idea of excavation helpful as well in marking the need to move beyond unidimensional gender analyses. The experience of feminist discovery—of uncovering oppressions and hidden strengths, piece by piece—gives us a felt knowledge of the possibility and promise of uncovering the specific dynamics of a range of social locations. Thus, it should help us understand the multiple projects of discovery that belong to various locations, and to make common cause with other analysts working to preserve, examine, and interpret the evidence of other hidden lives.

4   Talking and Listening from Women's Standpoint

Feminist Strategies for Interviewing and Analysis

THE RESEARCH generated by academic feminism—involving a new and careful attention to women's experiences—"brings women in" to theorizing. But this research also demonstrates how traditional paradigms have been shaped by the concerns and relevances of a relatively small group of powerful men. The dilemma for the feminist scholar, always, is to find ways of working within some disciplinary tradition while aiming at an intellectual revolution that will transform that tradition (Stacey and Thorne 1985). In order to transform sociology—to write women and their diverse experiences into the discipline—we need to move toward new methods for writing about women's lives and activities without leaving sociology altogether. But the routine procedures of the discipline pull us insistently toward conventional understandings that distort women's experiences (Smith 1987, 1989).

Feminist methodology should provide strategies for managing this central contradiction—strategies that will help us with the "balancing act" demanded of any scholar who attempts innovative research within a scholarly tradition. I use the term "strategies" to suggest that feminist methodology will not prescribe a single model or formula. Rather, I think of feminist methods as distinctive approaches to subverting the established procedures of disciplinary practice tied to the agendas of the powerful (Smith 1990a). In the discussion that follows, I pursue some implications of feminism for the production and use of interview data. I do not treat questions about the ethics of interviewing or relations with informants, which have been discussed extensively by feminist researchers (e.g., Mies 1983, Oakley 1981, Reinharz 1983, Stacey 1988). In many ways, my approach is solidly grounded in a tradition of qualitative sociological inquiry and in relatively conventional methods for conducting interviews. But I will suggest that feminism gives us distinctive ways of extending the methods of this qualitative tradition.

I begin with an observation central to much feminist thinking: that language itself reflects male experiences, and that its categories are often incongruent with women's lives. This apparent obstacle to expression, I will argue, can be turned to advantage through attention to research as activity fundamentally grounded in talk. Qualitative researchers of various sorts have become increasingly conscious in recent years of the obvious but mostly taken-for-granted feature of the data they collect: that interviews consist of talk (Paget 1983, Mishler 1986a). This new awareness is related to the insights of phenomenologists, who investigate the production of everyday consciousness (see, e.g., Psathas 1973, Darroch and Silvers 1983), and ethnomethodologists, who have taken as problematic the patterns of talk and interaction through which the members of any group constitute a shared reality (Garfinkel 1967, Heritage 1984). I will suggest that this new kind of attention to the language of research should be central to the feminist project. Assuming relatively standard procedures for interviewing, I will examine, as social interaction grounded in language, four aspects of work with interview data: constructing topics, listening, editing, and writing. My aim is to bring into the methodological discussion insights from feminist linguists about women's relation to language and to speech, and to examine, as aspects of social research, the processes of talking and listening "as women." My understanding of what it means to talk or listen "as a woman" is based on the concept of "women's standpoint" (Smith 1987, Hartsock 1981); the approach does not imply that all women share a single position or perspective, but rather insists on the importance of following out the implications of women's (and others') various locations in socially organized activities (see chap. 6 for a discussion of reading "as a woman").

WOMEN AND LANGUAGE

Language was an early topic for feminist researchers and by now there is a large body of research on women and language (for summaries, see Thorne and Henley 1975; Lakoff 1975; Miller and Swift 1977; Spender [1980] 1985; Thorne, Kramarae, and Henley 1983). These studies demonstrate how linguistic forms (the generic "he," for example) exclude women, and how vocabulary and syntax make women deviant. The names of experiences often do not fit for women. For an example that is simple and immediate, consider the difficulties that arise in an attempt to apply the terms "work" and "leisure" to most women's lives. Many of the household activities so prominent in women's lives do not fit comfortably into either category (see, e.g., Smith 1987:68), and many of women's activities, such as family, community, and volunteer work, are best described as "invisible work" (Daniels 1987). There are other examples— the terms "public" and "private," for example, construct a distinction that obscures women's "multiple crisscrossings" of fluid and constantly shifting boundaries (Saraceno 1984:7). Such disjunctures between language and women's lives have been central to feminist scholarship; presumably, there are many more to be revealed. Presumably, as well, the lack of fit between women's lives and the words available for talking about experience present real difficulties for ordinary women's self-expression in their everyday lives. If words often do not quite fit, then women who want to talk of their experiences must "translate," either saying things that are not quite right, or working at using the language in nonstandard ways.

To some extent, this kind of problem must exist for everyone: language can never fit perfectly with individual experience. My claim, however, is that the problems of what we might call linguistic incongruence must be greater for some groups than for others. Research on gender differences in speech provides some support for this claim, suggesting that, in at least some contexts, women face particular difficulties of speech. In mixed-sex dyads and groups, women are less listened to than men and less likely to be credited for the things they say in groups; they are interrupted more often than men; the topics they introduce into conversations are less often taken up by others; and they do more work than men to keep conversations going. Further, Candace West (1982) suggests that responses to speech are so thoroughly gendered that women cannot overcome these difficulties by simply adopting "male" styles: she found that when women did interrupt male speakers, they were more likely than male interrupters to be ignored, a pattern she speculatively attributes to a male presumption that women's speech can, in general, be treated as trivial. These and similar findings have been presented as effects of power relations between men and women. They can also be seen as manifestations of the special obstacles for women to speaking fully and truthfully.

Dale Spender, in *Man Made Language* ([1980] 1985), reviews and extends these ideas in ways I have found especially helpful. Beginning with the anthropologists Edwin and Shirley Ardener's (E. Ardener 1975a, S. Ardener 1975) idea that women in society are a "muted group," she traces the consequences of various ways that women are denied access to linguistic resources. The concept of "mutedness" does not imply that women are silent: in every culture, women speak, in a variety of forms and settings, and in almost all cultures, women are important transmitters of language, through their care and teaching of children. But just as muted sounds are audible but softened, women speak in ways that are limited and shaped by men's greater social power and control, exercised both individually and institutionally (and exercised to control less privileged men as well as women). Spender argues that distinctive features of women's speech should not be seen as deficiencies in linguistic skill, but as adaptive responses to these constraints on their speech. She also sees in language a potential source of power for women: she argues that woman-to-woman talk is quite different from talk in mixed groups—because women speakers are more likely to listen seriously to each other—and that it affords opportunities for women to speak more fully about their experiences. She argues, in fact, that consciousness raising, which might be understood as woman-to-woman talk systematized, is at the heart of feminist theorizing (see also MacKinnon 1983).

Spender's discussion of "woman talk" is optimistic; she emphasizes the value of communication among women, and does not give much consideration to its difficulties. In drawing on her discussion, I do not mean to imply that women always (or even usually) understand each other easily. While understanding and familiar comfort are benefits of some of the ways that women have come together, they are not guaranteed by gender alone. Women who are positioned differently learn to speak and hear quite different versions of "woman talk," adapting to distinctive blends of power and oppression. Failures of understanding abound. Statements from feminists of color, for example, reveal not only their difficulties speaking among white feminists (e.g., hooks 1981), but also the costs for feminist research of the exclusion of their voices (e.g., Collins 1990). At the same time, feminist scholars have begun to experiment with texts that reflect the conflict and messiness of talking and listening together (e.g., Joseph and Lewis 1981; Lugones and Spelman 1983; Bulkin, Pratt, and Smith 1984). Such texts hold the promise that, with careful attention, we can learn from each other about our differences as well as our common experiences.

These ideas from feminist linguistic researchers provide the starting point for my discussion of interview talk, which will focus on the talk that occurs in interviews conducted by women with women. (I do not mean to imply that the label "feminist" can be applied only to research conducted by women and about women, but this category does include most feminist research to date. The reasons for such a pattern deserve attention, but lie beyond the scope of this chapter.) Below, I discuss the ways that these perspectives on women's talk have influenced my own thinking about interviewing. Though I draw examples primarily from my study of the work that women do within families (DeVault 1991), I attempt to indicate as well how these ideas might be relevant to other projects.

CONSTRUCTING TOPICS

The categories available from the discipline construct "topics" for research that do not necessarily correspond to categories that are meaningful in women's lives. Female researchers, like other women, have become accustomed to translating their experiences into standard vocabulary. But to fully describe women's experiences, we often need to go beyond standard vocabulary—not just in our analyses, but also in the ways that we actually talk with those we interview. By speaking in ways that open the boundaries of standard topics, we can create space for respondents to provide accounts rooted in the realities of their lives.

My research, for example, examines household routines for planning, cooking, and serving meals. I thought of it, in the beginning, as a study of housework. But I was also motivated by a sense that the feminist literature on housework didn't fit my experience. Analyses that took the content of household work for granted left things out, and the parts left out were somehow what made the work not only burdensome, but meaningful and compelling as well. I wanted to study a single kind of housework in detail, and for a variety of reasons that were only partly conscious, I was drawn to the work of providing food. The term is awkward and sounds odd, and in fact, there is no term that says precisely what I meant. I meant more than just cooking, more than "meal preparation" (the efficiency expert's term). And "providing," of course, has traditionally been used for what the traditional husband does—it is linked to the wage that a woman transforms into family meals. Though I knew—in at least a preliminary sense—what I wanted to study, I had no concise label for my topic. Eventually, I began to call it "the work of feeding a family," and later, just "feeding." But in the beginning, as I started to conduct interviews, I told my respondents that I wanted to talk with them about "all the housework that has to do with food—cooking, planning, shopping, cleaning up." I used my questions to show them that they should talk very specifically— "Who gets up first?" "What kind of cereal?" and so on—and in spite of my worries about "topic," these interviews were remarkably easy to conduct. Almost all of my respondents, both those who loved to cook and those who hated it, spoke easily and naturally. Looking back, I can see that I identified, in a rough way, a category that made sense to my respondents because it was a category that organized their day-to-day activity. For women who live in families and do this work, feeding is a central task and takes lots of time. Strategizing about how to do it leads to the development of routines, to frequent rearrangements and improvisations, and to pride in the "little tricks" that make the work easier. The topic is easy for women (and for men who actually do the work) to talk about. Our talk happened in a way that I and my respondents knew and were comfortable with, because such conversations among women are often settings for discussing this kind of work. Chatting about the details of household routines is a way of finding out what someone else does, reflecting on one's own practice, getting and sharing ideas or solutions to common problems. Sometimes, in fact, my respondents were uncomfortable because our talk didn't seem like an interview: several stopped in mid-sentence to ask, "Is this really what you want?" "Are you sure this is helping you?" They were prepared to translate into the vocabulary they expected from a researcher, and surprised that we were proceeding in a more familiar manner.

The point here—that feminist topics go beyond standard labels—applies to other kinds of research as well. Elizabeth Stanko, as follow-up to her book *Intimate Intrusions* (1985a), conceived a study of women's strategies for avoiding assault (Stanko 1985b, 1990). Her aim is to examine a broad range of what we might call "defensive maneuvers"—not just learning self-defense, but choosing places to live, things to wear, routes for walking home, and times to go to the laundromat. There is no label that includes all of these—and the category is probably one that men would be less likely than women to understand. But when Stanko, as a female researcher, says to women that she is concerned with "the things we do to keep safe," she taps into a set of activities informed by knowledge and strategizing that make up a meaningful category for virtually all women in our society. (Though, of course, the practices and conditions of the experience vary tremendously—in this instance, urban women are probably more at risk and more vigilant than others; and affluent women certainly find it easier to avoid risk than those with fewer material resources.)

Marianne Paget (1981), as part of a study of the practice of committed artists, has written about a barrier to creative work that she could see in the stories of women artists but not in those of men. She uses the term "ontological anguish" to refer to the conflict between these women's intense commitment to the creation of high art, and their learned sense that, as women, they are not supposed to participate in making culture. The artists themselves do not identify this problem. Paget sees it in their accounts of becoming artists—accounts that they provide in response to her questions about the work they finally came to do. This example suggests that researchers do not have to begin with a conception of expanded topic. Paget began with an interest in how artists do their work; she discovered that in order to explain their art, women artists have to tell about getting over a barrier. Paget allows them to tell their own stories, gives a name to the barrier they describe, and through her analysis makes it a phenomenon that we can examine and discuss.

The household work process that I analyze and the defensive strategies that Stanko studies are activities that most women learn to take for granted, activities that are normally only partly conscious, learned without explicit attention. Similarly, Paget discusses a sort of "problem with no name" for women artists, a problem they experience in various ways and can talk about indirectly, but do not ordinarily label. The promise of feminist ethnography is that we can elicit accounts and produce descriptions of these kinds of practice and thought that are part of female consciousness but left out of dominant interpretive frames, shaped around male concerns. When this kind of topic construction is successful, we recognize the thinking that emerges from the analysis—we know the experience—but we are also surprised and learn something new. The analysis produces the "aha" or "click" of consciousness raising that has been central to the development of feminist thinking, and that serves as a pointer toward a new way of seeing the world.

Conversation analytic researchers have investigated the construction of "topic" in everyday talk, and their findings help to illuminate the examples I have discussed by demonstrating how topics are produced collaboratively. Boden and Bielby (1986), for example, report that elderly conversation partners use a shared past as the basis for constructing conversational interaction in the present. And Maynard and Zimmerman (1984) report that unacquainted speakers often work at establishing areas of shared experience. In their study, conversation partners often developed topics out of the shared features of their immediate setting (the oddness of an arranged encounter in a social psychology lab). But speakers also investigated each other's categorical memberships (e.g., "sophomore" or "sociology major") and experiences (attending a recent concert) in "pretopical" talk aimed at constructing a "sharedness" that could lead to topic development. Paget (1983), emphasizing the "conversational" character of intensive interviewing, discusses how an interviewer and respondent collaborate in a "search procedure." It is the interviewer's investment in finding answers, her own concern with the questions she asks and her ability to show that concern, that serves to recruit her respondents as partners in the search: the things said are responses to these words of this particular researcher. The researcher is actively involved with respondents, so that together they are constructing fuller answers to questions that cannot always be asked in simple, straightforward ways.

I claim here that a feminist sociology must open up standard topics from the discipline, building more from what we share with respondents as women than from disciplinary categories that we bring to research encounters. In order to do this, researchers need to interview in ways that allow the exploration of incompletely articulated aspects of women's experiences. Traditionally, qualitative researchers have conducted interviews that are "open-ended" and "intensive," seeking to avoid structuring the interaction in terms of the researcher's perspectives. But eliciting useful accounts of women's experiences is not simply a matter of encouraging women to talk. Most members of a society learn to interpret their experiences in terms of dominant language and meanings; thus, women themselves (researchers included) often have trouble seeing and talking clearly about their experiences. What researchers can do is to take responsibility for recognizing how the concepts we have learned as sociologists may distort women's accounts. We can return to activities conducted in specific settings as the sources for our studies, and ground our interviewing in accounts of everyday activity—in accounts of how particular women actually spend their time at home, for example, rather than a previously defined concept of "housework." Dorothy Smith (1987:187–189) suggests that when we ground interviews in this way, we find that social organization is "in the talk" and that we can mine the talk for clues to social relations. This kind of interviewing, which does not begin from topics established in the discipline, will be more like everyday "woman talk" than like survey research.

LISTENING

I have argued above that since the words available often do not fit, women learn to "translate" when they talk about their experiences. As they do so, parts of their lives "disappear" because they are not included in the language of the account. In order to "recover" these parts of women's lives, researchers must develop methods for listening around and beyond words. I use the term "listening" in this section in a broad sense, to refer to what we do while interviewing, but also to the hours we spend later listening to tapes or studying transcripts, and even more broadly, to the ways we work at interpreting respondents' accounts. (I do not, however, attend to comparative aspects of analysis, which involve bringing together interpretations of multiple interviews.)

Spender's discussion of the special features of "woman talk," cited above, emphasizes the importance of listening. She notes that listening has been neglected in communication research in favor of research on speech, and she suggests that this imbalance results from the fact that those who control knowledge production are more concerned with airing their views than with hearing those of others (Spender [1980] 1985:121–125). Spender argues that women (like members of other subordinate groups) are highly skilled at listening—to both men and women (see also Miller 1976, 1986)—and that women together can more easily cooperate in understanding each other than speakers in mixed groups. Presumably, these ideas have relevance for woman-to-woman interviewing, even though the interview setting is structured, and more artificial than everyday talk. When women interview women, both researcher and subject act on the basis of understandings about interviewing, and both follow the rules (or negotiate a shared version of the rules) associated with their respective roles. But changes in the role of researcher, based on incorporating rather than denying personal involvements, have been at the heart of many discussions of feminist methodology (Reinharz 1983, Stanley and Wise 1983). In fact, it is sometimes quite difficult for female researchers, and especially feminists, to maintain the role prescribed by traditional methodological strictures. Ann Oakley (1981), for example, explains how impossible it was for her to be an "ideal" interviewer in her discussions with pregnant women: she wasn't willing to respond, "I haven't really thought about it" when interviewees asked questions such as "Which hole does the baby come out of?" or "Why is it dangerous to leave a small baby alone in the house?" Many of these discussions suggest that women interviewing women bring to their interaction a tradition of "woman talk." They help each other develop ideas, and are typically better prepared than men to use the interview as a "search procedure" (Paget 1983), cooperating in the project of constructing meanings together.[1]

When this project involves the recovery of unarticulated experience, as so much feminist research does, researchers have another resource: they can listen for the everyday processes of "translation" that are part of women's speech. When I use the term here—as I have been doing rather loosely so far—I mean to refer to the various ways that women manage to deal with the incongruence of language in their everyday speech. Often, this means using words that are familiar and "close enough" to experience for most purposes, relying on listeners to understand—for example, calling "housework" whatever chores must be done at home. Sometimes, too, translation means trying to develop a more complex meaning, trying to respond more fully to questions that are not quite appropriate. In these cases, it may mean saying part of what is experienced, groping for words, doing the best one can. As an interviewer who is also a woman—who has also learned to translate—I can listen "as a woman," filling in from experience to help me understand the things that are incompletely said. As a researcher, my job is to listen for these translations, and to analyze the disjunctures that give rise to them. These linguistic phenomena provide "clues" to women's experiences (Frye 1983:xii).

In my research on the work of feeding a family, I was concerned with uncovering neglected aspects of women's experience of housework. I wanted to examine those parts of the work of planning, cooking, and serving meals that women rarely think about, but have learned from their mothers and from ideologies of family life—those parts of housework that actually produce family life day to day. I asked the women in my study (and the few men who took major responsibility for cooking) to describe their daily routines in some detail: what they cooked and why, how they planned and managed family meals, when and where they bought food, and so on. As the interviews progressed, I became increasingly fascinated with some characteristic features of my respondents' talk. They spoke very concretely about the mundane details of everyday life, but they often said things in ways that seemed oddly incomplete. They connected topics in ways that were sometimes puzzling, and they assumed certain kinds of knowledge on my part ("Like, you know, the Thursday section of the newspaper," an implicit reference to the fact that many U.S. newspapers include recipes and features on food and diet in their Thursday editions). I coded my data in the traditional way, noting when respondents mentioned "topics" such as "planning," "nutrition," and so forth. But in many cases, the analysis really began with a particular phrase that seemed to demand investigation. I began to pay more and more attention to the ways things were said. I was especially interested in difficulties of expression—those fascinating moments when respondents got stuck, and worked at articulating thoughts they were not used to sharing: "It's kind of hard to explain. . . ."

One woman, talking about why she worked so hard at organizing regular meals for her family, told me:

> My husband sees food as something you need to live. But—I don't quite know how to describe it—I really have an emphasis on the social aspects. I mean, the food is an important part, but it's kind of in that setting.

As we talked, this woman was trying to formulate the principles that guide her activities. It is difficult because she doesn't have appropriate words. She knows what she means, but expressing it is new. Another woman echoed her idea, in a similar way:

> The initial drudgery is what you dislike. Actually going shopping, doing all the planning, chopping, cutting, what have you. And of course cleaning up. But you do it for the good parts, you know, you get enough of the good part to keep doing it.

There are words for the physical tasks, but not for the interpersonal work that is more important for this woman—the activity she summarizes, somewhat puzzled herself, as "the good part." Again, it is clear that her experiences are inadequately coded in standard vocabulary, and that she must work at saying what she means.

Another example: although most women told me that they didn't really do much "planning," several of my respondents referred to an immediate, improvisational kind of thinking they do while shopping. They did not know quite what to call this process. One told me: "Most of the time, I kind of plan when I'm at the store, you know? Like OK, we have chicken Monday, pork chops Tuesday—I be kind of, you know, figuring out in my mind, as I shop, what's what." Another explained: "My husband likes to just get in and out, and then that's it. Whereas me, I like to look around, and just think, you know."

These kinds of comments do not constitute "good quotes" in the conventional sense: they are halting and rather inarticulate, and seem hardly to have any content. Typically, I think, they would be discarded as containing little information about what these women do. I used these women's words somewhat differently, however: not as straightforward accounts of "what happens," but as hints toward concerns and activities that are generally unacknowledged. Often, I believe, this halting, hesitant, tentative talk signals the realm of not-quite-articulated experience, where standard vocabulary is inadequate, and where a respondent tries to speak from experience and finds language wanting.[2] I tried to listen most carefully to this kind of talk. As I began to understand what these women were saying, I also began to see more clearly how standard vocabulary—the managerial term "planning," for instance—really doesn't describe what they do. I could also begin to see why the term doesn't fit: the concept of planning makes organizational sense where there is a separation of conception and execution, but housework has traditionally been organized so as to join not only conception and execution, but also work and the personality of the one who does it.

As I began to look for these difficulties of expression, I became aware that my transcripts were filled with notations of women saying to me, "you know," in sentences like "I'm more careful about feeding her, you know, kind of a breakfast." This seems an incidental feature of their speech, but perhaps the phrase is not so empty as it seems. In fact, I did know what she meant. I did not use these phrases systematically in my analyses, but I think now that I could have. Studying the transcripts now, I see that these words often occur in places where they are consequential for the joint production of our talk in the interviews. In many instances, "you know" seems to mean something like, "OK, this next bit is going to be a little tricky. I can't say it quite right, but help me out a little; meet me halfway and you'll understand what I mean." (It is perhaps similar to the collaborative use of "Uh huh" to sustain extended stretches of talk, noted by Schegloff 1982.) If this is so, it provides a new way to think about these data. "You know" no longer seems like stumbling inarticulateness, but appears to signal a request for understanding. The request was honored on the woman-to-woman level, as I nodded, "um hmm," making the interview comfortable, doing with my respondent what we women have done for generations—understanding each other. But I fear that the request is too often forgotten when, as researchers, we move from woman talk to sociology, leaving the unspoken behind. In some sense, this is a betrayal of the respondent—I say I understand, but if I later "forget," her reality is not fully there in what I write.

Finally, there were bits of speech that just seemed odd to me, that I wanted to understand. In one interview, for example, I asked what the evening meal was like. The reply was a long one; we had been talking about this woman's own parents and how they ate, and her answer gave information about her own childhood as well as the patterns she and her husband have developed. Eventually, I asked her to explain how their "family style" meals were different from those of her childhood. Again, her answer was long and specific and moved beyond the question. Her husband serves the meat, but not as well as her grandfather and her father did; this bothers her sometimes. Then she went on:

> And the service is important. You know, how the table is set and so forth. We probably, again when I was growing up we never had paper napkins except when my dad was out of town. We do now, have paper napkins, although we have cloth napkins and I like it. What I would like—maybe I will but probably not—but at one point where we lived we had cloth napkins and everybody had their own napkin ring, and that way you didn't have to keep changing the napkins.

She went on to talk about other things, but I was haunted by a fragment of this excerpt: "What I would like—maybe I will but probably not—," which struck me immediately with its off-hand poignancy. The question, for me, was why anyone would say such a thing, what context produces this remark. Later I began to see how this woman was doing her work as we talked; she was, momentarily, musing and strategizing about the kind of meal she wished to produce for her family. What happens in her talk? Telling about her family routine, she mentions napkin rings, and thinks that she would like to use them again. Her wistful, automatic thought that she will do something different (again, not quite planning, but something akin to it) reveals her sense of how the material trappings of meals can become foundations for more emotional aspects of family life. And her brief comment also contains clues to the fate of her own preferences and desires: she plans and wishes, but she also recognizes that she alone is responsible for doing the work, and that in the end she will have limited time and make choices that reflect the priorities of others. I certainly could not see all these things when I noticed this remark, but I knew at least that there was something more to be said about this oddly contradictory phrase. As I thought about it, it brought back the time in my own life when I thought I might save my marriage by making better salads. And when I began to look, I found this kind of thinking in the comments of others as well.

As the last example suggests, researchers' own experiences as women serve as resources for this kind of listening. While other feminists have noted the value of personal involvement in interviewing, even researchers who value involvement have talked of it in a mostly unanalyzed way, as experience rather than as an element of method. If feminist researchers are to move toward a more disciplined use of the personal, we need to make the process one that we can consciously adopt and teach. We need to analyze more carefully the specific ways that interviewers use personal experience as a resource for listening. Here, I briefly discuss my own approach and a related example. What they have in common is a focus on attention to the unsaid, in order to produce it as topic and make it speakable.

My procedure, which I have illustrated above, involves noticing ambiguity and problems of expression in interview data, then drawing on my own experience in an investigation aimed at "filling in" what has been incompletely said. The point is not simply to reproduce my own perspective in my analysis; the clues I garner from this kind of introspection are only a beginning and should lead me back to hear respondents in new ways. What produces the analysis is the recognition that something is unsaid, and the attempt to articulate the missing parts of the account. The interpretive process is analogous to reading a narrative account, placing oneself in the narrator's position and referring to an implied context for the story that is told. It is a process that is being studied by analysts of reading and narrative, and the work of these theorists should provide one way of conceptualizing this kind of listening (for sociologists' discussions of narrative, see, e.g., Smith 1983; Mishler 1986a,b; DeVault 1990; Richardson 1990).

A related approach to "personal listening" can be seen in the work of Dorothy Smith and Alison Griffith, who have studied the ways that mothers' activities are shaped by the organization of schooling (Smith 1987, Griffith and Smith 1987). They interviewed mothers about what they do to help their children in school—how they get them dressed and there on time, how they teach them "basic skills," how they manage children's experiences with teachers and the institutions of schooling. Griffith and Smith have written about the ways that they have used their experiences as resources for analysis. They were aware from the beginning that their personal histories as single mothers provided impetus and direction for the study, and that they used a commonality of experience with their respondents to develop interview questions and to establish "rapport" and move the interviews ahead. But they also report that their analysis was furthered by noticing and using a particular sort of emotional response to some of their interviews. Griffith, for example, tells about returning from an interview with a middle-class, full-time mother who deploys an impressive range of material and educational resources to further her children's development. Her fieldnotes ask:

> And where was I in all this? I was feeling that I hadn't done my own mothering *properly*. I had let my children watch T.V.; they'd never been taken to a Shakespearean play; when I was upset with the school, I have never managed to make things better for my children and indeed, at times made it worse; etc. In other words, my mothering, in relation to other women's mothering, appeared to be less than adequate on almost every count. As a consequence, I was finding the interview process very difficult emotionally. (Griffith and Smith 1987:94)

The reaction is understandable, and might simply be treated, sympathetically, as one of the pitfalls of researching personally meaningful topics. But Griffith and Smith go beyond this kind of recognition to analyze the unnoticed matrix of social organization that constructs both the interview talk and their emotional reaction to it. They report that reflections on this kind of reaction led them to see a "moral dimension" to mothering, and to trace its sources in social organization. Analysis does not end, but rather begins with the recognition of their own emotion: Griffith and Smith went on to look for, and found, other illustrations of this aspect of mothering in the accounts of those they interviewed. But their own experience helped them find these clues to the social organization of mothering (see also Rothman 1986 on deep emotional response and its relation to the analysis of amniocentesis experiences).

Any competent listening depends on various kinds of background knowledge. I have argued above that woman-to-woman listening can be based on a particular type of unspoken knowledge. Of course, this kind of listening is not simple. It is certainly not guaranteed in any woman-to-woman interaction. Riessman (1987), in an analysis of a middle-class Anglo interviewer's misunderstandings of a Puerto Rican respondent, provides a sobering account of one woman's inability to hear another. Asked to explain how her divorce came about, the respondent provides an episodic narrative in which a series of exemplary vignettes answer the question. The interviewer, expecting a story with a linear temporal organization, is confused, and interrupts the account repeatedly in an attempt to elicit the sort of narrative she expects. It is not only a frustrating encounter, but a striking example of how difficult it can be to hear things said in unfamiliar forms, and how damaging when respondents are not heard. But Riessman's analysis of this mishearing also suggests that, with awareness and effort, it is possible to analyze such problems in the service of more skillful listening. The critical point is that feminist researchers can be conscious of listening as process, and can work on learning to listen in ways that are personal, disciplined, and sensitive to differences.

PRESERVING WOMEN'S SPEECH

I have suggested above that researchers can use women's speech to provide clues to analysis. This kind of analysis proceeds through attention to typically unnoticed features of talk, and is therefore made possible by methods of data collection and recording that preserve such features. In this section, I discuss several issues of "editing," a term I use to refer to the decisions researchers make about recording, transcribing, and excerpting from conversations with informants. Though these are usually thought of (if thought of at all) as mechanical or technical issues, researchers are increasingly aware of their substantive relevance. Each decision about these matters results in saving or losing aspects of interview talk, and some approaches to analysis depend on aspects of talk that are routinely discarded by other analysts. Concretely, the questions include: Should interviews be tape recorded? How should they be transcribed? What would constitute a "complete" transcription? When excerpting from transcripts, what (if anything) are we allowed to change? Should we "clean up" quotations? How? And why or why not? My aim in what follows is not to prescribe any particular version of transcription or presentation. Rather, I want to call attention to the questions, survey some possible answers, and suggest that for feminist researchers, "more complete" representations of talk can provide a resource for analysis built on distinctive features of women's speech.

Standard handbooks on qualitative methods stress the importance of exhaustive recording of conversation in interviews and field settings, but devote relatively little attention to methods of recording conversation or writing about it. Bogdan and Taylor (1975), for example, who discuss such issues in more detail than most authors, recommend that fieldworkers avoid taping; they provide some hints for remembering dialogue, and they suggest including records of "dialogue accessories" such as gesture, tone, and accent, but they also reassure the reader that fieldnotes need not include "flawless reproduction of what was said" (pp. 60–61). They do suggest that researchers tape-record intensive interviews, because subjects' words are important and the situation is artificial anyway, but they omit discussion of transcription techniques. Presumably, students learn how to deal with these matters through experience and oral teaching, and by reading exemplary texts. The Bogdan and Taylor book, for example, teaches about these matters implicitly through the inclusion of exemplary fieldnotes and finished research reports.

Fieldworkers in the symbolic interactionist tradition adopt a variety of solutions to problems of collecting and representing talk as data: some rely on memory rather than tape recordings (and indeed, some work in settings and adopt roles that make recording impractical), while others advocate taping interviews (often citing, in addition to the analytic utility of this technique, the benefit of easier concentration on the face-to-face interaction instead of on remembering what is said). Transcription, in this tradition, is typically viewed as a mechanical task, often assigned to subordinates in the research enterprise, though many researchers do acknowledge that the transcription process can afford rich insight. While some qualitative researchers insist that transcripts should include everything that is said (often mentioning, for instance, the importance of recording the interviewer's questions), many seem to edit out some material at this stage. Lillian Rubin (1979: Appendix), for example, defends the practice of organizing edited transcripts in terms of previously developed categories of interest rather than as verbatim records of the interview (though she does listen to entire tapes as she proceeds with the analysis). Further, the interactionist tradition in qualitative methods is virtually silent on methods for recording particular features of talk, taking for granted, for the most part, the adequacy of standard English spelling and punctuation. Excerpts in published reports tend to be brief—a few sentences from the respondent surrounded by analytic comment—and usually seem to have been "polished" by the sociologist, since they read more smoothly than most ordinary speech. Researchers routinely indicate that they have changed respondents' names and some details of their lives in order to protect their subjects' anonymity, but they rarely report in detail on which details they have changed and how.

In a rare discussion of these issues, Bob Blauner (1987) discusses the problems of editing "first-person" sociology. He notes that oral history and life history researchers have been more self-conscious about editing than most qualitative sociologists. Perhaps because the talk of informants is so much more prominent in their texts, life history researchers seem more conscious than others that they must make decisions about how to condense long hours of conversation, whether and how to represent dialect and nonstandard grammar, and how much commentary to add to their subjects' words. Though Blauner limits his discussion to "personal document" texts—intended to present findings through extended personal narrative rather than through a sociologist-author's analytic discussion—every researcher working with interview data makes these editing decisions.

Blauner argues that the particular features of an individual's speech often have substantive significance. (Interestingly, his examples focus mainly on the ways that African American speakers mix standard and Black English, and might be seen as linguistic phenomena corresponding to the ones I have claimed are important in women's speech.) Reporting on his own editing, he describes himself as having "some of the folklorist's purism" with respect to language and expressive style, but also as being "very free as an editor" (Blauner 1987:50). He almost never changes any words when he quotes his informants (though he sometimes adds or deletes words to clarify meaning), but he condenses and eliminates material in ways intended to bring out the meaning and sociological relevance of a particular story. He also eliminates repetitive speech,[3] and, like most sociologists, changes personal names and details of identity in order to protect the anonymity of informants. Blauner also reports that many life history researchers edit their informants' words in order to encourage more respectful reading. Usually, the worry is that readers will be prejudiced, or simply distracted, by speech that reveals lack of education or a particular regional or class background. Blauner cites the example of Robert Coles, who translates slang and vernacular into standard English in order to highlight the content rather than style of respondents' speech.

These approaches, while emphasizing the importance of respondents' own words, also give the researcher much authority as translator and mouthpiece. The researcher, relying on her understanding of respondents' meanings, represents their words in forms that fit into sociological texts. Typically, this means interpreting, condensing, excerpting, and polishing respondents' talk. One rationale for such transformation emphasizes its benign intent: the researcher's purpose, often, is to secure a hearing for respondents who would not otherwise be heard. The purpose of editing is to cast talk into a form that is easier to read—and more compelling— than raw interview documents, which are often lengthy, rambling, repetitive and/or confusing. Another rationale emphasizes the redundancy of talk: the researcher should include only as much detail as needed to illustrate the analytic points to be made. (Howard Becker, for example, argues that tape recording interviews is usually unnecessary, explaining that he is confident of remembering those details that he needs to make an analysis [personal communication]. My work as Becker's student convinced me that I could remember "enough" from interviews to write sound and interesting sociology, and I repeat his advice to my own students, though with more ambivalence. However, my discussion elsewhere in this article

suggests that memory is often inadequate.) Both rationales show that editing, though usually relatively unnoticed, is an essential and consequential part of the routine practice of producing a particular kind of sociological text.

Such "routine practices" must be thought of as the solutions to problems of representation accepted by a community of interpreters (Becker
1986a). They are neither right or wrong for all time, but represent solutions that are relatively adequate for the purposes at hand. I have suggested above, however, that feminist researchers—whose purposes often
include disrupting routine practice—might do well to adopt a reasoned
suspicion of standard solutions to representation problems. I have argued
that one purpose of feminist research is to recover and examine unnoticed
experience, and that standard language and forms are likely to be inadequate for describing those experiences. Standard practice that smooths
out respondents' talk is one way that women's words are distorted; it is
often a way of discounting and ignoring those parts of women's experience
that are not easily expressed.

Conversation and discourse analysis provide models for representing
talk much more completely. Conversation analytic researchers (see, e.g.,
Schenkein 1978, Atkinson and Heritage 1984) aim at discovering the re-
curring features of talk and interaction that produce the orderliness of social life; they take talk as the primordial grounding of social interaction.
Analysis focuses on the significance of conversational features as minute
(and as typically unnoticed) as indrawn breath, elongated vowel sounds
and hesitations as short as one-tenth of a second. Discourse analysis
(e.g., Fisher and Todd 1983, Mishler 1986a) is typically based on longer
stretches of talk, but involves a similarly close attention to the details of
talk and storytelling. Feminists working in these traditions (e.g., Fishman
1978, West and Zimmerman 1983, Todd and Fisher 1988) have attended
to the significance of gender as it both produces and is produced by the
social relations of talk. Their work is especially useful for the kind of analysis I propose here, because they show, explicitly and in detail, the kinds
of obstacles to expression that women confront in everyday interaction.

Researchers who rely on these approaches work with very detailed
transcripts, which look more complicated than standard text and are usually rather difficult for the uninitiated to read. In the case of conversation
analysis, they are based on a system of notation developed by Gail Jeffer-
son (described in Schenkein 1978:xi–xvi); some researchers use other,
generally similar notation systems (see, e.g., several different levels of detail in the papers brought together by Todd and Fisher 1988). Although
the form of such a transcript gives many readers the impression of a technical, "objective" approach to talk, insiders to the tradition view tran-

scripts more provisionally. For these researchers, the talk itself is central; they work primarily from tapes, they play tapes when they present their work to others, and they view transcripts as subject to continual criticism and revision as they "hear the talk" more completely. Transcribing itself is a subtle and difficult craft, learned through apprenticeship and experience, and practiced improvisationally. Notation systems change as researchers attend to previously neglected features of talk.

Conversation and discourse analysts aim to study talk as it actually happens, and they certainly come closer than those who simply translate talk into standard written English. However, one of the important lessons to be drawn from conversation analysis is precisely how difficult it is to hold and study "the talk itself." While these technically sophisticated notation systems capture many features of talk left out of more conventional representations, they cannot be thought of as "complete." So far, most of them leave out gesture and "body language" (but see Goodwin 1979, Goodwin and Goodwin 1989), as well as subtle aspects of talk that have not yet been noticed and notated. They seem most useful (or at least are most used) for studying the form rather than content of speech. In addition, these systems often have the effect of obscuring the individuality of speech. Because transcripts in this form require large investments of both production time and space in articles, analyses are based on relatively short fragments of speech, usually too short to give a sense of a speaker's characteristic style of speech. One might argue that the difficulty of reading a detailed transcript has the beneficial effect of forcing the reader to study respondents' talk more carefully than when it is represented in standard English. But because these transcripts require such concentrated reading, accent and dialect are often less effectively conveyed than through variations on more standard writing.

No transcription technique preserves all the details of respondents' speech, and no technique will be adequate for every analysis. My intention here is not to propose that feminist researchers must follow analytic programs emphasizing the details of talk, but rather to encourage strategic borrowing from these approaches. In my research on housework, for example, I did not begin with the intention of studying women's speech. I was not trained as an analyst of talk, and I did not use any specialized method for transcribing discourse. But I worked carefully from tape recordings. Without the tapes, I would not have been able to reproduce the hesitation and uncertainty of speech that have so interested me since I finished the interviewing. I doubt that I could have reproduced the delightfully individual accounts built around the significance of particular brands of breakfast cereal or particular cuts of meat—these stories contained too much detail about items too ordinary to remember with confidence. I think I would have remembered hesitation as a general phenomenon, or the fact that respondents often referred to particular preferences, but I needed their exact words as evidence, in order to show readers, in some detail, how they spoke about these matters.

As I worked with the interviews, I learned from conversation and discourse analysis to attend to the details of respondents' speech. I did not systematically transcribe details of dialect, pauses, or emphasis. But as I transcribed, I developed the rudiments of a system for preserving some of the "messiness" of everyday talk. I inserted ungrammatical commas to indicate hesitation mid-sentence. I included many (though not all) of my respondents' "um"s and "you know"s; I indicated outright laughter, but I had not yet learned to hear more attenuated out-breaths as signals of emotion. I transcribed the often confusing process of self-correction (e.g., "And I'm a lot more concerned about—well, I shouldn't say concerned, I should say aware, of what I eat."). In these ways, I recorded more of the inelegant features of my respondents' talk than is customary in the kind of interview study I conducted, and the transcripts retained at least some of the distinctiveness of women's talk about housework.

When I began to write about these interviews, I first selected illustrative excerpts that were clear and concise, and I felt free to do minor editing that made them clearer or more euphonious (eliminating a superfluous phrase, for example, when the meaning of a statement was clear). As the analysis developed, however, I became aware of the power of respondents' actual, often puzzlingly complex language. I began to search for more confusing rather than clearer speech, and I stopped editing excerpts. The halting, unedited excerpts I produced required more analytic comment, of a different sort than I had previously provided. I began to attend more carefully to the small features of respondents' accounts, and to how their stories were situated in longer stretches of discourse. I returned, sometimes, to the original tapes, listening for and transcribing more details of the talk. Instead of relying on the routine practices of the interactionist tradition I had learned, I developed editing strategies that preserved and exploited distinctive features of respondents' talk.

Paget's work provides another example of strategic borrowing, and suggests that editing actual talk may be one of the ways that conventional sociology has suppressed emotion. In her study of artistic work (Paget 1981, 1983), she relies on a system of notation that preserves many features of naturally occurring speech: false starts and hesitations, rhythm and accent, periods of silence. In the analysis, she uses these features of the talk as signals of emotion. For example: the artist informant tells a story of long, hard times, and finally, some success. Paget presents a long excerpt from the interview transcript, and uses the sound of her respondent's

speech to pinpoint the artist's account of a turning point in her development: "THHEN. . . . . . . sl(h)owly i started to meet other artists. . . . ."
(Paget 1983:84). As she develops the analysis, Paget summarizes the artist's
story, and also explains how she herself understood its significance: "Then
things in general got much better. 'THHEN' (line 1212) is said with special
dramatic effect. It is like a beacon" (Paget 1983:87). Paget attends to both
the content and structure of speech. In her approach, features of speech
like pauses and emphasis provide clues to emotion and meaning, and these
in turn are building blocks for the analysis. Knowledge, Paget says, "ac-
cumulates with many turns at talk. It collects in stories, asides, hesitations,
expressions of feeling, and spontaneous associations" (Paget 1983:78).
The researcher preserves the emotion in respondents' talk, and displays it
for readers. "Had I edited these exchanges," she explains, "freed them of
the odd and essential noises of talk's presence, I would have reworked
meanings. The transcript would move forward in an orderly and formal
manner. But the dynamic construction of what was said would be gone"
(Paget 1983:87).

There is increasing evidence of a fruitful interchange between traditional
approaches to qualitative sociology and the newer insights of conversation
and discourse analysis (e.g., Mishler 1986a, Moerman 1988, Boden 1990).
There is also evidence of a heightened awareness of transcription in linguistic research (see, e.g., Ochs 1979), and especially at the borders between conversation analysis and other qualitative approaches (e.g., Mishler
1984). Feminist work should be an important site for mutual influence.
For conversation and discourse analysts, attention to the characteristic difficulties in women's speaking provides one route toward showing how the
primordial "social doings" of talk and interaction form the "scaffolding of
social structure" (West and Zimmerman 1987:129, 147). For feminists
working in more conventional qualitative modes, these approaches call
attention to the importance of talk and its organized complexity, and provide techniques for capturing and using talk in analyses of interview data.

WRITING ABOUT WOMEN'S LIVES

Social scientists have become increasingly aware that writing is not a
transparent medium with which researchers simply convey "truths" discovered in the field, but itself constructs and controls meaning and interpretation. In anthropology, a well-developed movement has grown up
around the analysis of ethnographic texts, and has begun to stimulate
its own feminist critique (see Clifford and Marcus 1986; Mascia-Lees,
Sharpe, and Cohen 1989). A similar focus has begun to develop in sociology as well (Brown 1977; Richardson 1988; Van Maanen 1988; Hunter

1990; and, with respect to feminist writing specifically, Smith 1989), though it has been less focused and coherent than in anthropology, perhaps because sociologists write in a variety of genres. Here, I will discuss just one aspect of sociological writing, the issue of "labeling" women's experiences. But broader questions about writing should be on a feminist methodological agenda. As we modify traditions for data collection and analysis, we will need to experiment with forms and texts that allow us to fully express the insights arising from transformations in research practice.

Feminists have long been aware that naming is political—the labels attached to activities establish and justify their social worth—and that women's activities have often been labeled in ways that serve the project of controlling and subordinating women (Frye 1983). When researchers write about women's lives, whatever our methods of collecting and analyzing interview data, we confront the dangers of mislabeling that can result from the use of language that does not fit. A feminist strategy in sociology, then, must extend to the language of our texts: we must choose words carefully and creatively, with attention to the consequences of naming experience.

As housework and child care have become legitimate topics for sociologists, for example, researchers have faced the vexing problem of labeling the unpaid work of raising children. Standard vocabulary forces a set of unsatisfactory choices. Suzanne Peters (1985) discussed these problems when she organized a group of sociologists to meet and share research on "motherwork." By selecting a label that referred to mothers, she chose explicitly to "capture a certain element of present social reality . . . (that women mostly raise children)" (Peters 1985:16). But she also recognized that any vocabulary used to describe these activities should be treated as provisional, and she invited participants in the working group to explore the implications of this and other labels. By using the term "motherwork," for example, with its gender specificity, we might be denying even the possibility that men can do this work. We might be leaving out lesbian and gay couples who raise children. By using a single, coined term, we might be universalizing the experience, implying that an activity exists that is somehow the same everywhere and in all times. And what are the implications of talking about "work"? The concept does for mothers' activities what it had earlier done in research on housework—calls attention to the time and effort involved in mothering, and its social and economic significance. But it might also obscure "important emotional aspects of mothering, which include creating relationships and cherishing individuals" (Peters 1985:19).

The problem is familiar, perhaps for all researchers, but especially for feminists exploring previously neglected experiences. But the problem is often defined rather narrowly, in terms of choosing a single word or phrase that will serve.[4] The assumption is that the researcher can, with reasonable care, make decisions that are politically or analytically correct, and then forge ahead, armed with the proper concept. I want to argue instead for a strategic imprecision—that researchers are not well served by deciding exactly what to call mothers' work, and that we would do better to use several different labels, sometimes more or less interchangeably, and sometimes to refer to subtle shadings of meaning that we are just beginning to interpret. This strategy recognizes that different labels will capture different parts of the reality we are working to construct. I developed such an approach in my study of housework, though I did not start out to do so. I began with the notion that I would eventually find a term for the neglected, invisible part of housework that I was most concerned with. As my analysis developed, I used a variety of labels—"family work," "caring," "the work of coordination" or "interpersonal work"—trying to indicate how thought and the construction of relationships are part of housework, but stubbornly resisting suggestions that I could capture what houseworkers really do with a term such as "management." Increasingly, as my understandings grew more complex, I gave up the search for a single label, and simply worked at producing a fuller understanding of women's household activity.

Now, I understand this problem as another manifestation of the uneasy fit between language and women's experiences. If the language is "man-made," it is not likely to provide, ready-made, the words that feminist researchers need to tell what they learn from other women. Instead of imposing a choice among several labels, none of which are quite right, feminist texts should describe women's lives in ways that move beyond standard vocabularies, commenting on the vocabularies themselves along the way (see, e.g., Reinharz 1988a). Instead of agreeing on what to call women's activity, we should make our talk richer and more complex—we should use many words, and put them together in ways that force readers to imagine the reality we're describing in a new way—to taste it, try it out, turn it over, take it apart. In discussions of household and family activity, labels like "work" and "emotion" are words that channel thinking, leading the mind down old, familiar roads. And that should not be the effect of a feminist text.

There are unexpected barriers to putting this strategy of rich and complex description into practice. Many readers of social science, accustomed to more conventional analysis, are confused by a shifting vocabulary. Copy editors, whose job includes checking manuscripts for consistency, enforce the routine practice of obscuring complexity under concepts derived from (or developed in opposition to) disciplinary frames (for some examples of problems with editing and feminist discourse, see Paget 1990). These problems suggest that feminist researchers must continue to discuss these linguistic difficulties very explicitly whenever we write. When using a multilayered vocabulary, quite different from those typically anchoring sociological analyses, we will need to alert readers to this strategy and intentions informing it. We will need to prepare the reader to read in new ways—not to expect neat re-definitions, but to settle in for a much longer process of shaping new meanings.

These last comments point toward the construction of an audience for feminist research as an aspect of feminist method. Texts work and move because they are read. But audiences must learn how to read texts, especially those that are "different" because they stretch and extend rhetorical convention (see chap. 8). This problem pulls writing toward the conventional, as authors strive to communicate effectively with audiences that exist. But a more transformative solution would involve more explicit attention to methods for reading innovative texts. Part of the task of feminist writing, then, should be to instruct a newly forming audience about how to read and hear our words.

DISCUSSION

I have argued that language is often inadequate for women. Its inadequacy surely takes multiple forms for women in different locations. Often, our relations to language are contradictory, because we are both subject to, and also working within, a loosely coordinated ruling apparatus (Smith 1987) with oppressive consequences for others besides women. Talk and interaction are thoroughly gendered, but women do not share a single experience of oppression through talk or a single culture of resistance. Instead, we share multiple versions of both oppression and resistance. There remains in this article an unresolved tension between an insistence on the importance of gender and a recognition of cross-cutting differences among women. I have relied on suggestive metaphors of language as "man-made" and of resistance through "woman talk," both of which are too simple if taken too literally. I acknowledge that difficulty here as a way of pointing to aspects of these methodological projects that need fuller development.

In spite of obstacles to women's expression, language is a resource to be used, and in use, there are many possibilities. While much feminist research in linguistics is designed to show how language and the organization of talk contribute to the subordination of women, it also shows, often, how skillfully and creatively women speakers circumvent and subvert the processes of social control, whether they do so by "talking back"

(hooks 1989) or "telling it slant" (Spender [1980] 1985). It is quite difficult for most women to be speaking subjects—harder than for men—and
that is true both for women as our research subjects and for us as researchers when we write and talk about our work. But women in different places
and positions have long traditions of working at self-expression and understanding, using the language to talk about our lives, and working at
listening. Professional training as sociologists and the routine practices of
the discipline encourage us to abandon these traditions of "woman talk"
in favor of a more abstract, controlled, and emotionless discourse. I have
meant to suggest that as we construct feminist discourses in sociology, we
can instead recognize those distinctively female traditions, borrow from
them, and build upon them in our practice as researchers.

5 Ethnicity and Expertise

Racial-Ethnic Knowledge in Sociological Research

SCIENCE, IN its traditional construction, aims for abstract knowledge—timeless and universal—and the science-based professions draw their legitimacy from an abstract and impersonal notion of expertise. The objectivity of science has, however, been challenged in recent years, partly through the introduction of "outsider's voices" whose claims provide new perspectives on knowledges previously taken as unproblematic (see Harding 1991). These critics assert that social position matters in the constitution and application of scientific knowledge; their writings are generating increasing interest in the significance for scientific work of the structured inequalities of racial-ethnic positions and cultures,[1] as well as those associated with gender, sexuality, and social class (Fausto-Sterling and English 1987, Gould 1981, Haraway 1989; and for social science, Collins 1990, Ladner 1973, Stanfield 1994). In this chapter, I join this chorus of challenge to the traditional view of science, arguing that attention to racial-ethnic dimensions of social organization will produce a more complete and accurate science. I pursue this claim through attention to racial-ethnic dynamics in the analysis of interviews I conducted and reflection on strategies I used as a white researcher to understand the situation of interviewees of African descent. The examples I will discuss also illustrate some of the ways that race and ethnicity are significant in the science-based field of community nutrition work.

The literature on qualitative research methods has been much concerned with questions about the effects of researchers' identities on their studies: classic fieldwork discussions often consider the advantages and disadvantages of "insider" and "outsider" status with respect to the group under study (e.g., Hughes 1984, Merton 1972, Wax 1979, Baca Zinn 1979). More recently, as research on gender issues has become increasingly race- and class-sensitive, feminist researchers have addressed similar issues, considering how the cross-cutting ties of gender and other oppressions work to facilitate or obstruct qualitative research (e.g., Edwards 1990, Oakley 1981, Riessman 1987); however, the fieldwork tradition—like American culture more generally—has been relatively silent on the significance of race-ethnicity in the analysis of data. The idea of eschewing preconceived hypotheses reinforces this lack of attention to ethnicity. Anselm Strauss (1987), for example, writes that a "traditional variable" such as race must "earn [its] way into the grounded theory" (p. 32). I mean to identify a problem with taking Strauss's guideline too literally.

This analysis arises at the intersection of these two strands in my training as a sociologist. On the one hand, my research is driven by a commitment to making visible the oppressions of race, class, and gender; on the other, by the qualitative methodologist's dictum, that we must allow our findings to "emerge from the data." Strauss and others following the conventional fieldwork wisdom seem to suggest that race and ethnicity will be readily apparent, if they are relevant in a research situation. I will argue instead that race-ethnicity is often relevant, even when it does not appear explicitly, on the surface of everyday talk. Talk is often full of oblique references and resonances that could make race and ethnicity relevant. Listeners who have the requisite interpretive competences can hear and understand meanings located in social contexts where race and ethnicity (like gender) virtually always matter. Others may simply miss some part of an informant's meaning.

Discussions focused on insider/outsider identities—especially the earlier ones—are concerned primarily with "access" to the research setting or "rapport" once there, and they seem to assume that the researcher's identity mediates access and rapport (or doesn't) in a relatively direct way.[2] In this analysis, I argue that achieving access and rapport is only a beginning. I will argue that researchers should treat questions of racial-ethnic positioning as integral to the developing analysis in a qualitative study and that "hearing" race and ethnicity in our talk with informants requires active attention and analysis rather than passive listening and recording. This approach is consistent with an interactionist perspective influenced by ethnomethodological studies—a perspective that aims to treat gender and race-ethnicity as ever present, though often unacknowledged, dimensions of the terrain on which social relations unfold—and with more recent methodological discussions based on such assumptions (e.g., Chase 1995, Riessman 1987, West and Zimmerman 1987).

Catherine Kohler Riessman (1987), for example, arguing that "gender is not enough," provides a compelling illustration of how easily racial-ethnic dynamics can be missed in interview studies and suggests that in feminist research, "[cultural] barriers to understanding are particularly consequential, for they reproduce within the scientific enterprise class and cultural divisions between women that feminists have tried so hard to diminish" (p. 173); however, she also points out that many cross-cultural conversations are at least partially successful and that close analysis of interview data provides a "second chance" for making meaning. Rosalind Edwards (1990), too, suggests that understanding and acknowledging differences in racial-ethnic positioning will construct a more productive basis for interviewing across racial-ethnic groups than will asserting a disingenuous claim to commonality. The analysis that follows is meant to extend these insights.

THE STUDY

The data discussed here come from a larger project concerned with the social organization of knowledge and work in dietetics and nutritional counseling. This predominantly female field of work includes hospital dietitians; community and public health nutritionists; and professionals who work in settings such as corporations, government agencies, health clubs, and the media. In the larger study, I am concerned with how fields of work and authority are constructed and how gender is implicated in these constructions (see DeVault 1995). This professional group has been relatively unstudied by sociologists of work; it is interesting both because the field is more diverse and less firmly subordinated than most "women's professions," and also because of the social and cultural significance of food and nutrition policy.

The study is based on fieldwork I began in 1981 and have carried on in several waves since then in three different cities and a variety of settings. My method, based on Dorothy Smith's conception of an "institutional ethnography" (1987), involves using interviews with practitioner-informants to learn about their field of work and about the social relations they are drawn into through their training and the organization of their daily activity. Smith uses the term "institutional ethnography" to refer to an investigation that explores the embeddedness of particular actors in a "ruling apparatus" or "regime" (G. Smith 1990) that coordinates their activity. The aim of research is to understand and disclose the social relations of the ruling regime (or, as George Smith [1990:636] puts it, "how people's activities are reflexively/recursively knitted together into particular forms of social organization"). In my study, the individual nutritionists I interviewed are not, as individuals, the focus of interest; rather, I am concerned with illuminating the organizing contexts that shape their activity—the positions constructed for them as professionals and the opportunities and constraints those positions provide.

Typically, the work of a particular setting depends in various ways on the invisibility of some activities that are nonetheless essential to it. In order to make visible these unacknowledged activities, this research strategy begins with close attention to the people who work in particular settings: the idea is that their knowledge and practices should serve as a point of entry for analyses that look beyond official, ideological accounts of what happens in the setting. This type of research is "institutional" because it examines coordinative processes that emanate from sites beyond local settings, situating local courses of action within broader administrative discourses (in this study, the abstractions of scientific professionalism). The research is "ethnographic" because of its commitment to investigation and description of these organizing relations, as they intersect with people's activities in particular local settings; Smith describes this aspect of the method as a commitment to showing "how it works" (D. Smith 1987:160).

Institutional ethnographies can be based on various types of data, and a single investigation often draws material from more than one source. One requirement, however, is some kind of investigation that reveals the perspectives of practitioners in the setting in considerable detail. In this study, I have used a version of narrative analysis (Riessman 1993) to uncover practitioner's experiences and perspectives. Narrative analysis in sociology has developed from the insight that people often make sense of their lives (in interviews as well as everyday life) by telling and interpreting stories. This insight suggests that interview researchers might usefully attend more carefully to the coherent narratives produced in interviews that traditional methods of analysis are likely to obscure (as when they are cut apart to illustrate themes that appear across interviews [Mishler 1986a]). Studies in the narrative mode are usually based on groups of interviews, like more traditional interview studies, but analyses develop from close readings of a smaller number of individual accounts, which are studied in depth in order to preserve their internal integrity.

In order to produce narratives for analysis in this study, I conducted interviews with thirty-five food and nutrition practitioners.[3] I asked each to tell me "the story of your career," and I urged them to give detailed accounts of their increasing knowledge of the field and the decisions they made over the years about training, certification, and work. Here, I work primarily with a single narrative—that of an African American woman, Janetta Thompson,[4] a registered dietitian who worked in an urban WIC program.[5] Although I do not analyze extended excerpts from interviews with other participants, I read Thompson's interview against the background of data from the larger study; thus, I refer below to general features of interviews with European American nutritionists and more specifically to the stories of two other professionals of African descent who were part of the larger sample.

LISTENING FOR RACE-ETHNICITY

Janetta Thompson's account of her professional history begins, in some ways, much like those of the European American nutritionists I interviewed; issues of race and ethnicity appear gradually and more explicitly as our talk proceeds. As this interview ended, I remarked that, while I had heard some of the same things from other community nutritionists, I had not talked much about race with anyone else. Unsurprised, Thompson responded, "Because you don't have that many people like me in the field."

Her comment states a well-known fact about her field (which is approximately 89 percent white [American Dietetic Association 1991]), but it also invites reflection about that fact, in its suggestion that the underrepresentation of "people like her" has consequences for understandings of the field. Her comment also identifies a methodological problem I faced — although informants "like her" are particularly important for a thorough analysis of the field, it is likely to be more difficult to find and interview them than it is to interview European American professionals. Of the several refusals to my requests for interviews, all but one came from women of color. I respected the reasons (as I understood them) for their reluctance: they were overburdened with work, usually in communities with far more needs than resources, and their responses revealed some skepticism about my purposes and my competence to write about their experiences. I realized early on that I would have to recruit these informants with particular care (as suggested by Cannon, Higginbotham, and Leung 1988; and Edwards 1990). In this context, my use of narrative analysis is in part a response to the challenge of learning as much as possible from a single woman's story. The point here is not that I could not or should not interview more women of color, but rather that it may be unnecessary and even exploitative to refrain from analysis until the researcher feels she has a large enough sample of accounts from those in underrepresented groups. (Indeed, African American feminists suggest that they are called on to do far more than their fair share of "explaining" to others; see Rushin's "The Bridge Poem" [1981]). I would not want this argument to be taken as a proviso *against* including many individuals from underrepresented groups in informant groups, but rather as a suggestion for an alternative approach to sampling issues, and especially as a challenge to the notion that "adequate" samples are always large and relatively homogeneous. (For discussion of a different approach to these issues, linked to a more survey-based logic and therefore more appropriate for some research questions, see Cannon, Higginbotham, and Leung [1988].)

In the analysis that follows, I discuss several excerpts from my conversation with Janetta Thompson. I use a transcription convention adapted from Paget (1983): the end of each line marks a brief pause in the speaker's talk. A hyphen signals a briefer hesitation within a line, and an ellipsis indicates that I have omitted some material from the transcript. My intention is to give the reader a sense of the cadence of our talk and to encourage attention to the development of meaning over time. Presenting the interview material in this form requires more space than the conventional format; it is meant to signal for readers the significance of Janetta Thompson's account. I hope it conveys, and also produces in the reader, a sense of respectful attention to her words and to the interview as our mutual search for the meanings of her experience (cf. Paget 1983).

Recruitment: "You Don't Have That Many People Like Me in the Field."

Here are some excerpts from the beginning of Thompson's career history, as she starts to tell her story:

When I got into the field, back then,
I had never considered nutrition as an option.
In fact, when I considered what I would do in high school,
you know, when I thought of nutritionists, dietitians, I thought of the
    school lunch-room lady.
I didn't know what nutrition was, so far as the field was concerned.
When I was in college I majored in chemistry,
and then I was going to go—
you know, not quite into medicine, because I really wasn't that interested
    in that,
but research and such. . . .
My last semester of college I realized I didn't want to go into chemistry,
    for sure. . . .
So I started going on informational interviews,
my last semester of college, and
talked to people who used chemistry in other ways,
than just in a lab, you know.
And I wanted to go into health.
So I checked with folks who were in environmental health,
forensic chemistry- and such and such.

Some features of this account repeat themes found in the stories of other nutritionists. For example, Thompson's description of her orientation toward the field is quite typical and describes a confluence of motives that often leads to nutrition: she is interested in science, but that interest is tempered by a desire for contact with people in her work and for opportunities to be of service to others. This construction of a career choice seems related to gender, more typical of young women's thinking than young men's. In the stories of other dietitians and nutritionists, there was evidence of quite explicit gender channeling. Many of the white women I interviewed reported choosing nutrition work earlier than Thompson, before they entered college or at the point of declaring a major. Many were steered toward the field by relatives: they were pointed toward professions and instructed—quite directly in many cases—that some professions were for men and some for women. Thompson's choices were shaped in somewhat different ways.

For Janetta Thompson, finding nutrition was fortuitous. As she continues, she tells a story of coincidence:

Then I, um
(pause)
a woman at the school said she knew someone who worked in a community health center.
And I got really excited about that, because I wanted to work in- in a, sort of like an inner-city kind of thing.
That's where I'm from, [Eastern City],
and I wanted to work with people who were like me, in a sense.
So I went on an interview at the [Westside] clinic, in [the city].
And- it was nice, you know,
everyone knew each other there, and knew their patients.
And
I was just so excited, and
the woman,
she happened to be in the WIC program.
And I- had never heard of WIC before, I had never,
you know, but anyway—
But I was just so excited!
So I went back to school, and
about two days later, I got a phone call from [someone else],
at the [Southside] health center in [another neighborhood].
And she said they had an opening for a nutrition assistant, and would I be interested in applying? And I said, "Sure!"

Two aspects of this excerpt deserve close attention. First, it contains talk that circles around race, though without making it an explicit topic. Thompson speaks of wanting to work "in a, sort of like an inner-city kind of thing," and goes on to explain that this means working with "people who were like me." Without securing a fixed meaning for these words, she provides a clue to the significance, for her, of the community health setting. She was "really excited about that" and her repetition of the phrase "just so excited" reinforces her point. It is important also to note her hesitations, as she marks time while thinking how to say these things, in this context, and especially to me, a relatively unknown white woman, and a professional, as she is, though in a different field. At this point in the interview, we have spoken face to face for no more than five minutes. It is perhaps too early in our conversation for race comfortably to become an explicit topic.

This excerpt can also be analyzed to uncover the organization of "coincidence" in the story. In Thompson's subjective experience, and in her telling of the story, the visit to the health center and the invitation to apply for a job are fortuitous, but there is certainly more than chance at work here, and to show what it is one must look beyond her account. What Janetta Thompson encounters as she begins to look for work is an organization that embodies a philosophy of community health care, an organization that is part of a network with a particular history. Her recruitment into nutrition work depends on this expression of the field and its fit with her interests and commitments. This kind of encounter figures in the stories of other nutritionists as well: a substantial group, especially a few years earlier, entered the field because of their developing political commitments, sometimes even growing out of work in radical organizations such as Black Panther kitchens or clinics. In Thompson's story, there is no doubt an additional dynamic in the organization of coincidence, although she does not mention it herself: Thompson's cultural and ethnic history gives her a kind of expertise that will allow her to work effectively in a multiethnic community setting; the organization needs the knowledge and skill that comes with her background.

Janetta Thompson enters the field as an assistant; it will be several years before she decides that she wants to be a nutritionist, and several more years before she is able to obtain professional credentials that match the work she has begun to do. When she eventually reaches the point of certification, she is blocked by the supervisor of her internship. Eventually, she files a successful affirmative action complaint; even so, she must make other arrangements to obtain her certification. Almost ten years after entering the field, she becomes a registered dietitian.

As I talked with Thompson, I realized that if I were going to include the perspectives of nutrition workers from a range of racial-ethnic communities, I would have to extend the scope of my "sample"—and my understanding of "the field"—beyond the formally credentialed nutritionists who work in community settings. Through Thompson's sponsorship, then, I interviewed two Caribbean women who worked in nearby program sites, one as a clinic administrative worker and the other as an assistant who does direct counseling in the WIC program. Their stories of entry confirm and deepen the analysis that I have begun to develop from Thompson's story.

Both began their accounts, like most of the others I interviewed, by telling of initial interests in science and food. One had earned an associate's degree, in her country, in home economics (she began in agriculture, but like many U.S. women, she was steered toward the field considered more gender-appropriate), and she had worked for ten years as an extension agent. After she came to the United States, she worked in an insurance office. She came to nutrition work through her experience as a WIC participant, when her husband was laid off and they needed assistance. She told of trying to hide her skills ("I thought you had to be kind of ignorant of nutrition to be on the program. . . . So I was going in and trying to act like I didn't know anything about nutrition."), and, with hindsight, she laughed about being "discovered" by a counselor who encouraged her to apply for a job in the program. Eventually, this woman completed a bachelor's degree, though not in nutrition, and moved into a WIC administrative position. When she told of inquiring about a nutrition degree, her story was one of discouragement and rebuff: she was "turned off" when the best-known program in the city was unresponsive to her need for a loan and told her "only negative things."

Another woman came to the United States with an interest in nursing, and began work here in a factory. She trained as a nurse's aide and worked as a home health worker for many years. She considered going to school for nursing, but decided against it: although she'd enjoyed her work, and especially her brief training in nutrition, she was discouraged by a friend's tale of investing in a college degree and then repeatedly failing the nursing registration exam. When she decided she needed more money, she trained as a secretary, and then—fortuitously—heard about an opening for a nutrition assistant in a community setting where her cultural background would be an asset. When I interviewed her, she had been doing the job for several years, providing direct counseling for participants with no special nutritional problems, and she had been engaged in several special projects: at her own program site, she had rewritten diet guidelines for participants from her native country, and she was also serving on a state task force organized to produce training materials incorporating more ethnically specific nutrition information.

There are two things to notice about these three career stories, taken as a group. First, there is a pattern in what is easy and what is difficult for these three women to achieve. They are fortuitously slotted into positions that appeal to them, located in communities they care about and involving work they believe in. In all of these cases, the job finds them; they are recruited by WIC staff, and they all tell stories of recruitment as welcome coincidence. What is difficult, once they enter the field, is to achieve the credentialed status that would allow full participation and professional status. They are "mentored" into a range of lower-level positions and then blocked from advancement by the formal credential-based organization of these work settings. The mentoring they receive is quite different from that which appears in the stories of white women who entered the field in more conventional ways and accumulated credentials more quickly and easily.[6] While these three women's stories should not be taken to represent the experiences of all women of color entering professional fields, they certainly suggest one dynamic of recruitment that would help to explain a racial-ethnic pattern of representation common in all professions, the progressive "whitening" of the ranks as we look upward in professional hierarchies.

Practice: "Knowing the Nuances"

Near the end of our conversation, I ask Thompson about her placement in community nutrition. I explain that I'd been wondering, as I got ready for this interview, whether she chose to work in public health, or whether there is some channeling process that places people of color there more often than in other areas. I comment that it's clear by this point in our conversation that she has chosen her work, but that I am still wondering about the general question. She responds:

I *chose.*
You know why I chose this?
I figured,
you know, I wanted to go into the health care field, it's true.
But I think,
why should people
from the outside
always be the ones coming in
for Black people?
Why can't
some of us- stay?
You know, why can't we as nurses, doctors, nutritionists—
I mean, at that time I wasn't thinking about nutritionists, but, psychologists—
why can't we be here?
Why do we have to import so many folks?

You know,
who- may or may not,
I mean, they may really- be sincere about it,
but they may not really- know the nuances,
you know?

In this excerpt, Thompson is willing to speak more explicitly about race than before. She discusses her concern about professionals from "outside" who work in the Black community, but the rather tentative character of her speech (her slight hesitations as she characterizes these professionals: "You know, who- may or may not, I mean, . . .") and the qualification she adds ("they may really- be sincere about it") indicate that she speaks with an awareness of the difficulties of talking about race and ethnicity— an awareness of entering what Susan Chase (1995) labels a realm of "unsettled discourse." Thompson constructs the competence she is concerned with here as a matter of "knowing the nuances."

This suggestive phrase raises questions: What does it mean to "know the nuances" of community work? And how does such knowledge appear in the constitution of professional expertise or professional training? Thompson's reference to knowing the nuances suggests a kind of working knowledge that contrasts rather sharply with the textbook account of ethnicity in this profession. In most professional materials, as in North American discourse more generally, European whiteness is taken as the norm. The core knowledge base of nutrition counseling is typically presented as free of ethnic marking; special chapters or articles deal with the dietary patterns of racial-ethnic "others" as deviations from this norm, noting modifications of standard practice that these differences require; thus, although ethnicity may be acknowledged as relevant to practice, it is treated as a factor to "add and stir" in relation to the abstract principles of scientific nutrition.

By contrast, Thompson gives an account of a more grounded practice: she insists on the complex specificity of racial-ethnic differences and explains that learning about and responding to these differences is an ongoing process. When she discusses her clients' backgrounds, she emphasizes specificity: "So far as culture is concerned . . . instead of lumping— you can't lump all Caribbeans together." And a bit later: "Even among Hispanics. People from Puerto Rico eat very differently from people from Cuba, and so on." She provides examples, showing how simple translation is inadequate: foods have different names in different islands, for instance. I ask her to talk about how she learns the significance of these differences, and how she trains staff. Here too, her answer is about a learning process, and she begins with a specific illustration from a workshop

they organized in her program, where paraprofessionals from the local
ethnic community brought food to share with other counselors:

And we had
the food!
Right there, so we could see it.
You know, I used to think,
when they said they had bread in the—
no, they had soup in the morning—
I thought it was like, chicken noodle soup, you know, wet.
No, it's not chicken noodle soup.
But a woman said, "No, you put bread in it."
So I thought, "Oh, it's like French toast?"
She said, "No," you know.
So I learn from- clients,
one on one,
my staff, who are- you know, multi-ethnic,
um,
reading,
listening, you know,
and asking questions, and,
and
clients,
a lot of them say, "Oh, I'll cook you this dish."
They never do (laughing).
Even though, sometimes, we do go
over to someone's house, you know- and eat, or whatever.
Because they insist, you know.
But, um
(pause)
I don't know, just—

[DeVault: Staying open to stuff, it sounds like. And looking for it, wher-
     ever]

And asking questions, if you're confused,
instead of letting something go . . .
I don't know, I'm not perfect.
And I learn so much, but there are so many gaps,
and I sometimes feel frustrated, you know?

A final excerpt from this interview shows what I believe is another aspect of knowing the nuances, by pointing to Janetta Thompson's commitments—to those aspects of her work she cares deeply about. This excerpt

also suggests how these concerns can fade from view in the discourses of the profession. While working as a nutrition assistant, Thompson started course work toward a master's degree (a route toward certification for those without a college major in dietetics). She knew she wanted to stay in a community setting, and she concentrated on community nutrition. Telling this part of her story, she explains in more detail her special interests in the field at that time:

And I figured,
since I worked with people who were from all- over the world,
I would- sort of specialize in
that too.
Because I used to get upset when,
even when I hadn't finished my degree,
I would have people from Haiti, or whatever,
being told about a diabetic diet.
And it was very inappropriate,
the way they were told to eat,
they were given a list of American foods,
and told,
"OK, you should eat less rice, you get to eat bread, blah-blah-blah."
And they may not have liked bread, but they loved rice.
So why can't they eat more rice and,
you know, the exchanges, and things like that.
So I used to get very angry.
I wouldn't show my
client that I was angry, but I would get *very* angry.

In order to explain, she presents a narrative from her professional experience. The account is framed by her emotion; it starts with getting "upset" and ends by announcing that she was "very angry" (though she didn't show it). These quite explicit markers of feeling emphasize the importance of this account; it tells what she cares about.

This excerpt also reveals how little space there is in the profession, as formally constituted, for the expression of Thompson's concerns and competences. Most obviously, she mentions the suppression of her anger, but more subtle effects of the organization of nutrition work can be seen in how this telling works: Thompson explains that she will "specialize in-
. . ." At this point, there is a very brief pause in her speech. She stops, and thinks how to say what she means, because what she wants to do in her field is not neatly packaged as a specialty. She has introduced her concern, explaining just before that she has worked with people from all over the world, and she goes on to say it is "that" that she cares about. But the

profession does not provide a ready term for the work she wants to do; thus, she tells about it through a series of stories like the one excerpted above.[7]

ETHNICITY AND EXPERTISE IN NUTRITIONAL SCIENCE

Darlene Clark Hine (1989) argues that "all professions look different when viewed from the black woman's angle" (p. x), and her history of African American women's participation in nursing, *Black Women in White*, provides compelling evidence for that assertion. Hine documents a long tradition of women's health care work in and for African American communities, a history of exclusion from white institutions, and the development of an extensive network of parallel institutions for African Americans. She discusses Black nurses' strategies for gaining access to the profession, and their debates about integration and separatism. She reveals a rich history that has been virtually invisible in official accounts of nursing and distinctive experiences that are still largely unacknowledged. My analysis here represents one response to her charge that race and ethnicity should be part of the analysis of any women's profession, even if the field appears predominantly white. In this analysis of Janetta Thompson's narrative of her career, I have begun to see the outlines of an analysis that attends to the racial-ethnic dimensions of professional work in dietetics and public health nutrition.

Dietitians and nutritionists work with food, and food is strongly connected to culture—and, therefore, to race and ethnicity. These professionals are certainly aware of these connections, yet their history is an inauspicious one: the standard story from outside the profession emphasizes the attempt to impose a bland "American" diet on a succession of immigrant populations (Levenstein 1988, Shapiro 1986). Further, this story is often told in ways that present nutritionists as rather ridiculous, oppressively moralizing dispensers of authoritative knowledge. My analysis has examined this kind of issue from a somewhat different angle. I have suggested that working within the frame of professionalism makes it difficult to attend adequately to the cultures of race and ethnicity and tends to hide the ways in which at least some nutrition professionals (like Janetta Thompson) work with a sensitivity to culture and ethnicity. Further, I have suggested that women with knowledge of ethnic communities are often recruited into subordinate positions, where they do essential work without gaining access to the benefits of full professional status. (Although the workers discussed here shared a cultural background that seems to contribute to their perspectives on these issues, several of the white public health nutritionists I interviewed shared these kinds of concerns and commitments, although they were expressed in different ways. The dynamics of their somewhat different locations remain as topics for further analysis.)

To the extent that nutritional counseling is conceived as a traditional profession, it must find its base and its legitimacy in knowledge conceived as abstract and impersonal. Within this frame, the local particularities of phenomena arising from race and ethnicity are construed as "extra" kinds of information that might modify or specify more general kinds of knowledge. In practice—on the job and in the actual operation of nutrition policy and programs—race and ethnicity are immediate, apparent, and strongly consequential. Clients come to nutritional counseling with attitudes and beliefs toward food and eating that are intimately linked with their ethnic backgrounds. Knowledge about ethnicity—especially local and particular knowledge of ethnic communities—is essential to the conduct of the work. Such knowledge enters the community health setting in several ways, partly through the creation of paraprofessional roles and the knowledge and commitments of professionals like Janetta Thompson (see also Gilkes 1982).

This argument suggests that a science determined to ignore culture and ethnicity is flawed and that science-based knowledge and practices will produce more robust truths when they incorporate knowledge of the cultural contexts of human life. Such a claim is troubling, for many, and perhaps risky given the linked histories of science and racism. When scientists have attended to racial-ethnic differences, their work has often reified racial categories and bolstered claims of essential differences among racial-ethnic groups. On the other hand, abstract science has often been a powerful weapon in struggles against prejudice and racism, a weapon that many are loathe to discard. Sociologist Ruth Frankenberg (1993) sees this dilemma in the context of overlapping cultural discourses of "essentialist racism"; "color-blindness" (which she analyzes as color- and power-evasiveness); and "race cognizance," an attitude that insists on taking account of the autonomy of different cultural groups and the social structural inequalities that organize group relations. In Frankenberg's scheme, the "color-blind" discourse can be seen as a formulation that is usefully critical of earlier essentialist understandings of race-ethnicity, but one that achieves that usefulness by obscuring the dynamics of group differences related to culture and power. Iris Marion Young (1990), in an analysis especially relevant to this study, argues that the hierarchical organization of professional work relies on a "myth of merit" that insists on the irrelevance of racial-ethnic differences. The problem with such a color-blind formulation of merit-based standards is that it ignores the political process through which work skills and qualifications are defined and organized into a hierarchical system.

My analysis of nutrition work begins to reveal such a hierarchy of knowledges and positions. Within the profession as a whole, the abstract science of a hospital model competes with the more socially grounded public health perspective that informs community nutrition.[8] Within the public health sphere, too, knowledge of particular ethnic patterns is typically construed as "social" rather than "scientific." Some kinds of knowledge are privileged, as "expertise"; some are viewed as subordinate, useful but "extra"; and some kinds of knowledge are discounted and exploited without acknowledgment, even though they are essential to the day-to-day work of the setting. Such a view of racial-ethnic competences as outside the core of professional expertise supports the construction of a system in which racial-ethnic "others" are concentrated in subordinate paraprofessional categories. As in nursing (Glazer 1991), the hierarchy of professional positions appears "fair" because of its basis in training and credentials, while racial-ethnic (and social class) hierarchies are reproduced through systemic inequalities in access to top positions.

In presenting this critique of conventional practice in dietetics and nutrition, I wish to state clearly that I do not mean to undertake this analysis as a distanced observer, passing judgment on a flawed profession from a position of moral superiority. I do not mean to single out food and nutrition fields as uniquely vulnerable to the critique offered here; there are certainly related problems in most of the sciences, and especially in the health care professions. Further, I am interested in the dilemmas of food and nutrition professionals in part because they mirror and illuminate the challenges facing sociologists as we remake our field in the current moment. Indeed, my primary message is for sociologists conducting qualitative research, and the methodological implications of my analysis will be discussed in the next section.

ETHNICITY AND EXPERTISE IN SOCIOLOGICAL METHOD

I have relied on close analysis of an interview with an African American nutritionist to disclose aspects of the racial-ethnic organization of her professional field. I have suggested that the racialized context organizing her career was only occasionally made an explicit topic in our conversation, even though its influence is pervasive. This absence in explicit talk is only partly a matter of rapport with the interviewee. I do believe that this interview shows evidence of increasing confidence and trust, so that we talk more explicitly about race near the end of the interview. The main point, however, is that talk is often shaped by racial-ethnic dimensions of social organization without bearing explicit marks of that influence. The lesson for the qualitative researcher, I believe, is that analyses will often be strengthened by an attentive and knowledgeable search for the effects of racial-ethnic constructions and inequalities in the lives of those we study.

The conventional wisdom of the qualitative tradition directs the researcher to enter the field with few expectations or assumptions and to build analyses on themes that arise from subjects in the field. Of course, operating as a "blank slate" has always been impossible, and the commitments of many qualitative researchers working in this tradition have sometimes produced quite sensitive analyses of the processes underlying racial-ethnic inequalities (e.g., Anderson 1978, Ladner 1971, Liebow 1967, Rollins 1985, Stack 1974, Wellman 1977, and Zavella 1987, to list only a few). The problem with the conventional wisdom, in my view, is that it makes attention to such inequalities "optional," and leaves unacknowledged the awareness and knowledge that make such analyses possible. Within the field of research methods (as in nutrition work), professional expertise is constituted abstractly, in terms of neutral techniques for analysis; it does not necessarily include the kind of knowledge that would help researchers identify and understand the effects of a racialized social context.[9]

In making the analysis presented here, I have relied on a broadly ethnomethodological understanding of conversational interaction to make sense of the interview as a jointly constructed verbal encounter, as well as drawing insights from the accounts of cultural "outsiders" who have written about the vicissitudes of speaking in various cultural contexts. I have assumed, for example, that conversation is always located: we always speak to and for particular partners or audiences in particular moments. In addition, I rely on the idea that speakers in any oppressed or marginalized cultural group learn distinctive skills that "tailor" speech for different cultural contexts (see hooks 1989, especially chaps. 1–2, 11, 22–33; and Jordan 1985). With other insiders, one can assume certain kinds of understanding that cannot be taken for granted elsewhere. When speaking with outsiders, then, one is often "deciding" (though the term implies too much deliberateness) whether to make difference an issue. If ethnicity is not made explicit, for example, outsider listeners may miss its significance entirely; when it is, there are other difficulties, including vulnerability to various kinds of challenge ("prove it") and misunderstandings that speakers no doubt often judge not worth it. In some situations, leaving truths unspoken may be understood as a kind of resistance to outsiders' unwelcome intrusions.

When I interview an African American nutritionist, she is certainly making these kinds of choices as she constructs her account. She makes judgments about what I can and cannot understand and about the wisdom of making race visible.[10] One important influence here, I think, is a general presumption in much everyday talk that race and ethnicity are irrelevant, that these differences should not matter. This presumption may have particular force when the topic is professional life, a terrain where the official story claims that knowledge and merit transcend ethnic and cultural differences (Young 1990). The conceptual frames of professional work organization make space for race and ethnicity, but only in rather circumscribed forms and spaces.

These observations suggest questions for the researcher: With respect to the interview analyzed here, for example, do I know enough—about the nuances—to understand and interpret Janetta Thompson's account? How did my knowledge—and perhaps more importantly my ignorance—shape our interaction and then my reading of the interview data produced in our encounter? I view my interview with Thompson as a relatively successful one, in which we were able to talk in ways that were useful, for me at least. I think it helped our unfolding interaction that we were both young professional women. We were able to laugh and nod as we spoke about the importance of mentors, for example, and about our conflicts and discomforts with them. I think, also, that as the interview went forward—as I displayed an openness to what she said and some degree of understanding—Thompson became increasingly willing to talk explicitly about race as an aspect of her career story. But, of course, she would no doubt tell somewhat different stories to different interviewers. I cannot know for sure how those stories would have been told, but I can analyze the story we produced with an awareness of the positions from which we both spoke. In pursuing such an analysis, as well as in conducting the interview, I will be most successful if I consider carefully what knowledge I need for a rich and robust interpretation and how my access to that knowledge is either facilitated or limited by my own particular location and history. I should consider not only how Thompson's story might have differed had she told it to an African American interviewer, but perhaps more importantly how I can find and analyze race and ethnicity in the stories of the white nutritionists I interviewed, many of whom never spoke about it explicitly. As I know more, I see this absence more clearly and it calls out for further analytic attention. (For an example of one small beginning toward such analysis, see the discussion of hospital kitchen supervisory work by white nutritionists in chap. 7.)

Both of the analytic approaches I have adopted here—institutional ethnography and narrative analysis—depart from the most common approach to qualitative analysis, the constant comparative method of grounded theory analysis. While grounded theory analysts are typically interested in social processes abstracted from particular contexts, the methods I have used here are attentive to the coherence of individual courses of action in local settings. The generalizability of the analysis comes not from the claim that actions and experiences are similar across settings, but from a focus on the social relations that organize those local settings and action within them. These methods may be especially useful in addressing issues related to racial-ethnic positioning, since they allow consideration of an actor in context rather than only as representative of a social category. Rather than searching for generalizable differences among categorical groups, the aim is to understand how a member of such a group is caught up in the social relations of her context. While it is necessary to recognize that the particular experiences produced by these social relations may vary, we can be confident that analyses will have general significance if the focus is on the relations producing varied experiences, rather than on the experience itself. In this analysis, for instance, my claim is not that all, or even most, African American nutritionists will share Janetta Thompson's route to professional work in an inner-city clinic. Instead, I mean to expose the conditions that surround her choices at crucial moments and the contexts that organize her daily practice on the job. This kind of analysis is, in Dorothy Smith's (1987) words, "open 'at the other end,' where it is tied into the extended relations of the political economy" (p. 170): While I have begun to reveal one aspect of the professional "regime" in nutrition work, my argument about that regime opens further questions, pointing my analysis in the larger study (and, of course, other investigators) toward consideration of how other individuals, in the same or somewhat different ethnic-cultural positions, enter and negotiate the same set of social relations.

My aim here is not to make pronouncements about appropriate methods of interviewing and analysis, but to invite deeper and more thoughtful reflection on these issues as they arise in the analysis of qualitative data. I mean to challenge the ostensibly passive stance toward our data that has been traditional in qualitative research and to encourage more vigorous, sustained analysis of the structured organizing effects of ethnicity and gender in the stories we are told. I wish to close with two suggestions for interview research sensitive to the play of race-ethnicity. First, I recommend careful and detailed analysis of talk, understood as jointly constructed interaction unfolding through time. This kind of analysis, drawing from recent perspectives on narrative and conversation, can move the researcher beyond questions of "access" and "rapport" as these are typically conceived. It provides a method for developing a particular kind of "meaning in context" (Mishler 1986a), a grounded and particular analysis of interview encounters that take place within racialized social institutions. My second recommendation is for what I would label a light- rather than heavy-handed approach to the interpretation of interview data. I have treated the transcript of my interview with Janetta Thompson as a text to be presented gently, even somewhat tentatively. Her words were spoken to me in a moment when we came together; I grasped, at the time, at least some of what she meant, and I have worked at deepening that understanding through sustained attention to her interview and by investigating the context that has shaped her story and its telling. I put forward an argument, but since my argument focuses on how cultural differences complicate interpretation, it would be self-negating if it claimed a final, objective truth. My call for tentativeness should not be taken as weakening my analysis. Instead, as Collins (1990:236–237) suggests, the acknowledgment of locatedness and partiality in this kind of analysis can move it toward a stronger and more credible kind of truth.

IV. THE SELF AS RESOURCE

FEMINIST EPISTEMOLOGIES suggest that personal perspectives are valid and perhaps even essential elements of any systematic attempt to know the social world. This idea comes from the critique of abstract knowledge claims that obscure interest and partiality. Feminists and others in opposition to ruling regimes often want to ask, "Who says?" The question suggests that they in turn should be willing to reveal their own authorship when they proffer competing claims.

Standard social science formats hide the personal and particular. Even beginning students have been schooled—if only through the media and early education—in the idea that authority resides in abstract and impersonal claims ("It was found . . ."; "The researcher saw . . ."; and so on); as a result, many social scientists hesitate to use the first person (see Krieger's [1991] interviews on this topic), let alone to reveal biographical and subjective detail. Given such conventions, making personal material more visible often stimulates strongly negative reactions, including trivialization and dismissal. Despite these problems, feminist social scientists have used personal reflection and testimony in various ways: as wellsprings for scholarly creativity, methods of generating data, touchstones for evaluating knowledge claims, and elements of new formats for reporting research, to name only a few. Their experiments contribute to a growing repertoire of strategies for working with personal material, and also to the development of audiences prepared to read social science texts in new ways.

The chapters in this section illustrate two versions of personal/reflexive research strategy. They use the self, as Susan Krieger suggests, as "resource rather than contaminant" (Krieger 1991). "Novel Readings" examines the situated character of reading, combining analysis of published book reviews and critical articles with my own reading of a single novel by Nadine Gordimer. It is presented here as an experiment in the use of personal response as part of an archive for analysis. I wrote this article while working as part of a research group studying modes of representing society (following the approach outlined in Becker 1986a); my intent was to show how various reading communities make sense of a text that travels through widely varying political scenes and societies. I did not set out to experiment with the use of personal material as data, but my thinking was much influenced by my own reading experiences—especially by the powerful role of novels in my feminist development. As I worked toward an analysis, it seemed sensible to make visible this source of my thinking (and illustration of my point), so I began to devise a way to use myself as a datum.

When I submitted this article for publication, reviewers seemed somewhat perplexed: some were dismissive, others interested and sympathetic but concerned about convention and rigor. Through a lengthy process of review and revision, I was interested in readers' complaints and misreadings of my intentions, some produced by ambiguities in my early arguments and some, I believed, by their expectations arising from standard sociological practices that I meant to challenge. It amused me—given the article's focus on the conventions of genre—when as a final requirement for publication I was asked to add a table: the text would at least look a little more like a standard sociological article. I was willing to comply and enjoyed the challenge of presenting these ideas in a form that would be unusual but still acceptable in a mainstream journal.

"Whose Science of Food and Health?" is more straightforwardly reflective. It considers the professional status of sociological researchers and how that status affects our research on other professions. When I wrote this chapter, I was much influenced by feminist writing about the power exercised in any representation of others (e.g., Stacey 1988, Patai 1991). As I conducted interviews, I wondered how participants would feel about my interpretations, worried about exploiting their willingness to speak, and brooded about whether my research would seem worthwhile to them. I became increasingly aware of how my topic connected to my own concerns (with roots I could find in family history, generations removed), and I pondered what those connections meant. It seemed only fair to make these reflections more visible, but I wanted to do so without making myself the center of the writing. The article, therefore, was an attempt to combine personal reflection with empirical investigation.

6   Novel Readings

The Social Organization of Interpretation

MANY SOCIOLOGISTS of literature and some literary critics, recognizing that cultural works are produced in social context, have argued that novels can be taken as sociological data and used as indicators of prevailing attitudes and social relations. The conventions of literary realism (Watt 1957) and the avowedly sociological aims of at least some novelists provide some warrant for thinking of novels as portraits of social conditions. This view, however, has always existed in tension with the position that novels should be taken as primarily "literary" or aesthetic expressions rather than as representational texts.[1] Recent work in literary theory makes any simple application of a "representation" approach highly suspect, for most current theorists question the possibility of any straightforward portrayal of an empirical reality "out there." These writers suggest that any representation is partial, selective, and constructed, and they emphasize, in various ways, how texts are shaped by conventions and traditions of writing, by the psychodynamics of desire and repression, by the cultural hegemony of ruling elites, and even by features of language that cause texts to subvert their own apparent meanings. In the light of this new thinking, the impulse to read a novel for information about society begins to seem hopelessly naive.

We know, however, that, as human beings live their lives, they often adopt epistemological stances that theory suggests are naive.[2] While sociologists should be wary of mistaking novels for information, readers are not so constrained. Readers of at least some kinds of novels seem to use fictional accounts in making sense of the world, or, at least—to limit the claim to more easily observable manifestations of the phenomenon—they feel entitled to use fictional portrayals as a basis for their own assertions about society. The case I discuss below provides one example: I examine readings that make a novel the basis for discussion about politics and social relations.[3] Whatever the theoretical status of the novel as representation, this kind of interpretive activity is an important focus for a sociology of literature, especially one that aims to connect with a long-standing sociological concern for the understanding of meaning.

Sociologists working in an interactionist tradition examine the variety of ways that human beings make sense out of their encounters with others, solving problems collectively. Texts, in this perspective, can be thought of as objects that people use and refer to in interaction, "props" in the drama of human life. But texts are objects with a special character because they convey complex meanings.[4] It is possible, of course, to analyze cultural works as props without attending to their meanings, and much important work in the institutional branch of the sociology of culture has been based on such an approach.[5] However, I want to suggest that there is also room for a sociological approach that does not ignore the text as story and can account for the ways in which the stories that texts convey become meaningful for individuals and are carried into their interactions with others.

This article is part of an ongoing series of studies that focus on the processes of "telling about society" (Becker 1986a). These studies extend Becker's insight that artistic production is collective activity and assert that any mode of representation is best understood as the product of concerted activity. Genres as diverse as documentary films, statistical tables, factory records, novels, and the stories that people tell about their everyday lives all have in common that they are produced and used in social settings. Within these settings, individual makers and users learn conventions that guide the production and interpretation of any text. General problems—what will constitute "adequacy" or "misrepresentation," for example—must be solved with respect to any form of representation but arise differently in various settings. Solutions to these problems are collective agreements that are "good enough" for the purposes at hand in a specific time and place. Thus, conventions develop and change through disputation and agreement about responses to the problems of representation and interpretation. Texts of various sorts enter larger discourses, or continuing "conversations," mediated textually, among participants separated in time and space (Foucault 1972). These discourses constitute the textual traditions within which both makers and users of representations operate. An important feature of this approach is a focus on activity as well as text—a concern with the joint activities involved in producing representations and the activities that develop from using representations: how readers, for example, interact with others after reading.

Interpretive activity has become a focus in recent literary theory as well, as some critics have begun to include readers in their studies of texts and to emphasize the active character of reading (see Tompkins 1980). This new attention to readers has both resulted from and reinforced the hermeneutic criticism of the idea that any fixed or correct meaning lies waiting to be discovered in a text or that interpretation can ever be independent of history and location (Wolff 1977). It also seems to emerge from a new diversity within cultural elites, the result of groups traditionally outside the dominant culture—women, racial minorities, and those on geo-graphical margins—becoming more active and visible in the production of cultural works, in audiences, and in scholarship about literature and art. These newly visible participants in cultural discourse have begun to provide new readings of cultural works, suggesting that, in the past, those with authoritative voices have provided only partial interpretations. In the face of this increasing diversity, theorists of interpretation are beginning to look for ways to theorize both the accuracy of interpretation that re-sults from knowledge of cultural convention and the divergence that arises from the located character of any interpretation.

Griswold (1987) has proposed a sociological model for understanding how cultural works enter into the "fabrication of meaning" in different social contexts. Drawing on the concept of "interpretive communities" (Fish 1980), she shows that novels are read differently in different societies by examining the divergent evaluations of West Indian novelist George Lamming produced by reviewers in the West Indies, Britain, and the United States. I begin with a similar observation, though I focus on the divergence that can result from other dimensions of difference among readers, within and across societies. Griswold suggests that the differences she demonstrates result from the shared concerns and presuppositions of different societies, and she goes on to argue that works with "cultural power" are those with the capacity to elicit different readings. I set aside such evaluative questions about texts and focus on contexts for reading in order to examine in more detail the processes of interpretation that pro-duce divergent accounts of the meanings of cultural works.

I will discuss readings of a single novel—*The Late Bourgeois World,* by Nadine Gordimer ([1966] 1982). My aim is not to explicate the novel the way a critic might or to discuss its sociological content but to examine the accounts of different sorts of readers in order to analyze the bases and limits for different interpretations. In deference to theorists of representa-tion, I do not assume that the novel is a straightforward representation of some social reality; I will, however, attend particularly to readers' discus-sions of the novel as representational and to their uses of the text in dis-cussing the social setting it represents. As I examine different readings, I will show how interpretation is collective activity: varying interpretations do not simply depend on individual insights but rather emerge as groups with particular interests acquire voices in discourses about similar texts and collectively develop and learn new interpretive frames. I will focus especially on an analysis of the differences produced by "gendered read-ing" in order to display the phenomenon of "reading as a woman" and to show how it can influence the interpretation and evaluation of at least some cultural works.

METHOD

My approach involves treating interpretation as learned, socially orga-nized activity.[6] To make sense of any text, readers must have competence in the conventions associated with different kinds of texts (Culler 1980) and must bring appropriate conventions into play (Smith 1983). The skills involved are not just those of combining sounds and sentences but also of recognizing and applying rules for understanding different kinds of texts, from bills and parking tickets to poems and short stories (and see McCoy 1995 on photographic texts). Most members of literate societies learn the skills of novel reading in various ways: as children, they learn "reading a story," and in high school English classes they study more sophisticated techniques (e.g., finding themes). Readers of specialized subgenres (e.g., romances, mysteries, and science fiction) learn conventions associated with these genres, either from repeated experience or from the communi-ties of readers within which they pass information about books (Radway 1984). Those who pursue literature professionally learn quite specialized methods of reading fiction (Kolodny 1981); others who read serious nov-els pick up some of these skills more casually—from the *New York Times Book Review,* for example.

I assume that all readers construct meanings from the novels they read and that they often make explicit arguments about these meanings. Re-viewers and critics do this professionally and quite formally; they make printed claims about novels in newspapers, journals, books, and so on. Lay readers presumably read less instrumentally, for entertainment or general edification, and draw conclusions they rarely articulate to anyone else. Still, they too construct meanings and carry them away from the nov-els they read. Sometimes they tell others about books they have particu-larly liked or disliked; in order to do so, they tell stories about these novels and why they are or are not worth reading. It is these kinds of formal or informal constructions of a novel's meaning that I take as data for the analysis to follow.[7]

I examine three kinds of readings. To study examples of professional readings, I examine reviews that appeared in 1966–67 when *The Late Bourgeois World* was first published and scholarly articles written during the mid- to late 1970s. These published sources were located through book review indexes and the *MLA Bibliography;* they are shown in Ap-pendix A, "List of Sources" (p. 233), and identified by parenthetical itali-cized letter when I refer to them in the text.[8] In addition, I examine as a lay reading my own account of the novel (not written down at the time of reading but articulated retrospectively in the course of studying the pub-lished sources and developing this analysis), with attention to my own biography and social position. Using a comparative analytic approach, I examine such questions as: How do different readers tell what the story is about? How do they describe the characters? What weight do they give to political content or to the fact that the narrator is a woman? What are their complaints about the book? I use the answers to these questions to illustrate different readings and as evidence of the processes that produced them.

AN EXAMPLE: READING *THE LATE BOURGEOIS WORLD*

Before presenting my analysis, I will provide a brief summary of *The Late Bourgeois World* for readers unfamiliar with the novel. Since it is *my* summary, it must be suspect as a text against which to read my discussion of varying interpretations. This apparent difficulty in fact illustrates the kind of interpretive process I will highlight in the analysis. Any account is partial and should be read as such. However, users of the conventional formats tend to accept them, routinely, as "adequate" for the purposes at hand (Becker 1986). The awkwardness of including a plot summary in this article points to distinctive features of sociological and literary analyses. Literary scholars typically adopt a convention that assumes that readers have read the primary texts they discuss; when they discuss texts that are part of a shared canon, they do not need to recount plots.[9] Sociological convention, on the other hand, requires that a scholarly article include some display of the data on which the analysis is based, and this convention has shaped my decision not only to include a summary but also to quote rather lengthy passages from the novel in later sections of this article.

In the analysis that follows, I present my own, located account (of a novel I have selected) as one among others, and I apply to my own account the same analytic tools applied to the accounts of others. In order to assess the effect of my predispositions on both summary and analysis, one could (and ideally should) read the entire novel, as well as the reviews and scholarly articles I will discuss. In any case, it should be clear that I cannot make decisions about how to identify and describe the novel without engaging in the kind of selective representation of the novel that I will analyze later.[10] The problems of trusting my representation are especially evident here because the data I display are atypical and do not fit well into such conventional sociological formats as tables, equations, or excerpts from fieldnotes. But, of course, these more standard representations of data—like all representations—are also partial, selective, and constructed by the analyst.

The Novel

The Late Bourgeois World, a short novel by Nadine Gordimer, was published in 1966. It is the story of one Saturday (which turns out to be the day of the American astronauts' space walk), told by a white South African woman. The day begins as Liz, the narrator, sits at breakfast with her lover, Graham, and receives a telegram telling her of her former husband's suicide. During the day, she visits her son, Bobo, at his boarding school to tell him about his father's death; shops; goes to see her grandmother in a nursing home; and meets her lover again in the late afternoon. As she does these things, she thinks about her former husband, Max, who was the son of a prominent South African politician; became a revolutionary; went to prison; and eventually testified against his coworkers in the movement. Liz also considers her own present life, which she has put together within the limits of what is possible; she has found work that is not immoral, but she sees few opportunities for any effective action. Later in the evening, she cooks dinner for Luke, a Black activist from her more political past. He asks for her help, and, after he leaves, she goes to bed considering whether she should use her grandmother's bank account to receive illegal funds for his organization. She seems to be leaning toward this course of action as apparently the only one open to her.

Divergent Readings

When *The Late Bourgeois World* was published in 1966, Gordimer had a reputation as a serious novelist; several of her previous books had been well received. As a result, the new novel was reviewed in major newspapers and journals of opinion aimed at a literate general public. The reviewers who produce such short articles are a diverse group; according to Coser, Kadushin, and Powell, "they range from hacks . . . to literary craftsmen of distinction" (1982:309). Some are on the staffs of the publications they write for, while others are writers or academics known to editors through personal networks or previous reviewing work. Despite this diversity, reviews combine relatively standard elements: some kind of descriptive summary and some sort of evaluation, whether "a sauce of flowery adjectives" or "serious critical judgments" (Coser, Kadushin, and Powell 1982:309). Reviewers respond to books relatively quickly and think about them in terms of issues of the time. Griswold (1987) suggests that they construct reviews from two sources: their own responses to a text and their expectations about readers' responses, taking the latter more or less for granted.

Reviewers of *The Late Bourgeois World* took the representational character of the novel as a starting point. Their reviews typically begin with some statement of what the book is about, and these comments describe the book as portraying some real South African situation. One writer (*j*) suggests that Gordimer "puts a smear of South African society under the novelist's microscope"; another calls the book a "slim, nervous novel about tensions in racially torn South Africa" (*i*); others say that it portrays the "life and thoughts of a liberal white woman in South Africa" (*c*), the "white suburban world in South Africa" (*f*), and a "climate of fear" (*g*).

Most reviewers, as they discuss the novel in more detail, continue to assess its representativeness. One refers to the mood of Liz "and, one guesses, of the hundreds she must broadly typify" (*e*), and another (*m*) relates the hopelessness he sees in the novel to an actual historical event: the imposition of the Ninety Day Law in South Africa (which allowed the government to keep dissenters in prison for extended periods without any trial). Hoyt W. Fuller, writing in the *Negro Digest* (*d*), says the story "illuminate[s] the waste and erosion of the South African soul"; he is one of only two reviewers who take the representational character of the novel as extending beyond its immediate setting in his claim that "South Africa is the United States at the penultimate step in its evolution toward the complete and unapologetic racist society." (The other [*j*] suggests that Gordimer is concerned with "the divisions set up by all aggressively fearful societies.")

Some reviewers take Gordimer to task, criticizing her work of representation. One questions the book's accuracy, claiming that this is important "in a book which is, to an uncertain extent, documentary." He explains: "When I showed this novel to a South African exile, the son of an imprisoned African leader, it made him unhappy. He feels, and his views are both considered and important, that the book shows very little real knowledge of the resistance movement, is inaccurate about the South African Communist party and is composed of 'European scenes with South African peculiarities imposed on them'" (*g*). Others are more ambivalent about the importance of representativeness in characters and setting. One complains that Liz is "unlike any real person," adds that this "wouldn't necessarily matter," but ultimately rejects the portrayal as stereotypical (*m*).

To be sure, such comments do not fully represent these critics' analyses of the novel. However, the fact that these kinds of statements seem necessary even to begin a discussion of the book testifies to the assumption (recognized or not) that lies behind them—that the story, though fictional, is an account of a real-world situation that can be referred to in more general terms. These summaries, which have a deceptively straightforward, descriptive appearance, may be casually produced, but they represent considerable conceptual work on the text of the novel. Accepting that the novel is an account representative of some real setting, the critics have made decisions, in these summary comments, about what setting—and which of its aspects—the novel should be taken to portray.

But now consider another reader: a young American sociologist, a woman and a feminist, socialized to politics during the 1970s, a participant in the academic branch of the women's movement. I read *The Late Bourgeois World* in 1983, almost twenty years after its initial publication. I recognized, of course, that it is a story of South African life and politics (or at least some segment of South African life and politics), and I was interested in the book as a portrait of a situation with global implications. However, I read novels not professionally but for my own purposes, and I was particularly interested in the novel because I felt it told the story of a woman whose life in some ways resembled my own.

I read *The Late Bourgeois World* as the story of a "free woman" like those I knew from Doris Lessing's *The Golden Notebook* ([1962] 1973).[11] Alone, and rather introspective, Liz has a consciousness of her own situation as a woman that combines awareness of social constraints and of the kinds of freedom she can make for herself. She makes choices deliberately, constructing a pattern that may be unconventional and imperfect but is at least chosen with awareness and thought. Like many women whose experience does not quite fit traditional patterns, she often wonders just how her life is to be explained.

I recognized Liz's connections to others as relations typical of women's usual locations in society. She remembers her ex-husband and his wealthy parents; spends companionable time with her lover, a prominent liberal lawyer; takes care of her son and her grandmother. These relationships give her a particular view of "the late bourgeois world." Although not at the center of political and social events in her country, she has a knowledge of those in power that is characteristically female because she has been connected with such people through family roles.

I was interested in Liz's relationship with her lover. They have established patterns and their own rituals of being together. But there are also unspoken but definite limits to their claims on each other, and they maintain scrupulously independent lives. Since theirs is not a clearly defined, conventional relationship, any small piece of interaction can become part of its construction. I saw in their conversation that they were watching themselves as a couple in order to understand the ground rules, and I saw that Liz was aware of herself observing the relationship and evaluating it even from hour to hour.

I read many of the political scenes in the novel as yet another case consistent with the feminist critique of Left groups—pointing to a division of labor that assigned leadership roles to males and support work to females—that emerged during the late 1960s as part of the development of the women's movement. During Liz's marriage, for example, her husband, Max, was prominent in their political circles but acted in erratic and undisciplined ways. Liz held two jobs in order to support their child and worked on "backroom stuff" in their groups. In spite of his irresponsibility and her real contributions, both thought of his activity as the important political work and of her role as being merely supportive.

Finally, I noticed that Gordimer's political scenes display an awareness of the sexual undercurrent to many political interactions, another theme in feminist portraits of the Left. As she serves dinner to her activist friend, Liz notices how they flirt with each other as a way of getting to the business of the evening. She realizes that he is trying out sexual strategies in the hope of enlisting her aid.

My reading of *The Late Bourgeois World* was more specific than the accounts given by most general reviewers. I recognized, with them, that the novel portrayed the situation of a white South African liberal in the mid-1960s. However, I read the novel additionally, and with more interest, as a view of the particular situation of a white South African liberal who is a woman. My purpose here is not to privilege my own reading of this novel but to point out that "I"—a reader located quite differently from the early reviewers—read the novel in a very different way. How, then, is my own reading located? I am a lay reader of novels, although I am one who reads with a sociological interest in gender. Since the early 1970s, particular novels—some that were part of the early women's studies curriculum and others that were passed informally among my friends—have influenced my developing feminism. I have talked and argued about these books, and, in some cases, I have read feminist critics' discussions of them. Through such activities, I have learned to notice whether and how novels portray female experience, and I have become more trusting of my own (feminist) responses to texts. I experience this way of reading as a reliance on a personal response, but it is more accurately identified as the adoption of a new set of practices. It means learning to read in a new way—relying on the "authority of experience" (Diamond and Edwards 1977) instead of on conventional wisdom.

My reading was structured in part by the same text read by the early reviewers but also by my experience as a woman and by an interpretive frame that permitted the use of my gendered experience. Earlier in this article, when I began to discuss my reading of the novel, I explained, "I read *The Late Bourgeois World* as the story of a 'free woman' like those I knew from Doris Lessing's *The Golden Notebook*." I wrote this sentence without any special attention, thinking only that it was shorthand useful for introducing my more detailed comments. But as I did the analysis, I came to see just what the comment is shorthand for: it points to the fact that I had at hand a method of reading that shaped my interpretation.

With a new interpretive frame, the novel makes sense in a new way. The early reviewers wrote in the mid-1960s, before the women's movement became a political force, and their writings reflect the unconscious but pervasive sexism of the time. Often, their problems in making sense of this story of a woman's life influence their critical evaluations. They notice, of course, that the novel's narrator is female, but most read this aspect of the book as a problem. Some seem primarily concerned with the story of Liz's ex-husband, a familiar character with a history they recognize. One, for plot summary, tells Max's story and then adds curtly that Liz, Graham, and Bobo "live on" (k).[12] Another remarks, ambiguously, that "Max's past is a blatant story. In a subtler, more casual way we become involved with Elizabeth in the present" (f); while "blatant" may suggest a criticism of Max's story, the reference to a "casual" involvement suggests a distanced reading of Liz's. One reviewer asserts, "The girl herself—blunt, cool, resilient—is hard to identify with" (h). Other commentators seem disappointed in a slightly puzzled way, but their comments too hint at some lack of empathy. For example, one wrote: "Somehow this novel did not affect me as powerfully as I might have hoped. I found it just a bit too tailor-made and I felt that the very evident feminine sensibility grew at times overwrought. Perhaps South Africa is too dark and sticky a mixture for us to take in a cut-glass phial" (a). Toynbee, writing in the *New Republic*, places *The Late Bourgeois World* in the series of modern English novels whose heroes are disillusioned, but fundamentally good, men. He notes that "a major point of interest" in Gordimer's book "is that we are now shown a female version of this very familiar male character." However, he says nothing about any consequence of this difference and, in the end, concludes that Liz is "too much of a fictional stereotype," and therefore "a familiar bore" (m).

These critics do not seem to like Liz, as I did. They describe her as "disillusioned" (e), "burnt-out" (i), "attractive and intelligent" but also "zombie-like" (d), and "egocentric without suspecting it" (e). They seem puzzled by the relationship with her lover, Graham, instead of being interested in it as I was. They tend to ignore this aspect of the story, and the infrequent comments they do make suggest that they lack interpretive frameworks for the relationship: they use phrases like "love affair," but then add that the affair is "half-hearted" (g) or "fairly uninvolved" (l), or leaves the couple in a "moral limbo" (d).

Two aspects of Liz's story were summarized by these reviewers in ways that reflect common stereotypes of women, and these stereotypes seem to have influenced their judgments of her. First, Liz's thinking about whether or not to help the activist group is described as more mystical than rational. One reviewer says that she goes to bed "in a haze of philosophic speculation" (*a*); others that she is "irresistibly tempted" (*n*) toward reinvolvement, makes a "half-passive" decision (*m*), or is seen "teetering on the brink of political action" (*g*). Some adopt a more general tone of psychologizing to explain the characteristics they do not understand in Liz; one refers rather mysteriously to "something in herself which welcomed the whole ambience of despair" (*m*).

Finally, Liz's attitude toward Luke, the Black activist, is interpreted by most of these reviewers as blatantly sexual, in a way that misses what I saw as the subtlety of Gordimer's comment on the inevitability and ambiguity of relations that are both political and personal. Where I saw Liz noticing the sexual undertones in her interaction with Luke and watching them play their respective roles, most reviewers saw her as seeking involvement in a much simpler way. One reports that she goes to bed "debating the possibility of becoming involved in a love affair with the young African" (*c*), and another, that "Soon, too, she is likely to sleep with her Negro politician" (*a*).

So far, I have displayed two ways of reading *The Late Bourgeois World,* one of which accepts and highlights the narrator's femaleness. My account made Liz's situation as a woman a point of interest in the novel and, in the interpretive process, drew on experiences of being female. I have also suggested, however, that this kind of reading depends on an interpretive frame that develops over time, intertextually. Reading as a woman is not a method associated unproblematically with being female; women do not read this way "naturally" or consistently (Culler 1982, Schweikart 1986). Typically, in fact, when women are taught to interpret texts (especially literary texts, which are more explicitly taught than popular genres) "correctly," they are taught to read from an ostensibly gender-neutral viewpoint. In the past, at least, this has usually meant constructing responses to cultural works in terms of questions and assumptions built on male concerns (Kolodny 1981). Given such training, women may notice aspects of texts that men do not but may not be able to articulate a fully developed interpretation incorporating these elements. Feminist scholars have referred to the general phenomenon as an experience of being "sliced in two" (Rowbotham 1973:40) or as producing a "line of fault" in women's experience (Smith 1987), and feminist literary theorists have discussed women as "resisting readers" (Fetterley 1978) who have a "bifurcated response" (Schweikart 1986:43) to male texts. Indeed, at least one[13] of the early reviewers I have discussed was a woman (*c*), and her reading is suggestive of just such a double consciousness of Gordimer's text; she does label the novel unambiguously as the story of a woman's life—an indica tion that she could at least notice Liz in a way that many of the male reviewers could not—but, like the male reviewers, she is dissatisfied with the story, and her complaints echo those of her male contemporaries.

During the next decade, another group of professional readers—literary scholars—began to write about *The Late Bourgeois World*. These critics represent a group of readers positioned somewhat differently from the early reviewers. They are mostly employed in college and university departments of literature (or sometimes are training for such positions), where they teach courses and do literary scholarship. Though academics sometimes write the kind of review I have analyzed above, when they write as scholars they write in a different genre. The critical texts they produce (articles in journals and book-length monographs) have significance within two different but related sets of activities. First, each published article is (potentially, at least) part of a literary discourse and, usually, of one or more of its specialized segments. This body of interpretations becomes a canon itself, commenting on the canon of literary works. The extension of this interpretive literature is the aim of criticism in a general sense, and critics refer to this literature in order to give their articles meaning and justification.[14] In addition to their status as intellectual products, critical articles have significance for professional reputations and careers: they are the currency constituting the basis for recognition, through employment, promotion, tenure, professional honors or awards, and the informal contacts that lead to further opportunities for professional advancement. Within this set of activities, publications acquire value through their placement within the discourse; they appear in more and less prestigious places, receive favorable or unfavorable (or, quite often, negligible) notice, and are cited more and less frequently by later scholars.

Critical articles are less concerned than reviews with summary and evaluation and more concerned with the interpretation of literary texts; they explicate, analyze, contextualize, debunk, deconstruct or reconstruct, sometimes responding as much to the secondary critical literature as to the primary texts. They are built on theoretical rationales for critical work, and the users of different theories constitute "schools" of academic criticism. Critics have usually learned one or another of these critical approaches (or some combination of them) and rely on its assumptions and techniques, even though the theoretical underpinnings of criticism may be implicit in their articles rather than sharply defined. The kinds of literary approaches considered legitimate at any time are subject to collective definition through controversies within the discourse. These features of academic writing about literature mean that critical articles represent a kind of reading that differs from the readings found in reviews in general periodicals. While reviewers respond quickly to new novels, literary scholars develop interpretations with more care and present them in the form of longer, more pointed arguments about specific questions. Reviewers and scholars address different questions for different audiences; reviewers are concerned quite generally with whether a book is of interest to a general public, while critics address questions that are of significance to a more specialized colleague group and assert that the text is worth studying as well as reading.

The literary canon—that group of books that scholars write about—is defined over time through the collective activities of this occupational group; that is, the critical works accepted as central to literary discourse define the canon through their subjects. The discourse is partly a debate over which works should be included. Generally, older literary works are more clearly in or out of the canon than contemporary texts; they have withstood the test of time and "speak to many ages." However, the composition of an established body of literature (e.g., "19th-century novels") is always subject to renegotiation, as scholars "discover" writers previously ignored or new reasons for attending to the work of writers previously considered uninteresting (as when feminist critics write about unsung women writers, for example). When a critic writes in the 1970s about a relatively new novel like *The Late Bourgeois World,* the decision to do so contains an implicit assertion that the novel should be considered a text worthy of study.

These aspects of the academic context are reflected in the critical discussions I will analyze. In order to locate their discussions in this special discourse, academic critics frequently frame them with reference to literary traditions. One discussion of Gordimer and Lessing, for example, identifies their work as belonging to a European tradition of "critical realism" and compares them with Turgenev and Conrad (*o*).

These special features of critical writing, however, do not constitute the only differences between the critical pieces on *The Late Bourgeois World* and the earlier general reviews. (In fact, there is substantial overlap in this respect, reflecting, no doubt, the overlap in the groups who write in these different genres: many of the general reviews include references to the kinds of theoretical frames that are more explicit in critical texts—e.g., Toynbee's reliance in his *New Republic* review [*m*] on the tradition of the modern English novel.) A more marked contrast between the early reviews and later critical pieces lies in the way later analyses link the novel to social issues of the more recent historic period. Most of the critics who chose to write about *The Late Bourgeois World* (Haugh [*p*], who pans the book, is the sole exception) had explicitly political aims. Writing during a time when political issues in South Africa have changed and the women's movement has become a social force, these commentators come to the novel with quite specific political concerns and make these concerns explicit in their interpretations.

Three critics (*q, r, s*) developed antiracist analyses of *The Late Bourgeois World*. One article, by Parker (*r*), appeared in a book of literary criticism with the overtly political aim of gauging the extent to which South African novelists have been "sensitive to" antiracist movements. This piece shows signs of being written by someone much more familiar with the details of the South African scene than the general reviewers: in his summary, the author explains that Max kills himself "by driving his car into Table Bay harbour" (instead of simply "drowning himself" [*c*]); that he was the son of "a respected United Party politician" (instead of a "prosperous and condescending" politician [*a*]); and that Luke is "of the Pan-Africanist Conference" (instead of simply a "young African" [*c*] or "Negro politician" [*b*]).

Parker is also concerned with a political issue that does not show up so specifically in the general reviews, the question of white involvement in the Black resistance movement. He contends that Gordimer deals with this issue through the character of Luke, the Black activist, who is, for him, one of the three main characters of the novel. He sees Luke as a "representative of the new politics" that "rejects white involvement, except for specific purposes."

This kind of reading refers to an issue that was becoming increasingly important in South Africa in the mid-1960s, when *The Late Bourgeois World* was published. The optimistic multiracialism characteristic of the opposition movements of the 1950s had subsided in the face of strong repressive measures. Black political parties had been outlawed, and the sharp differences in the difficulties faced by Black and white activists were making joint political activity less and less feasible. Parker, writing in 1978, seems less concerned than the earlier reviewers with the story of Max, an activist typical of an earlier time, and attends instead to the elements of *The Late Bourgeois World* that seem relevant to this newer political problem.

Gerver (*o*), writing in the same year, developed a reading with an explicitly feminist focus in an article that appeared in a literary journal's special issue devoted to "Women Writers of the Commonwealth." Gerver emphasizes a theme she describes as a particularly feminist concern: the "drive towards integration of private and public life." Unlike the general reviewers, who seem barely to notice Liz, she insists on making the "development of the woman narrator" the center of the novel, and, when she does so, she sees "the beginning of a movement towards serious commitment to revolutionary activity." She highlights Liz's relationship with her son, almost completely unmentioned by other commentators, and concludes that: "Gordimer has opened up new territory for exploration in her emphasis on the possibility of a woman's commitment both to a child and to a revolutionary cause" (o). Rather than focusing on Max's story, she emphasizes the fact that Liz is living on her own. When she summarizes the plot, she pays particular attention to aspects of the story that suggest independence: "Elizabeth's final commitment is made after she has freed herself from her husband. Acting entirely on her own, Elizabeth commits herself, albeit fearfully and in the midst of uncertainties" (o). Although she echoes in some ways the general reviewers' distaste for Liz—finding her a "shadowy" and "rather shallow" character—she still makes Liz a more active protagonist than do any of the other writers. Her plot summary has the action of the novel developing from Liz's "insistent examination of her responses to the suicide," and she argues that Liz finds "a personal vitality in political action." Gerver, like the other critics, has a political agenda and writes about Gordimer's novel as a book about politics. However, instead of responding to changes in the South African scene as most of the other critics did, she lifts Liz's story out of the South African context altogether and makes Liz's situation as an activist woman central to her reading.

In summarizing these different readings of the novel, I wish not to argue that *The Late Bourgeois World* is a feminist or a political novel of a particular sort but to show that there are multiple possible interpretations, and divergent uses, of such a novel. I have examined the statements of three kinds of readers: the early general periodical reviewers (mostly male), literary scholars (also mostly male, but including one woman with a feminist agenda), and "I," a lay reader, but one who also has an explicitly feminist interest in the novel. These readers' accounts of the novel, discussed above, suggest the emergence of three kinds of readings. The features of these three readings are summarized schematically in table 1.

There are several sources for the differences in these readings. The professional interests of reviewers and scholars have oriented them toward different audiences, shaping their readings as accounts for a general public or for more specialized (mostly, in this case, more politically committed) colleague groups. And the historical context for reading has changed since the novel's publication, producing new frames of reference for interpretation (Jauss 1970).[15] The early reviewers understood the novel in terms of South African racial politics of the 1950s and early 1960s and focused on Max as the center of a story of white activism. By the mid-1970s two kinds of changes had occurred: a self-conscious Black activist movement had emerged in South Africa, and the women's movement had brought

TABLE 1: Three Readings of *The Late Bourgeois World*

	Thematic Focus	Attitude toward Narrator
Early "liberal" reading: Early reviewers—10 men, 1 woman, and 3 unattributed reviews, plus 1 later male scholar..................	Human tragedy of South African setting	Liz an "odd" and "difficult" narrator
Later readings: Antiracist—3 of 4 male scholars.................	Conflicts between European liberal humanism and emerging Black activism	Liz accepted as central character but without attention to the details of her life
Feminist—1 female scholar plus female lay reader,"I" ...	Distinctive limits and opportunities for contemporary women activists	Liz a point of interest in her own right, attention to her situation as a woman

an increased awareness of women's distinctive experiences and concerns. Most of the male readings from the 1970s respond to the political changes; the critics who deal with the novel are more interested in Luke and his challenge to white activism than in Max. The women's readings from the 1970s and 1980s respond to feminism, interpreting *The Late Bourgeois World* as a portrait of distinctively female experience. Reading as a woman produces an interpretation different from those of the mostly male readers who came before.[16]

Some theorists of reading, noting this sort of divergence, suggest that texts are "re-created" (Wolff 1981) with each reading and that each reading produces "new meanings" (Bleich 1977), so that there are "many texts," perhaps as many as there are readers. I assume, more straightforwardly, that readers always encounter the same text, which is, after all, a reproducible physical object. The problem in developing a theory of reading, then, is to explain in more detail how it is that readers can use the same text to construct such different readings.

Constructing Accounts of the Novel: Sources and Limits of Divergence

We can begin to see how these different readings of a single text have been produced by thinking about how these professional readers and I developed our own stories of what the original novel is about. Formally or informally, we made our own representations of the text, tied to evidence from the text. We were constrained by the text, but we also made choices as we developed interpretations, and these choices were influenced by the questions and background information we brought to our readings.

Becker (1986a) contends that making any representation involves at least three kinds of activities: selecting the elements to be included from whatever is to be represented, translating the selected elements into standard kinds of parts that will contribute to the new representation and its intended uses, and arranging these new elements in a format prescribed by convention. In this section, I will apply this framework to the process of interpretation by examining the processes of selection, translation, and arrangement as they contribute to the construction of the accounts contained in these reviews and critical articles—and underlying my own, less formal response to *The Late Bourgeois World*. The analysis will not address the micro-level processes of interpretation that enable readers to make sense of the words on a page. Rather, I will focus on the social processes that follow sense making, as readers construct understandings oriented toward wider arenas where they will use the same novel for different purposes in different settings.

Selection and translation.—*The Late Bourgeois World* includes a scene in which Liz visits her son, Bobo, at his school to tell him of his father's death, and an extended reminiscence about her family's earlier life together and Max's irresponsibility. Here is a brief sample from her visit with Bobo:

> Like most boys Bobo has a feeling for cars akin to the sense of place, and when he gets into the car I can see that it's almost as if he were home, in the flat. He noses through all the old papers that collect on the shelf beneath the dashboard and looks for peppermints and traffic tickets in the glove box. I am often called upon to explain myself.
>
> He was sitting beside me touching a loose knob, probably noting with some part of his mind that he must fix it sometime, and he said, "I don't suppose it was painful or anything."
>
> I said, "Oh no. You mustn't worry about that." Because all his life, he's been made aware of the necessity to recognize and alleviate suffering; it's the one thing he's been presented with as being beyond questioning, since the first kitten was run over and the first street beggar was seen displaying his sores. (p. 17)

I read these passages as familiar portraits of experiences associated with the roles of mother and wife and as important information about Liz and the shape of her life. But most of the other readers I have discussed treat these passages as unimportant. Only one of the reviewers or male critics discusses Liz's son, and for him this aspect of the story represents the use of "warmed-over materials": "the woman in an odd, cold relationship with a teenage son from a past marriage, once more disposed of in a boys school" (*p*). He does not include this information about Liz's experience as mother in his own version of the story; in his view, the inclusion of such details in the novel was a mistake.

These readers are more likely to notice Max, the former husband, but not the ambivalence with which his political and personal characteristics are portrayed. They mention such information casually, labeling Max a "good lover but unsatisfactory husband" (*a*) or an "ineffectual rebel" (*c*), but do not make these aspects of his character a central part of the story. Only one links Max's life to Liz's in even an oblique way, by explaining that Liz, "a reluctant camp follower at first, more and more had to wear the pants in the family" (*n*). These readers do not select these story elements, as I did, in order to put together an argument about male and female responsibilities and conflict. They mention these parts of the story, then, only as unimportant, superfluous details.

For the feminist critic (*o*), as for me, these passages describing family ties are of key importance. Gerver uses every hint of Liz's family responsibilities, weaving them into a story about the difficulty of combining mothering with political work. She selects these passages as central elements from which she draws the following conclusion: "[Elizabeth] has a son, for whom she feels totally responsible, and whose care has previously limited her political commitments. . . . In the past this conflict has been unresolvable, but, once her son has fully understood and adhered to her own absolute repudiation of white domination in South Africa, she finally sees herself as free to take serious risks" (*o*). This reader places at the center of the story what is clearly a peripheral element for the other, mostly male, readers. She chooses to include these parts of the novel in her account of it because she has come to the novel with a concern for a particular issue: "how two of the most dominant concerns of our time—the struggle of revolutionaries and of women for political and personal freedom—are inextricably connected with one another." Answering her question demands attention to the characters' personal lives. In addition, however, she translates these story elements differently from the other reviewers: she brings knowledge to her reading that helps her to recognize Liz's family responsibilities. Having been brought up female, she has learned the tasks assigned to women in her culture and knows (or can easily imagine) what it feels like to be responsible for children, even when they are not physically present. Male readers are less likely to have had primary responsibility for children and more likely to think conventionally about women's caretaking roles rather than attend to the detail in Gordimer's portrait of Liz as a mother—more likely therefore to read her son's attendance at a boarding school as being an abdication of family responsibility.

I paid particular attention to Liz's relationship with her lover, Graham. For example, I enjoyed passages like the following, detailing Liz's introspection and what I saw as a characteristically contemporary combination of romance and pragmatism in her attitude toward her lover. Liz has asked Graham to order some flowers for her grandmother's birthday, while she visits Bobo at school. Now, she returns home:

> The telephone was ringing as I came into the flat, but when I reached it, it stopped. I was sure it was Graham and then I saw a bunch of flowers under cellophane, on the table; he'd got the florist to send them here instead of to the Home. But my name was on the finicky little envelope—he had sent me flowers at the same time as he ordered them for the old lady. Samson the cleaner must have been working in the flat when they were delivered, and had taken them in. They were pressed like faces against glass; I ripped them free of the squeaky transparency and read the card: With love, G. Graham and I have no private names, references, or love-words. We use the standard vocabulary when necessary. A cold bruised smell came up from the flowers; it was the snowdrops, with their onion-like stems and leaves, their chilly greenness. He knows how crazy I am about them. And about the *muguet-du-bois* that we bought when we met for a week in the Black Forest in Europe last year. There is nothing wrong with a plain statement: with love. He happened to be in the florist's and so he sent me some flowers. It's not a thing he would do specially, unless it were on a birthday or something. It might have been because of Max; but good God, no, surely not, that would have been awful, he wouldn't have done it. We had made love the night before, but there was nothing special about that. One doesn't like to admit to habit, but the fact is that he doesn't have his mind on court the next day, on Friday evenings, and I don't have to get up next morning to go to work. (p. 33)

Passages like this one were unimportant for both the more explicitly argued feminist and political readings of *The Late Bourgeois World*. Its ambiguity does not fit well with the tightly drawn integration of political and personal that the feminist critic aims for and is simply irrelevant to the antiracist analyses. The feminist critic—surprisingly in an analysis concerned with personal life—never mentions Liz's lover. But she omits these parts of the novel because she has defined the feminist question about personal and political life narrowly, as a question of potential conflict between family responsibility and activism, and she constructs her argument to address that specific issue. The readers who make antiracist arguments only rarely attend to Graham's role in the story and, when they do, tend to see him rather simply as representative of a restrained liberal humanism that is increasingly meaningless in the South African situation. Each analysis presents a more specific story constructed from the novel, and neither constructed story requires the kind of nuance in Liz's relationship with Graham that Gordimer has provided in the novel itself.

The general reviewers pay considerably more attention to Liz's interactions with Graham, but they treat these parts of the novel as problematic. The relationship as portrayed is neither a marriage nor a love affair as conventionally understood, and these readers seem unable to understand it or to empathize with either Liz or Graham. Their references to the relationship have an uncomprehending, pejorative tone: it is a "companionable but inconclusive liaison" (a), a "cool and rather clinical sexual accommodation" (k). The terms in which Liz thinks of the relationship— "standard" rather than conventionally romantic vocabulary—seem to be one source of the trouble and also point toward the reviewers' more general complaints about Liz's voice. One commentator is bothered by what he reads as Liz's "impossible smart-mouth" and "bold use of four letter words" (p), and another concludes that Liz's "brittle stylishness begins to seem not heroically effortful but almost ruinously limiting" (e). One commentator (p) finds Liz's talk so discordant that he rejects her story entirely: "Good God, says the reader, cringing at the adolescent bravado masquerading as 'candor.' How can I believe this narrator upon any of the subjects in the novel: racial justice, white liberalism, revolutionary resistance, or any other endeavor, be it personal, social, or political?" For this reader and perhaps for others who are not so blunt, "The difficulties put in the way of the reader by this sort of narrator obscure the meaning of events, and interfere with the very necessary empathy of the reader."

These readers cannot translate Liz's relationship or her distinctive voice into anything that fits with the arguments they make from the novel. Again, we see in their comments an interaction between selection and translation. Because these scenes and thoughts make little sense to them, these readers do not make them part of their constructed accounts of the novel. At the same time, those who do not wish to include such elements in their own versions of the story cannot simply ignore them; in order to exclude them, they translate them as being irrelevant or as faulty writing.

The varying readings I have displayed are made up of different combinations of elements taken from the novel itself. The accounts we readers constructed could not include everything from the novel, so we had to select from all the elements that were there. Some of the differences in our selections seem related to a professional-amateur distinction. In my comments on the novel, above, I mentioned several of its aspects—Liz's relations with her son, her intimate life, and her everyday chores, as well as her political work—without any sense that I needed to make explicit connections among these different aspects of the story. The professional readers, required by their formats to produce more formal and tightly argued statements about the novel, seem less willing to incorporate diverse elements into their analyses. The early reviewers developed quick summaries of the novel and mentioned only those elements that made up their summaries, while the critics tended to focus on whatever story elements contributed to their discussions of particular issues. Other differences in our selections seem related to differences in background knowledge and show the interaction between selection and translation. Some story elements were important for female readers or for those with political experience and not for others. It was only when we were able to put some parts of the story in context, by reference to the experiences associated with our social locations, that we were likely to select these elements as important parts of our own accounts.

As we made these selections, we all omitted parts of the story. I, for instance, deemphasized Gordimer's lengthy portrait of Max's parents, which for the critics doing antiracist analyses was a crucial element in a condemnation of bourgeois society. And nearly all of us (Fuller [d] and Wade [r] being notable exceptions) omitted Gordimer's references to the spaceflight, which have a mystical and transcendent tone that none of us seemed very comfortable with. In theory (according to literary scholars), every part of a novel is significant. Actually, of course, an interpretation cannot include everything, or it would be the novel itself. Every representation is partial and "leaves out much, in fact *most*" of what it represents (Becker 1986a:126). Thus, an efficient account of a novel is one that includes just enough to make the argument a reader intends to construct.

Arrangement.—When readers summarize a novel, they must arrange the elements they have selected and translated so as to produce a summary story with its own plot. These processes of arrangement can be seen in readers' treatments of the final episodes of *The Late Bourgeois World*.

As the novel nears its climax, Liz meets with Luke, the Black activist, and he asks for her help. She cooks dinner, and they talk rather aimlessly as she wonders why he has come. Eventually, he explains that he is looking for someone to receive funds from outside the country for resistance work. They talk in the guarded way both are used to as a part of such conversations, carefully noting each other's reactions. For example:

> He went on looking at me, half-smiling, satisfied I couldn't get away.
> "You're not thinking of me!"
> It was absurd, but he saw the absurdity as another attempt at evasion, and made me feel as if I were concealing something by it. But what? It's true that I have no money coming to me from abroad, in fact nothing in the bank more than the small margin—which often dwindles into the red—between the salary I deposit at the beginning of a month and the bills I pay by the end. He laughed with me, at last, but beneath it, I saw his purpose remain; the laughter was an aside.
> "Ah, come on, Liz."

I told him he must be mad. I didn't know of anyone, anyone at all whom I could even approach. I said I was out of that sort of circle long ago—a meaningless thing to say since we both knew he wouldn't have come to me, couldn't have come to me, otherwise. But everything I was saying was meaningless. What I was really telling him and what he understood was that I should be afraid to do what he asked, should be afraid even if I knew "someone," even if I had some feasible explanation for money suddenly coming in to my bank account. We kept up the talk on a purely practical level, and it was a game that both of us understood—like the holding and flirting. The flirting is even part of this other game; there was a sexual undertone to his wheedling, cajoling, challenging confrontation of me, and that's all right, that's honest enough. (p. 86)

While they talk, Liz remembers her grandmother's bank account and realizes that in fact she could provide the help Luke is asking for.

As the novel ends, Liz lies awake that night considering what she will do. She thinks of the problems that might arise and what such an action would mean. And in the end, she seems to conclude that she should do this thing simply because it is the one possible action, for her. Her musings could be described, I think, as either simple or complex:

It seems to me that the answer is simply the bank account. I can't explain; but there is the bank account. That's good enough; as when Bobo used to answer a question about his behavior with the single word: "Because." Am I going into politics again, then? And if so, what kind? But I can't be bothered with this sort of thing, it's irrelevant. The bank account is there. It can probably be used for this purpose. What happened, the old lady asked me: well, that's what's happened. Luke knows what he wants, and he knows who it is he must get it from. Of course he's right. A sympathetic white woman hasn't got anything to offer him—except the footing she keeps in the good old white Reserve of banks and privileges. And in return he comes with the smell of the smoke of braziers in his clothes. Oh yes, and it's quite possible he'll make love to me, next time or some time. That's part of the bargain. It's honest, too, like his vanity, his lies, the loans he doesn't pay back: it's all he's got to offer me. It would be better if I accepted gratefully, because then we shan't owe each other anything, each will have given what he has, and neither is to blame if one has more to give than the other. And in any case, perhaps I want it. I don't know. Perhaps it would be better than what I've had—or got. Suit me better, now. Who's to say it shouldn't be called love? You can't do more than give what you have. (p. 94)

A paragraph later, the novel ends with a suggestion of the importance of her choice—in her own mind, at least—as Liz tells us, "the slow, even beats of my heart repeat to me, like a clock; afraid, alive, afraid, alive, afraid, alive . . ." (p. 95).

These passages have different places in the varying arrangements of story elements constructed by different readers. The general reviewers barely treat this series of events as significant. While some who ignore Liz's decision may have been, in part, avoiding giving away the ending as a requirement of their genre, several of those who do refer to these passages make light of the service Liz might render, labeling it "some kind of pointless atonement" (e) or "of dubious value and even of dubious decency" (m). Most of them are more interested in Liz's quasi-sexual interaction with Luke than in the content or consequences of their talk, and when they mention these scenes, they almost always refer to the likelihood of some future involvement. Their readings of these passages recall one of the familiar ways that men and women can misunderstand each other's sexual signals in everyday life: they ignore what Liz says and assume that, because she talks about sex, she must be wanting it.

These readers seem to have expected a more traditional story, with an active male hero, and very few of them make the shift that would allow them to see Liz at the center of the novel. One reviewer, who summarized the novel as having a "vague 'story line' about Max," concludes that the book "ends without an ending" (b). Max, of course, is hardly a classic hero, and these readers can see that he has a number of unheroic qualities, but they manage for the most part to incorporate these into the stories they make. Some continue to treat Max as heroic, minimizing his flaws, while others treat the entire book as "glum" (e) and "cheerless" (i). At the extreme (such an extreme, in fact, that I think it is a true misreading of the book), one critic, Haugh (p), invents a story about Max facing a crucial decision while in prison (a period Gordimer tells us nothing about) and "coming to some truths" about his political activity. Haugh, who would like to move the climax of the story to an entirely different place, believes that "[Max's] change of heart, properly perceived, is the heart of a novel, here another 'chance missed.'"

The feminist critic (o), in contrast, has no trouble placing Liz and her decision at the center of the story. Where the general reviewers read Liz's decision as somewhat mystical and almost accidental, she sees an important choice, firmly made. She constructs a story with Liz as an active protagonist who successfully resolves the issues raised in the novel: "This decision to commit herself, acting entirely on her own judgement, forms the close of the novel, as Elizabeth's fear at the risk she is taking brings her fully alive" (o).

The readers who developed antiracist analyses of the novel talk of Liz's decision in a third way. They empathize with Liz in a way that the general reviewers cannot, probably because they come to the novel already concerned with the kind of issue presented in her situation. They do see the decision as important and Liz as thoughtfully considering it. One describes her as "aware of moving forward, by this act, towards the future" (s), and another points out, "Elizabeth thus recognizes something unique—that if she wants to take part in the game, she will have to play according to rules over which she will have no control, and which may even change while the game is in progress" (r). These readers describe Liz as "recognizing" her situation; however, as the preceding example suggests, and in contrast to the optimistic feminist interpretation, they also emphasize the limits to what she can do. Although they read her decision as a climax for the novel, it is a pessimistic and unsatisfying one for them because it does not give a sufficiently active answer to the question it raises. One, for example, complains, "In the end, I suspect that Miss Gordimer has proved the first part of her epigraph from Kafka: 'There are possibilities for me, certainly'—but the rest of the epigraph: 'but under which stone do they lie?'—would seem to continue to elude her" (r).

Interestingly, part of the pessimism of these readers' interpretations echoes the general reviewers' focus on the sexual. They also emphasize the inauthenticity of the personal interaction between Liz and Luke. One points out that "Elizabeth has to admit, at last, that the notion of building bridges across the races, of the European liberal humanist code of cricket across the colour bar, is a chimera. She is forced to admit that ' . . . friendship for its own sake is something only whites can afford'" (r). And another contends that: "For [Elizabeth], the ugly truth is that she has nothing special to offer in terms of human relationships, and she is reluctant to accept the reduction of the situation between Luke and herself to a merely economic level" (s). These readers accept the terms of the question posed by Liz's situation, overcoming the barriers to empathy that kept so many of the general reviewers from identifying easily with a female narrator, but they are less willing—or eager—than the feminist critic to make Liz an exemplary model, and not so satisfied with the "answers" they find in the text.

Each interpretation of Liz's decision can be supported on the basis of some part of the text. Liz does think about her decision, but she thinks about other things as well, hazily. She does think of Luke in sexual terms, and she recognizes the limits that the South African situation imposes on cross-race friendships as well as on the kinds of effective action possible for whites. The novel does end with the suggestion that the decision to act is, somehow, linked with being "alive." But these same elements can be combined differently in different accounts, so that the novel "speaks" quite differently through the mouths of different readers.

I have not analyzed the arrangement of my own reading of the novel; by noting this missing piece of analysis, I mean to point out that I was not required to arrange my response in a conventional format. My own lay response was not an explicit one; indeed, I became aware of my own reading of the novel in large part through my reactions (surprise and annoyance) to the reviews and critical articles I found when I began to research discussions of Gordimer's work. As a lay reader, I had no reason to develop a fully crafted account of the novel—an argument responsive to a professional discourse, for example. I read the book, noticed and enjoyed the parts that interested me—admittedly for a variety of reasons—and remembered those elements from the text. My more explicit formulations (which are part of this paper) were triggered by my feeling that the reviewers had been unfair to Gordimer and developed out of my analysis of the sources of this feeling.

Discussion

That the same novel is interpreted differently by different readers is hardly a new or surprising observation. But this observation is being taken seriously in a new way in literary studies and in sociological theorizing about meaning and interpretation. I suggested in the introduction that this new interest arises at least in part from contemporary diversity in scholarly communities and cultural elites. All readers, of course, stand outside of texts and work actively to interpret them. But the interpretive traditions within which novels are written and read emerge from the continuing activities of groups of specific people. A tradition constituted largely through the activities of white, Western, male readers and writers tends to take the perspectives of such individuals for granted. Those who are outsiders to the tradition—different in some way from the particular person taken as the norm—are likely to be treated as odd and perplexing (just as the early reviewers treated Liz). As groups of these outsiders, previously on the margins of culture, put forward new interpretive claims, those at the center are challenged to reevaluate traditional methods of interpretation. Both outsiders and insiders are struggling now to sort out the implications of interpretive divergence. If different groups, positioned differently, make such different claims, how, in the future, will we think and talk about the meanings of cultural works?

One of my aims here has been to claim space for a sociological approach to issues of interpretation. I do not propose that sociologists should become arbiters of meaning or judges of aesthetic values. However, I suggest that examination of the processes of interpreting textual materials can contribute to the study of meaning, long a central concern of sociology. The approach I have meant to illustrate includes attention both to textual features that arise from the conventions of a collective tradition and to how these traditions prescribe (or allow) particular uses in context.

As we begin to see that novels are produced and read in contexts of collective activity, the concerted activity underlying all interpretation comes into view. We see that the construction of meaning through literary tradition and convention involves a kind of social interaction that is not so different from everyday sense making as the notion of culture might suggest.

Novels—and perhaps all literary texts—are "multivocal" (Griswold 1987). Different readers interpret the same story in different ways, and it is common for a single reader to find different things in the same novel read at different times. The relatively wide range of readings that characteristically evolve from a novel can be understood in terms of features of the genre and its use within a literary "world" (Becker 1982). The text of a novel is made up of many bits of detail, carefully observed, from an imagined world; a good novel succeeds through an extremely dense kind of presentation, achieved by "drawing out each incident through a copious presentation of its minutest components" (Ortega y Gasset [1925] 1968:77). Its design permits—even invites—the construction of multiple accounts of its meaning. In addition, a novel demands that the reader use experience as a resource for interpretation. There are "gaps" in the text, which produce the "indeterminacy" of the novel (Iser 1978). The reader must place himself or herself in the text and then draw on a stock of knowledge about the world in order to complete the narrative, filling in details that are necessary for understanding but not explicit in the text (Smith 1983). All readers learn this aspect of narrative reading, but each reader comes to a novel with a particular stock of background knowledge, shaped by experiences in different social locations. Each is likely to fill in a text somewhat differently, and many of the differences will be related to varying social positions.

These indeterminate texts are typically discussed in contexts where divergent interpretations are relatively unproblematic. Different accounts of a scientific article present a problem for scientists: articles are written to constitute "facts," and only one interpretation should be correct. Similarly, when zoning maps are interpreted differently by different parties, the divergence constitutes a dispute and must be resolved (Volberg 1984). Different accounts of novels, by contrast, are unsurprising. Critics read novels differently and take many of their differences as manifestations of varying but equally legitimate critical approaches. Many literary people even regard differing interpretations as evidence that a novel is "alive and potent and fructifying" (Lessing [1962] 1973:xxii). Lay readers have few occasions even to articulate their readings in any public setting, much less argue about them. Thus, most people who are involved in discussion of fiction do not expect to resolve divergent readings.

My discussion of three quite different kinds of stories drawn from *The Late Bourgeois World* does not necessarily imply that those who produced them used the novel irresponsibly; though different, most of the readings I discussed are sufficiently grounded in the text to be defensible. Given such room for divergence, then, what would constitute a misreading, and how would one identify it? I sometimes judged that readers had misunderstood particular details of the story (e.g., the several reviewers who seemed to think that Liz planned to take her grandmother's money and give it to the activists, instead of simply receiving money from outside the country in the older woman's bank account). And two commentators made arguments that I would argue are "true misreadings": Haugh (*p*) that the novel is about Max's change of heart while in prison, and Gerver (*o*) that Liz's son has "understood and adhered" to her political position as a result of their brief conversation. However, my selection of only these two arguments as really "wrong," when most of the reviews differed so sharply from my own reading, seems indicative of the kind of permission typically accorded to divergent readings of fictional accounts.

Becker (1986a) suggests that the concepts of "file" and "argument" are useful for understanding different ways of using representations. Some texts, such as scientific articles, are meant to be read as arguments, pointing toward a single conclusion by presenting just enough material and no more. Other texts, such as maps, are meant to be used as files of information that users dip into for their own purposes. No representation can be thought of in itself as an argument or file: a scientific article can be taken as an assembly of research results, as when scientists use data for purposes other than those for which they were originally collected, and a map can be taken as a political statement, as when people complain that it is drawn to make Europe and North America the center of the world. File and argument, then, do not refer to kinds of documents but to methods for using them. Conventional formats evolve in interaction with the typical uses of documents within the relevant communities of use. A scientific text, for example, is designed to lead to a single conclusion, and its form and stylistic features are meant to capture readers and lead them directly to the single idea the author intends (Latour 1984). No extra, potentially distracting, details should be included; although data are displayed, as are the features of a map, they are displayed along with explicit instructions for interpreting them as part of an argument.

If we think of typical uses of scientific articles and maps as the extremes of this continuum, it is clear that the usual approach to reading a novel must fall somewhere in between. A fictional text can be read as an argument, and usually is; however, it does not take the form of an argument but of observations of an imagined world. The conventions of literary realism mean that the fictional situation is portrayed in a way that includes much more than is necessary for any single argument. Readers construct arguments in their accounts of novels, drawing on part of the information provided in the text. They expect to do an active kind of reading, searching for evidence of some argument rather than for an explicit statement of it.

In part, then, I have shown here how varying responses are more characteristic of literary texts than of many other kinds of representations. But responses to fiction, like responses to any kind of representation, are shaped by collective conventions. Readers know how to attend to particular story elements and to recognize stories as examples of familiar genres. These kinds of skills, taken together, constitute methods for reading various kinds of texts. The early reviewers I have discussed, for example, knew how to read *The Late Bourgeois World* as a serious, modern, realistic novel—set in a "foreign" land, but with some sort of universal interest. The later critics shared this perspective in part but relied on other methods as well; they were more likely to read the novel as a book of social criticism. Lay readers would seem to have somewhat more freedom than professional critics to interpret novels in terms of special or individual concerns. But collective frames influence lay readers as well: my own reading of *The Late Bourgeois World*, for example, depends on the availability of a method of interpretation I learned from other novels and from feminist discussion of them.

I have argued, then, that reading is always socially located activity, shaped by history and a social-organizational context as well as by the social background of the reader. Given this located character of any reading, I also argue that the readings of cultural outsiders expand the possibilities for shared meaning. Reading as one who is located outside the dominant cultural frame (in this analysis, "as a woman," but also, potentially, as one disenfranchised in some other way) is a process that can challenge claims to universal meaning. It is a process of putting forward an understanding of a text that relies on a particular stock of cultural knowledge and experience, and it reveals the predispositions that underlie ostensibly universal accounts. Reading as an outsider, however—like reading itself, or indeed like "doing" gender or race (West and Zimmerman 1987)—is learned from a community. New readings develop from shared insights about texts, and these emerge publicly only when there are opportunities to articulate them. The case presented here shows that, while prevailing conventions for interpretation promote readings that assign novels to established traditions, groups of readers with different experiences can develop new frameworks for interpretation. For readers who do construct new interpretations, a novel may become a resource for supporting claims to new knowledge about society.[17]

This analysis has implications for understanding controversies about the evaluation of cultural works. Reading a narrative requires placing oneself in the work, but placing oneself in a novel is a complex process. Many of the early reviews I discussed show signs of the difficulties male readers had in placing themselves comfortably in *The Late Bourgeois World*. They lacked the background knowledge that would have helped them to be sympathetic to an intelligent and introspective single woman in the mid-1960s and seemed unable to translate her story into anything of interest. Instead of placing themselves in the narrator's position, they looked elsewhere for the meaning of the novel. As a consequence, they judged as flawed writing much of the material I took as being central and meaningful. Such responses illuminate a crucial aspect of the evaluative processes involved in the construction of reputation and fame for women writers (see Tuchman and Fortin 1984).

The analysis also suggests that, while texts do shape and limit readers' interpretations, we should be skeptical of discussions that rely too heavily on the power of something "in" the text. Griswold (1987), for example, suggests that novels have "cultural power" to the extent that they evoke multiple meanings while retaining "coherence." Her case study, an analysis of how the meanings drawn from the same corpus vary in different societies, suggests that the potentialities of particular texts vary for different interpretive communities. Yet she subverts her own analysis by attempting to measure the power of particular texts across societies; her own demonstration of divergent readings suggests that the more relevant question might be, Powerful for whom?

It is telling, of course, that the readings readily available to me for this kind of analysis did not include a Black African reading (though I quote a piece of one from [g] earlier in this chapter), an African feminist reading, or an Afrikaner reading, although one can imagine such accounts. The banning of the novel in South Africa shortly after its publication (the first instance of censorship of Gordimer's work) is evidence of an official reading with explicit political consequences. Elsewhere, *The Late Bourgeois World* has been taken up as a text removed from the setting that produced it. It has been read by different readers, at different times, in a variety of ways. Many of those readers understand it as an account of South African society, even though most of those who live in the situation portrayed have no voice in the discourses that surround its interpretation.

The interpretive processes I have discussed also have implications for the processes through which people understand one another. I have suggested that readers often look to novels for information about the lives of those unlike themselves. The richness of the observation underlying a realistic novel means that it includes information not readily available in other public forms and gives us a sense of seeing into a different world. But interpretations are conditioned by conventional interpretive frames and by the blinders associated with different social locations. Different readers of a novel read it differently in the light of what they already know. The things that I took away from *The Late Bourgeois World,* for example, seem mostly to have involved a heightened awareness of aspects of my own experience—things that I saw reflected in the imagined life of a woman with whom I have some things in common. The reviewers and critics I have discussed took up different themes, presumably relevant to their own experiences and agendas: with the single exception of the feminist critic, they focused on the stories of men in the novel or on political issues that they defined as human rather than specific to one gender. Perhaps, then, readers are typically likely to understand any text more in terms of their own concerns than those of others. Noticing this feature of interpretation, though, may in itself be a step toward constructing knowledge about the experiences of others, because it suggests that readers might consider what their own interpretations are missing and that developing meaning must always be a collective endeavor.

We see in this case study the dynamic tension of interpretation as process and the fundamentally social character of any interpretation. Both representation and interpretation necessarily operate through conventions, which develop and are learned through collective use. Conventions are continually subject to revision, and they change, as new traditions develop, through collective activity as well. I have pointed to a political dimension in the interpretive process, which means that "novel readings" can develop from the shared experiences and perspectives of social groups located differently from those who have previously monopolized interpretive authority. Although such new readings are often experienced as personal responses to cultural works, they depend on revisions of convention and can develop only as new interpretive communities emerge. Finally, then, this analysis recommends a profoundly skeptical approach to claims about the "correct" interpretation of any text, including the texts of sociology. It suggests that any interpretation, to be accurately characterized, must be thought of as the product of a located community of particular interpreters. And it insists on attention to the composition of interpretive communities and on an active receptiveness to the interpretive claims of outsiders.

7   Whose Science of Food and Health?

Narratives of Profession and Activism
from Public Health Nutrition

SCIENTIFIC KNOWLEDGE of food and nutrition is organized around a paradox—or at least the appearance of a paradox. The claims of science are, traditionally, presented as abstract, timeless, replicable, and universal.[1] The social activities of producing, distributing, and using food, on the other hand, are more obviously relational, contextualized, politicized, and embodied activities. As in many health-related fields, this disjuncture is managed, and at least partially obscured, by a gendered division of labor (Smith 1987:83–84). Nutritional scientists—historically, mostly men—develop "basic" knowledge of food and human sustenance, while professional dietitians and public health nutritionists—mostly women—are given the complex and often frustrating tasks of using the findings of nutritional science to solve problems in particular material settings. Authorized knowledge moves in one direction, from scientists "down" to practitioners, whose broader knowledge of food in the life-world is typically understood as mere application of general principles.

I begin with this contrast in order to call attention to the work of "intermediate" or "subordinate" professionals in the health care system—nurses, social workers, health educators, science and medical technicians, for example—workers who are mostly women and who are often left out of analyses of science and the production of scientific knowledge. This essay draws from my studies of one such group, dietitians and community nutritionists, in which I explore how these professionals are positioned in a complex network of institutions that organize the production and distribution of food (see also DeVault 1995, and chap. 5). I am interested in how they are drawn into these networks, how they are trained in the "authorized" knowledge of food and nutrition, and what they might have to contribute as actors at the margins of the institutions that organize and control food systems.

One of my difficulties has involved finding a comfortable "stance" toward this group. I became interested in food and nutrition work because it seemed to be undervalued work; even before I knew very much about it, I was interested in taking this field seriously—and that is still my intention. I wish to avoid the dismissive, humorous, or hostile tone that characterizes much writing on the less prestigious professions (see, e.g., Shapiro 1986, whose history of home economics is billed on the book jacket as a "droll" and "amusing" text that "deconstructs the marshmallow"). I believe that the pervasive sexism in societal views of professional work sometimes creeps into feminist writing as well, rendering us too ready to criticize women in the so-called "women's professions," and too easily inclined to see them in caricatured ways, simply as carriers and enforcers of dominant ideologies. As I learned more about the field of food and nutrition work, I did find grounds for critique. In fact, I would argue that dietitians and nutritionists do work in institutions where they are drawn into practices that carry and enforce dominant views of nutritional science (and a larger social order). But I will also argue that this observation captures only part of the practice and thought one can find among nutrition professionals.

In this chapter, I propose a feminist rationale for renewal of the long-standing sociological concern with professional socialization and work, especially in the so-called women's professions. In doing so, however, I wish to pay particular attention to the disciplinary "lens" of sociology, considering how the traditional concerns of the field have shaped approaches to these topics, and how we might see these concerns differently, bringing "subordinate" groups more fully into analyses of professional work. I will suggest that feminist studies in this area can work against the traditional sociological view—and thus supplement it—by calling attention to the gendered diversity of professions and to significant heterogeneity within professional fields.[2] I will illustrate such an approach with an analysis of how some public health nutritionists negotiated professional identities in a particular moment—the decade that spanned the late 1960s and early 1970s—when food and hunger were widely if only briefly understood as political issues. Their stories raise questions about professional socialization in the "women's" professions—about the selves that form during professional training, the curious mix of authority and deference that characterizes professional identities in these fields, and the possibilities for practice that challenge professional subordination. In pursuing these questions, I will rely on feminist methodological strategies that provide a foundation for the analysis: I will attend to the emotional dimensions of social organization and to dynamics of participation and exclusion.

PROFESSION AS A TOPIC IN FEMINIST STUDIES

Feminist scholars enter the academic world with an oppositional purpose: we bring new perspectives, and we intend to challenge the dominant modes of scholarship that have too often left women's experiences unexplored. In spite of considerable success in that project, we often find that becoming professional is an enterprise that leads in other directions, to some peculiar dilemmas. As we learn to be sociologists, nutritionists, historians, lawyers, theorists—as we accept the discipline of any field—we often find that we must struggle to sustain and act upon the feminist insights and intentions with which we began.

This observation points to the powerful effects of professionalism as a form of work organization. Becoming a professional means gaining a particular kind of authority; a professional is warranted to do particular kinds of work, to speak as an expert, to set policy. For these reasons, becoming a professional promises—for many of us—the opportunity to bring new ideas into public discourses, and perhaps the power to make change. But the process of becoming professional is inherently conservative. One is trained in the established paradigms of a profession, gains the competences associated with the field, and becomes a practitioner of a craft with its own canons and traditions. One also learns about disciplinary and professional boundaries and etiquette—one learns that the professional warrant to act depends on adherence to established modes of thought and practice.

In an early second-wave feminist essay, Mary Howell wrote about these potential contradictions in an article entitled, "Can we be feminists and professionals?" (1979). Professionalism, she argued, teaches elitism and can lead to arrogance toward "clients," while feminism begins with solidarity among women in all kinds of positions, and aims at the elimination of oppressive relations. Professionalism assumes that experts should control others, while feminism assumes that women should be in control of their own lives. And professional frameworks dictate particular, established agendas, while feminism calls for a focus on change and liberation. Howell did not insist that we leave professions; she noted that there are very few ways for women to work effectively outside of patriarchal institutions. She did suggest that we need to develop a keen awareness of our professional contexts, and that thinking through the difficulties of feminist action within established conventions, collectively, is a process essential to maintaining feminist understandings of these contradictory situations.

Berenice Fisher (1990), a feminist educator who teaches in a school for human service professionals, has also written about the experience and effects of professionalism, with special attention to fields that are predominantly female. Fisher is interested in the contradictory experiences of women who enter the human service professions, such as social work, nursing, and teaching. She points out that many women are drawn to these fields by the promise of economic independence and the chance to perform work they understand as socially valuable. As they move into these "women's professions," however, they discover that these promises are not fully met: they usually receive relatively low pay, they may have little control over their own work, and they are often located in bureaucracies that regulate their activities but provide little support for the work they want to do. Fisher's discussion of this phenomenon is titled "Alice in the Human Services"; by calling on the story of Alice in Wonderland, she calls attention to an aspect of the subjective experience of professional training and entry into a career—the sense we may sometimes have that we've entered a rather strange world, where things are not quite what they should be. In part, Fisher points to features of the women's professions that are widely recognized, related to their subordinate status relative to the "classic" professions such as medicine or law (see Stromberg 1988). But Fisher also urges that feminists look beyond these features of the women's professions and examine respectfully the perspectives and activities of women committed to these fields of work. She points out that, too often, these traditionally female professions are devalued by feminist as well as nonfeminist observers (though perhaps for different reasons). And her discussion suggests that women professionals respond actively to the constraints of their positions, and may resist or transcend conservative aspects of professional training in their actual practice.

Sociologists have produced a vast literature on the professions, characterized by particular ways of thinking about this form of work organization. While these studies are often useful, it seems important to notice the boundaries that are implicitly drawn by sociological studies of professional work. The theoretical apparatus that highlights some aspects of professional work leaves out others. For example, most sociological studies focus on the professional as autonomous expert, leaving out all those who support professional work. Even studies of women in "supportive" professions, like nursing or social work, often overlook "other women" in the lives of these professionals—women whose labor underwrites professional activity (e.g., domestic workers, paraprofessionals, and clerical staff).[3] Clients' perspectives are often left out of research on professional work. Sociological frameworks also seem to encourage analyses of the abstracted, formal features of professional work such as questions of status and control—characteristics of the work that can be compared across professions. Sociologists less often tie these formal features of professional work to their substantive aspects, considering the products and consequences of professional work as well as its organization. (I saw this effect in my own writing when one of my informants read an early paper from this study and exclaimed, "But there's nothing about food in here!")

Most important for this analysis, sociological studies of professional socialization typically proceed from the profession itself, asking, "How are good professionals produced?" Feminists are often more interested in the production of professionals who will resist the demands of male-centered professional standpoints. Indeed, as I have thought about these issues, I have begun to collect a "counter-literature" on professional socialization that reads the process rather differently, with a concern for its darker side and for individual struggles for authenticity and multiple allegiances as well as professional identity.

Virginia Olesen and Elvi Whittaker (1968), for example, in an early study of nursing students, provide an account of professional socialization as an intensely emotional process. Shulamit Reinharz addresses both the shaping effects of professional training and resistance to those effects in her autobiographical account, *On Becoming a Social Scientist* (1979). Susan Krieger's autobiographical essays in *Social Science and the Self* (1991) deal with similar struggles, compounded by the homophobia woven into the practices of professional institutions. Cheryl Townsend Gilkes (1983) writes about the careers of African American women activists who think of career mobility in terms of "going up for the oppressed," and who conduct careers that are organized by allegiances to their communities of origin rather than professional communities. Patricia Hill Collins's (1990) discussion of the work of Black feminist intellectuals points less directly to this kind of strategic use of the powers conferred upon individuals through professional education and credentialing. And in a review of Krieger's book (perhaps because she is writing less formally), Barrie Thorne (1994: 138) shares a dream that vividly expresses an aspect of professional socialization that rarely shows up in sociological studies:

> One night when I was in the throes of finishing my Ph.D. dissertation, I dreamed that I was in a line of people slowly marching toward a guillotine wielded by my advisor. As he chopped off each head, he declared, "I pronounce you my colleague." Just before it was my turn, I jolted out of the dream. It left me with disturbing thoughts about professional socialization as loss, conformity, even as a kind of violence to the learner.

These writings represent a feminist, "oppositional" strand in studies of professional socialization. While mainstream studies examine the process as one that fits the individual to the professional mold, these feminist writers treat the process as more problematic and variable, making more room for questions about the endpoint in the process, and taking account of individual or collective goals that might conflict with institutional ones. This approach makes profession itself problematic.

I did not plan my study of the nutrition professions with all these ideas in mind. However, I have come to see that my interest in the work of nutritionists is rooted not only in theoretical questions, but also in my personal and practical concerns—my own struggles to operate as a "feminist professional." These insights into my own feelings have helped me to read my informants' stories of becoming professional more closely, with greater attention to their hopes and struggles along the way. In the next section I begin an analysis of some of those stories.

NARRATIVES OF ENTRY

I have collected career narratives from thirty-five dietitians and nutritionists (for details about the sample, see chap. 5 under "The Study" and n. 3 there). I began each interview by requesting a career history: to most interviewees, I said something like, "I usually start by asking if you'll tell me the story of your career." I used the familiar term *story* partly out of a relatively unconsidered personal inclination toward informality; as I consider how the interviews unfolded, however, I believe the term also signaled my openness to complex and grounded narratives. Stories are entertaining, plotted, and full of contextual detail. They begin at the beginning, wherever that may be.

Informants sometimes seemed surprised that I asked for a story. In many interviews, I find in the transcript an opening "dance" of sorts, as we orient to each other as teller and listener, negotiating a way to begin. Often, I noticed signs that the teller was preparing: a deep breath or contemplative pause. Sometimes there was clear indecision, and an appeal for help: "You mean—way back?" I learned to help out with a gentle nudge: "Long story?"

Many narrators started in childhood, telling of interests and aspirations, family contexts, and their first thoughts and feelings about meaningful work and future lives. They talked about interests in food and its significance, sometimes in the context of a rich ethnic heritage, or about the importance of food in family lives, sometimes as an aspect of family illnesses. These stories of early interest must be interpreted with care; they are, of course, constructed retrospectively, and I do not mean to take them as unproblematic causal accounts. But they may reveal some of the meanings of a nutrition career that are not easily expressed elsewhere.

Informants' stories were told with emotion—pride, regret, affection for family and teachers, and sometimes anger, uncertainty, or disappointment—and the depth of feeling in these accounts took me somewhat by surprise. I feel now that I should not have been surprised by the feeling in these narratives; after all, my interest in these lives stems in part from my desire to understand my own too often submerged feelings about career and profession.

TWO WORLDS

My aim in interviewing was to elicit stories without imposing a structure. I asked many clarifying questions along the way, but I did not plan specific questions in advance. As the interviewing proceeded, I learned about the class and family backgrounds of my informants. Telling their stories, they provided the contexts those stories required, explaining along the way who they had been and where they had come from. The portraits that emerge hint at travel between two worlds: the richly social world of their families and communities, and a relatively unfamiliar world of professionalism.

As a group, these professionals came from stable, upwardly mobile, but not particularly affluent families. Raised primarily in the northeastern United States, they were mostly white, and the white women who mentioned ethnicity were of European descent (e.g., German, Irish, Italian). One of the thirty-five interviewees was African American, and three were immigrants from Asian or Caribbean countries. Many of their parents held working- and middle-class jobs that were relatively secure; they were bakers, government workers, nurses, and salespeople. Informants' families were relatively comfortable economically and expected them to go to college (sometimes as the first family member to do so), but they were careful about money. One woman recalled that she came from a family "that thought eating well was important"; then she laughed gently and added, "And eating economically, too."

The accounts convey a distinctive texture of family life. Several informants spoke of a closeness to family and community that was both comforting and confining. Gina Falcone explained, "I had been very protected in a family unit, in my little neighborhood in [a large city]—it was very neighborhood oriented."[4] Parents were very much involved in the women's decisions about education and work and urged them to consider professions, in part because they were oriented very practically toward work as a means of survival. One father "felt that his daughter should have a definite career. You know, a definite earning potential." And several informants reported that their parents advised them to choose fields where the pay is good and "there's always work." They also spoke of relatively traditional families, telling somewhat ruefully at times of their parents' views on appropriate work for women, and how they were quite explicitly directed toward "women's" professions.

When they talk of high school years (and even earlier experiences), many of these people describe themselves as school achievers, and they often mention an early interest in science. As they tell of moving toward college, they often convey the sense of entering a new world that is characteristic of social mobility stories. Dorothy Mancini remarked, "I had no notion what a college was." Another woman described herself as "the baby of the family" and "not a trail-blazer," but also indicated that one factor in choosing a college was her desire to move away from the family. And another explained that her small college was a good choice because it gave her the chance to "feel secure."

Gina Falcone's story gives the most vivid sense of movement from one world to another. Her Catholic high school provided little career counseling, and when she began to think about a career, she sought advice from "my teacher that I trusted." Then, she explains:

> I went to the public library in [the city], myself, and looked up lists of colleges. And I didn't even know about the library at that point . . . I squeakily asked someone whether—if they had such a thing.

Telling the story as an experienced professional, she wishes she had gone to Cornell University, a place that was "too intimidating" at the time. Instead, she relates:

> I found a little college in [a small town], which is where my family—my mother's family is originally from. It's a small Catholic college; I was not feeling very adventurous. And, well, maybe it was adventurous in a way [*laughing*], in retrospect.

Her choice was indeed "adventurous" for the young girl she was then; and it began to move her away from family and into a wider professional world.

These young women move from family and community toward the promise of professional work. But they enter a profession with a particular character, and the roads they travel do not always lead to the destinations they expect. They enter a "women's" profession, leading to positions with relatively limited authority and very short career ladders. Indeed, their comments about gender tracking often emerged as they talked of feeling blocked, or wondering whether to leave the field. They learn that pay is low and case loads high; that respect and adequate resources are hard to come by; and that "teamwork" means, in most settings, that they will do whatever is needed.

These young nutritionists also enter a field that is marked by continuing (if often relatively muted) tension between competing conceptions of the aims and scope of nutrition work. I entered the field as a researcher, in the mid-1980s, through contacts with nutrition educators who had an explicitly political and often activist orientation toward their professional work. As I expanded my view of the field, I began to see that these women operated in a larger professional environment whose strongest and most pervasive themes were quite different. As I read journals and attended professional conferences, I saw that the field relied heavily on a science mediated by agricultural interests and the food industry. At professional meetings, much of the research presented is subsidized by corporate funding; "snack breaks" and luncheons are sponsored by groups such as Pepsi, Kraft Foods, and the Pork Council. Those working in the field are not unaware of these corporate connections: they notice them, joke about them, and sometimes raise these issues for sustained debate (see, e.g., Tobin, Dwyer, and Gussow 1992). But these connections are mostly accepted as part of the landscape of the field, and they coexist with an understanding of "science" as the source of "objective knowledge."

Much of the work that these professionals do—and believe in—is work that they insist would not get done without support from industry. Thus, they "make do" with what they can secure: jobs are always vulnerable to shifting currents of politics; program planning is driven in part by agricultural policy and the supplies of surplus commodities it produces; and nutrition education often relies on materials produced by food corporations and commodity boards promoting particular products. Dietitians and nutritionists are aware of these dilemmas and compromises and come to understand them in various ways. Their standard practices, constructed in various times and settings in fragile niches on the margins of the powerful institutions of medicine, industry, and agriculture, are formed through both historical and moment-to-moment negotiations between nutritionists' own visions and intentions and their sense of what is possible (for more on this theme, see the case studies of professional practice in DeVault 1995). They carry on with the day-to-day work of feeding, educating, managing—doing their best to deliver food to patients and clients in need.

NETWORKS OF RESISTANCE

Within the larger professional field, there are pockets of resistance to dominant constructions of professional work, which provide other ways of seeing the landscape and conceiving of meaningful practice. Some people enter the field with commitments to other communities, and struggle to work in ways that honor those commitments that arise outside the profession. Some of those people find professional mentors who help them in that project and train them in a counter-tradition within the profession. The networks that sustain these counter-traditions grow and shrink in different historical moments. When I conducted career-history interviews in the early 1990s, students just entering the field were drawn most often by the promise of new developments in high-tech medicine and a cultural emphasis on "fitness." But a number of the mid-career women I talked with, especially those working in public health settings, talked of coming to the field with a strongly political orientation, born out of the political movements of the 1960s that, for a while at least, made food a political issue. Political activism outside the profession gave nutritionists the opportunity to expand a network of public health programs and institutions inside their field that they believed could provide sites for productive work with communities in need.

We can see how individuals encounter these networks by examining several moments in the career histories of three of these women. All three studied nutrition as undergraduate students between 1964 and 1974, a decade of political activism and possibility. Their stories show how a collective sense of doing nutrition work differently was woven into their careers. They give some sense of these women's struggles to find professional work that is meaningful and also show how meaning is constructed collectively, with like-minded colleagues and the institutions (however fragile) they create together.

Dorothy Mancini, for example, recounts a turbulent time in her college years. Her story is told haltingly, with much laughter marking her references to politics and the near "slip" in her career path, when she almost became an English major:

> I was much more together, I think, when I was in high school. When I got to college, everything fell apart. [*laughing*]
>
> DeVault: Yes, it's sort of a shock. What do you mean by that?
>
> Well—I was quite sure what I wanted to do before I got to college. [*laughs*] I got to college, I was no longer quite so sure, and almost became an English major. [*laughs—for several seconds*] Decided I did not like science. Um— that I much preferred to write and be on picket lines, [*laughs*] if I was in school. This was in the mid-sixties, and so, I almost dropped out, at the end of that first year. And I was going to transfer to arts and sciences. Um—I decided to stay.

Why did she decide to stay? As the story proceeds, Mancini's college years are told as a continuing struggle to stay on track. Basic science courses seemed less engaging than literature and politics, but those focused on food and nutrition were more promising, somehow:

> I finally started taking some of the nutrition courses, and biochemistry, and really liked that. [I ask why.] Well, the nutrition. I wasn't taking—I was sick of all these courses that didn't seem to make any sense, in any way, to—the kinds of things that I was interested in at that point, which was, you know, [*laughs*] civil rights, stuff like that.

She does not spell out exactly how things begin to come together, but the implication, I believe, is that nutrition courses deal with things that matter for people. In her senior year—in 1968—Mancini takes a course in public health nutrition, and here she encounters the beginning of a network of professional activism:

> My senior year they started teaching a course in public health nutrition, and—that was like magic. And that combined what I loved about nutrition, and what I loved about people, and communities, and sort of grass-roots teaching. . . . I got a very broad exposure to public health nutrition, because this was the first time they were teaching this course, and so, they were trying everything out. And we got out to elderly programs, and Headstart programs, and community health center programs . . . they got us to everything that was possible. . . .
>
> So that's how I learned about public health and community nutrition. And it really—that made sense to me, in terms of, well, I mean do I—I really liked it.

She goes on to say that the course was never again taught in quite the same way; in subsequent years, the teacher had formal credentials and didn't try to pack so much into the course. She doesn't use the words, but we can hear that the new political perspectives in the field have begun to be institutionalized. In that initial moment, however, public health nutrition is "like magic" for Mancini, and gives her professional life a clear direction.

For Gina Falcone, a similar struggle developed in the late 1960s, during the internship that typically follows a college degree and leads to professional certification. She, too, refers rather obliquely to politics as an element in her story; its significance emerges slowly and quietly. She begins by talking about the intense, continuing work—"abuse," she calls it— required in her "old-style" internship:

> We worked, one time, nine weeks in a row without a week-end off. And a lot of times I—one time I worked twenty-one days in a row without a day off . . . that was real student abuse. I mean, if they needed a pot-washer, you washed pots. It's not bad to—I mean, everyone needs to pitch in, I really believe in teamwork. But I felt so abused, in a lot of ways. It was a real tug of war inside me between wanting to be a good student and learn things,

and wanting to just run off, and explore my own life. And it was real hard to balance those two things, that growing up stuff.

She talks then about her teachers, stern but understanding; she appreciates that "they could have tossed me out, and I could have said, 'Well, I'll be a secretary.' [*laughing*] And be back at square one or something." And she talks about the other students, a highly-qualified group, and "quite a mix of people."

Then, very quietly, and with a comment that she is somewhat uncomfortable being taped, she mentions her involvement with a political group working in a newly established community clinic:

> I got involved in that. It was—again, trying to go beyond myself, get out of the four white walls, get to meet different people, of color, and experience. [*softly*] And, put my nutrition into action. You get to do that a little bit in your internship. But this was much more meaty, and [*softly*] I don't know.

In fact, her internship produced a crisis, and for a while she wasn't sure she could continue. She felt herself being drawn into a model of hospital dietetics—a model in which "counseling" can only mean a fleeting contact at a time of crisis—that seemed wrong in several ways:

> That's when I really realized that [*pause*] hospital dietetics was very limited. When people are scared, they take in a little bit. And then I noticed that doctors would give you discharge orders, right before the patient was discharged. And I spent so much time, handing out menus, and making sure that things were in order. Aaaghhh. I felt like what I went into it for was such a small piece of—of the pie, that it wasn't worth it to me. And I saw a lot going on in the kitchens [*softly*] that, I didn't really like. The way people treated each other.

Falcone's reference to how people "treated each other" alludes to the pervasive hierarchies of hospital life, organized not only through physicians' control of nutrition work but extending as well to the layers of support staff who contend over the conduct of more mundane aspects of institutional life. Her comment about the kitchen deserves closer examination:

> I saw a lot going on in the kitchens [*softly*] that, I didn't really like. The way people treated each other.

The kitchens are a site where nutritionists are required to exercise a particular kind of class-based (and in most settings ethnically-charged) authority. In the kitchens they cannot merely help and advise clients; instead they must be supervisors of a low-paid work force. Had it been the only one, I would have been puzzled by this fleeting reference to this kind of discomfort; it is rarely discussed explicitly in terms of class and cultural relations. However, the kitchen appears, fleetingly, in many career stories—it points to the part of the job that many of these young women do not enjoy, because, as they explain, it is often difficult to work with nonprofessional staff. Given this charged context, I believe we can read Falcone's soft aside as evidence of her resistance to the expectation that she will exercise this kind of authority. Her next sentences suggest that she is interested in another kind of authority, perhaps equally uncomfortable, but more worth pursuing:

> I was really observing a lot, and at the same time verbalizing what I was feeling. Those were very new and different things for me—[from] being in a small little family unit, where you didn't criticize authority [*smiling*]. So, for me that was—I just wanted to do other things with my life. I wasn't sure what that was, but I knew that hospital dietetics was not [it].

Falcone endures a period of confusion and uncertainty. A friend who is both professionally and politically active provides a sense of what might be possible. But she must try out several uncomfortable positions before she finds a community health center where she feels comfortable with the work she is asked to do.

Mary Ann Walter encountered the developing network of new public health nutrition programs during the early 1970s, in her first jobs in the rural communities of a southern state:

> The first thing was starting up the elderly feeding—you know, the elderly feeding programs.

> DeVault: That must have been fairly new then.

> It was, it was brand new. 1976. And—here I am, a—let's see, 1976. So I was twenty-five years old. And they give me this grant proposal, and about a hundred and twenty-five thousand dollars [*laughing*]. And—here get these feeding sites going [*laughing*]. You know, luckily, I'm the kind of person that, I don't know why, I'll take on anything. I usually don't—I have enough confidence, that I can do it. So I did. And um—I did that for two years, and it was a very good experience, I learned a lot.

Though she enjoyed this work, she "burned out" and, missing the personal contact of nutritional counseling, moved to a newly established WIC[5] program:

> If you know anything about the history of WIC, WIC was just starting back then. They'd finally got funds allocated. So it was a very exciting time, because [the state] was one of the ten states they originally surveyed, and said, major nutritional problems, you know, let's implement all these federal programs. And [this area] was one of the ten surveyed, so there was a lot of

pressure to get [it] on the WIC program, as much as possible. So I was able to—being, again, the only RD [Registered Dietitian] in this eight-county program—I was able to *really* do a lot. And I've always liked jobs like this, where I can kind of—given the lead, just go do it [*breath, and a little laugh*].

Working at these jobs, she met other public health professionals who had come to the area with the National Health Service Corps. They mentored her in a broader vision of public health practice:

These folks had all gotten their master's degrees, so they had kind of a, a broader scope on public health, public health nursing, public health nutrition. And—how it can impact on—well, eventually on the family, but— you know, just how it can impact on other health professionals, and the whole area, the region, you know, providing services, to groups. Which I've always found fascinating.

DeVault: So by a broader scope, you mean sort of taking all of the—the whole system into account? Or—

Right. And seeing how your piece fits in. And where you—what you really need to do to make an impact. I mean, one-on-one counseling's nice. But, you know—in the scope of things, you probably need to move up a level, in terms of policy, decision-making, you know, implementing training, you know, whatever it might be. Um—so it really expanded my horizons, beyond direct service.

All three of these women have continued working in various community health settings for over twenty years. They have sought and found ways to contextualize their work with individuals, broadening the scope of their professional practice. Their commitments to the work were nurtured and sustained because they found groups of like-minded professionals who were building fresh visions of meaningful work.

The community health networks these women encounter do not, of course, solve the problems of hunger and inequality. Indeed, the professional orientation of these programs—and the political trade-offs that produce them—tend to support definitions of these problems in terms of education rather than inequality (see DeVault and Pitts 1984). But there were some significant gains. Commodity food programs, the expansion of food stamps, and new programs to aid the elderly and pregnant women and their children did help to get food to people who needed it. And many community health centers have provided sites in which professionals could work with community advocates to improve nutrition and health services.

This network does not stay in place, however. By the time I began these investigations, in the mid-1980s, the Reagan administration had forced deep cuts in these programs. (Indeed, community nutritionists, based in the Society for Nutrition Education, were battling the American Dietetic Association, whose leaders approved the "fiscal responsibility" they saw in the administration's cutbacks.) It was no longer easy to find any job in a community setting, and certainly less inspiring to work there. By the 1990s there was even deeper pessimism about the future of these programs.

Under these difficult conditions, some of these practitioners continue their work in local communities. Some are fortunate enough to work in programs that give them considerable autonomy; they can do things like helping to obtain the equipment mothers need to feed their children more easily—a high chair, for instance. Others simply take charge of their own activity, giving advice about food and also making referrals to the public library or a GED program. Some are bound by tightly regulated programs that mandate only particular kinds of help in particular circumstances. In these situations, they may sometimes step beyond the bounds of professional propriety. An African American community nutritionist told me that she gets angry about the commercial foundations of the program she must implement, which she feels encourage some clients to believe that particular kinds of formula are essential for their infants' health. At times, she speaks very directly to her clients:

> Sometimes I come right out and say, "You know, I just hate this." [*hitting a spoon against the table, and emphasizing each word*] I say, "I hate this." I say, "You don't need all this stuff—"
>
> DeVault: You say that to them?
>
> Yes, sometimes. I say, "You see this food guide. Most of our food guides—all of our food guides have milk as the first thing." I say, you know, "The dairy industry is a powerful lobby." I say, "Milk is important." But I say, "Everybody can't even drink it," because people of color sometimes can't—you know, have that lactose intolerance.

She wants her clients to learn not only that milk is nutritious but, more importantly, "to manage their own stuff": to make their own informed decisions about how to keep their children healthy, rather than learning to depend unthinkingly on the products promoted through the program. Finally, some community nutritionists I interviewed during the 1980s and 1990s continue their political work outside of their occupational settings, by working with local groups, helping to run food banks and emergency pantries, testifying at legislative hearings, and organizing within professional organizations. These activities are organized by their conceptions of the professional mandate; they can be seen as individual expressions of a collective challenge to the dominant view of the profession.

My analysis of these stories highlights a challenge to one conception of science, an attempt by those working in local communities to "own" nutritional science. Toni Liquori's (1995) study of changing views of science and practice in the nutrition department at Teachers College provides another examination of a local version of this generational shift: she shows how, in some periods, faculty and students have been able to conceptualize food as "nurturance" (as opposed to more science- or industry-based conceptions of food as "nutrients" or "marketable products"). The challenges posed over these decades seem, in the 1990s, to have largely been absorbed and managed by dominant constructions of science and a medical model of nutrition work. Yet that dominant view itself is continually reconstructed in response to shifts in scientific and political contexts. Perhaps, then, we should see such changes in terms of an ebb and flow that includes the periodic reappearance of counter-traditions within the professions, nurtured through periods of "doldrums"[6] by networks of professionals who sustain alternative views.

CONCLUSION:
CLAIMING OUR OWN PROFESSIONAL PRACTICE

The career stories analyzed here point to recruitment and socialization to professional work as a process involving keenly emotional transformations of self. Though it has not been the dominant way of conceiving professional socialization, this idea is not entirely new. Virginia Olesen and Elvi Whittaker (1968) wrote about emotions in the professional socialization of nursing students: they suggest that an inner dialogue, in response to a series of depressions and elations, is key to the students' adjustment to the demands of nursing. More recently, feminist philosophers and social scientists have argued that emotion is always significant for knowledge production, and ought to be treated in a more focused way as a signpost to knowledge (e.g., Jaggar 1989; and see de Montigny 1995 for a powerful account of becoming a social worker).

Feelings are rarely explicitly made part of the official curricula of professional training. Individuals living through the process of training and socialization often experience these moments in relative isolation. Furthermore, professional training often produces, structurally, a kind of isolation from family and community. Thus, as new recruits to professional life, we learn to suppress many emotions. If we are lucky, we find networks of colleagues and create spaces—more or less formally—where we can work on reconciling our hopes and fears with the demands of professional work.

My intention here is to effect a small version of such a reconciliation, both in my own writing and in my analysis of those I studied, by examining professional work in a way that opens the concepts of sociological study to admit more of the complex lived experience of women professionals. I have attended to aspects of professional socialization that I believe are too often overlooked: the actual pathways from women's lives and communities into professional identities—pathways that are always more complex than they might appear, as well as more contingent and more deeply infused with emotion.

I hope that this approach represents at least a step toward developing an honest and useful stance toward the group I study. I mean to suggest that my researcher's "attitude" toward the field of dietetics and community nutrition must include an openness to the heterogeneity of the field, and the various ways that nutrition professionals position themselves within it. Rather than conceiving practitioners one-dimensionally, as mere carriers of the dominant ideologies of their field, such a view would provide for analyses that hold in our range of vision the landscape of the field, the competing views of subgroups within it, and the struggles of individuals to locate professional selves within the constraints of both that larger terrain and their local situations. Further, and extending the metaphor of "mapping," it seems necessary to consider my own location in a neighboring county. The point is not just that nutritionists and sociologists operate in similar environments because we are professionals, but that our practices connect us: just as these community nutritionists "work on" the food lives of their clients, I "work on" their stories. We hope that our work will benefit those we "work on," but we are also tied to professional settings with their particular constraints and demands. Acknowledging these connections does not provide any direct route to better practice, but it may help us to think more usefully about agendas and coalitions, and how our concerns might be aligned with those of women positioned differently in this complex of social relations.

V. WRITING AND RHETORICAL STRATEGY

IN GRADUATE school, I learned from Howard Becker that "no research is finished until it is written up"—and his adage still torments me when I think of unpublished papers in my file drawers. But writing is more than a simple report or conclusion to a project. Becker (1986b) and others (Katz 1983, Richardson 1994) point out that writing is a form of thought, shaping the ideas of researchers. Writing is also active, an operator of social relations (Smith 1990b). Recent work in science studies (following writers such as Latour and Woolgar 1979) has shown how scientific texts are designed to persuade and mobilize audiences. (Even elementary school science students learn that "writing up" an experiment is not a matter of simply telling what happened, but of fitting that narrative to a standard format; see Smith 1987:162). And the "linguistic turn" in the social sciences (reflected, for example, in the work of Clifford and Marcus 1986) has brought a widespread (and for social scientists, relatively new) recognition of the rhetorical character of our work. Feminists, like other scholars, have built upon these observations as sources for a lively literature exploring both the rhetorics of traditional research texts and possibilities for new formats.

Writing is a moment in the research process when the "balancing act" required of feminist investigators becomes especially perilous. Standard textual formats can be powerful instruments of persuasion, and feminist writers often wish to call on the power of such texts to convince. For some readers, any deviation from standard format threatens to diminish the persuasive power of the text. In the academic context, standard formats also prove to gatekeepers that the writer is worthy of membership; a "proper" text lifts the writer into the company of scientists, while one that is different may not. Despite these pulls toward tradition, many writers feel dissatisfied with standard formats. Often, research texts obscure personal experiences, objectify research subjects, and drain topics of emotion. (Since feminist and other oppositional researchers typically research topics of intense personal concern, it is especially ironic that they often feel compelled to write dry and dispassionate texts.) Further, writing choices link texts to different audiences and discourses: some choices seem more likely than others to challenge or reproduce prevailing modes of thought (Smith 1989). Thus, thinking of writing as part of the research process should heighten a scholar's awareness of audience, so that one considers carefully how a text will move readers, and toward what end.

The next three chapters take up questions about writing feminist texts. The first, an essay first published in 1990, examines two texts whose authors adopt different strategies for making feminist arguments. Its declarative title, "Women Write Sociology," was meant to insist on women's presence in the field, and therefore might be seen as the kind of "excavational" move I discussed earlier in this book. I also wanted to consider what made rhetorical strategies "successful" or not—but in a way that would question the judgments that produce disciplinary canons. I was angry while writing this essay, profoundly frustrated by the apparent disinterest of many male scholars in the feminist work that so excited my feminist circles. I wanted to cry out in protest, and for a while I wrote in two parallel computer files, using one for the "rage notes" (as I thought of them) that would be inappropriate in an academic piece. I imagined, at the time, including them as footnotes or along the margins of my text, but eventually, I found ways to translate, referring more decorously to the sources of my anger. Along the way, I decided that in this essay I would cite only women writers—a small act of resistance, to be sure, but one that pleased me. (When the essay was published, in a volume with eight others, I was the only woman author and my fourteen citations of women's writings nearly equaled the combined citations of women's writings of all the other authors.)

"Metaphors of Silence and Voice" was written collaboratively with Chrys Ingraham. It grew out of ongoing and always challenging conversation: we agreed on many points and yet often found ourselves arguing with surprising ferocity over differences that seemed small but consequential. Our mutual respect meant that each could push the other to think beyond initial formulations, or at least to try out thinking in different ways. In this essay, we examine the ideological underpinnings of a metaphor we both relied on, that referring to the "silencing" of women. Our intention is twofold: first, to examine the range and potential consequences of the silencing metaphor, and second, to demonstrate for social scientists the kinds of subterranean effects that any such metaphor can bring to analysis if it is deployed too simply.

Some of the caution we recommend shows up in my title for the last chapter in this section, "Speaking Up, Carefully," which is concerned with the search for "voice" but qualifies that goal with its aspiration toward careful speech. This short discussion piece was motivated in part by continuing discussions with other feminist ethnographers—at conferences in the United States and Canada—about potential risks of harming or exploiting women we studied. We often construed these issues as moral dilemmas, and I felt it might be useful to reframe them as questions of authorial voice. My intention was to avoid the paralysis sometimes induced by moralizing, and to seek ways of attacking the problem more positively as a question of practice.

8   Women Write Sociology
Rhetorical Strategies

A RENEWED interest in rhetoric has accompanied the recent "discovery" that language is used to persuade in every field of cultural and scientific production. The line of theorizing associated with this discovery emphasizes the crafted nature of scientific and social scientific analyses and the constitution of their claims of objectivity, and rhetorical analysis is being applied in a variety of relatively new ways (see, e.g., Hunter 1990). One aspect of this project should involve asking if gender matters—or better, asking *how* it matters, since several decades of renewed feminist scholarship tell us that it virtually always does. I will suggest, as well, that an analysis of rhetoric as gendered process will illuminate the social construction of "women's place" within intellectual communities.

Since the rebirth of feminism in the late 1960s, women in virtually every discipline have begun to search out the history of women's contributions. This fact in itself has significance for an investigation of rhetorical process, since it suggests the importance of a gendered tradition for those who would do intellectual work. These women have sought a rhetorical tradition that models distinctively female voices (as other nonwhite-male writers and thinkers have sought traditions in their voices). These investigators, though not all sociologists, have learned to do a kind of archaeological investigation that has taught them much about the sociology of communities of knowledge. Several general processes can be seen in the various inquiries (for example, Chicago 1975 on artists; Rossiter 1982 on scientists; Showalter 1977 on novelists; and Deegan 1981, 1988, and Reinharz 1988b on sociologists). First, there is evidence that at least some women practitioners seem to produce work "outside" or marginal to (that is, different from) the predominant male forms of their times—in other words, there is evidence of the development over time, with some continuity, of "female" traditions. (There is evidence as well that similar processes produce traditions of Black thought, and distinctively Black feminist thought; see, e.g., Collins 1990). Second, there is evidence of systematic segregation: women—no matter what the content of their work—have been channeled into particular spaces within disciplines, which, over time, have been defined as the subareas appropriate for women. These areas have simultaneously been defined as those that are least presti-gious—the simplest and least "interesting" subfields. Finally, there is evi-dence of a process whereby the gap between men's and women's concerns and relevances interacts with gender segregation to systematically influ-ence judgments of scientific and aesthetic quality and importance. Hence, women practitioners do not develop the reputation necessary for active and continuing participation in their fields, and disappear from the his-torical record more quickly, and for different reasons, than male counter-parts (Spender 1982, Tuchman and Fortin 1984, Tuchman 1989). These processes shape the construction of disciplinary canons. Too often, men have presented accounts of male experience as accounts that are gender-neutral. Texts about women's experiences—when they exist—have been read as minor revisions, works that merely add small pieces to the overall picture.

Rhetorical processes—like all social interactions—are deeply gen-dered. Speakers and listeners produce and respond to statements on the basis of deep but usually unnoticed understandings of gender. In general, women's right to speak (or write) authoritatively is attenuated and circum-scribed. For a woman to do scholarly work means speaking in arenas not normally conceded to female speakers. When women are trained as soci-ologists, for example, they are trained to think and speak in the manner of the disciplinary tradition. They learn that, if they are to be heard, their texts must enter a discourse whose contours reflect male perceptions and concerns. The readers whose judgments are influential—the teachers, edi-tors, reviewers, and colleagues who will incorporate and perhaps extend their work—have, in the past at least, mostly been men.

Women have opportunities to view the world from standpoints that are distinctively female. Of course, individual women in sociology do not all take up distinctive women's concerns and issues. Some attempt to posi-tion themselves as knowers outside of gender. But others—more and more as a community of feminist scholars has emerged—have embraced the position of marginality and have sought to give it fuller expression. These writers who address distinctive women's concerns face special prob-lems of audience. They write as sociologists, building upon the insights of a sociological tradition and intending that their texts should become part of that tradition. Many of them, however, also intend that the inclusion of women's voices should transform the discipline. In order to enter the dis-course, they must show how feminist concerns are instances of established sociological concerns, producing texts that fit into a sociological tradition. But if their texts fit too well they may subvert their own transformative project. These observations suggest several questions: To what extent is it possible to examine women's experiences in terms consistent with the established discourse of sociology? Through what rhetorical means do researchers who write about women "translate" so as to facilitate the entry of texts into a male-dominated discourse? How do the rhetorical conventions of social science influence readings of research reported by women?

The rhetorical analyses now under way in the social sciences typically adopt a method whereby recognized classics are examined in order to reveal elements of presentation and to specify how the language and style of the research report convey meaning. These studies examine rhetoric when it works smoothly and well; they bring to light the craft (presumably only partly conscious) that makes these works convincing and powerful. Indeed, it is hard to imagine another way to proceed, since rhetorically unsuccessful works are likely to disappear. But what makes a classic? In using terms such as *successful* or *unsuccessful* we take up a standpoint within an intellectual circle created and maintained by male scientists writing to and judged by their male colleagues. One might also ask on whose terms these works have been successful. With what kinds of readers have they succeeded? And perhaps most troubling, what can be said about works that might have spoken to those who have had no voices in the discourse? Presumably many of the documents we would like to examine have been lost or destroyed. And much of women's social theorizing has perhaps gone on elsewhere—in novels and poetry, or kitchen-table conversation, for example. Any search for a feminist tradition in sociology must begin cautiously, with skepticism toward the "data" that are available, but with confidence that suspicion arms us to understand more than is evident to more sanguine investigators.

FOR EXAMPLE

During the 1970s and 1980s, a community of active feminist scholars began to influence the conduct and reporting of sociology. Dale Spender (1982) suggested at the time that this activity was not so unusual as we thought—that women have for many years produced distinctively feminist thought, and that women's writing has often been suppressed, sometimes in vicious, personal ways and sometimes through the routine practices of the intellectual world. I am concerned with routine practice and its implications for contemporary feminist research. In the discussion that follows, I will examine two books by sociologists who have written about women's experiences: *Men and Women of the Corporation* by Rosabeth Moss Kanter, and *The Mirror Dance* by Susan Krieger. Both were relatively early feminist books (Kanter's was published in 1977, Krieger's in

1983), written by women whose concerns were shaped by the women's movement and feminist scholarship. Both are case studies of groups, and both aim to illuminate continuing sociological concerns through the case-study method. Kanter, in *Men and Women of the Corporation,* examines the work lives of male and female employees (including executive wives) in a large firm. She is concerned with the relationship between organizational structure and behavior: she argues that in any organization, opportunity, power, and group composition shape the way individuals respond to their work situations. Krieger, in *The Mirror Dance,* examines the lives of women who participate in a loosely structured, primarily lesbian women's community in a midwestern town. She is concerned with the relationship between community and identity: she argues that in any community, similarity provides a basis for community but also makes it difficult for individuals to maintain their individual identities. Both studies are based on extensive involvement in the settings they describe, including interviewing and participant observation.

In spite of these similarities, my discussion will focus on differences in these authors' approaches to topic and method. While both authors frame their data in terms of continuing traditions of investigation, Kanter's topic is more amenable to placement in a predominantly male tradition. She does a thoroughgoing translation that makes "the women's issue" a special case of more general organizational concerns, and her rhetorical strategy draws on the social significance of the corporation, a traditionally male arena, to highlight the significance of her research. Krieger, concerned with the experiences of women in a relatively closed and largely invisible community, works with a topic that cannot be attached so easily to established traditions, and her presentation emphasizes the particularity of the group she studied. Although both studies are based on fieldwork, they are written with different assumptions about method as well. Kanter adopts the voice of authoritative sociology—a sociology of variables and theory that provides a single interpretation for the reader. Krieger aims to explore a new method for the presentation of field data, and she adopts an unconventional mode of presentation—one that emphasizes voice and pattern, and requires a kind of reading unfamiliar in sociology.

Kanter's book is widely known and read—quickly becoming a sociological "classic"—while Krieger's is less widely circulated and known. One temptation in this analysis will be to read Kanter's as the "successful" effort at placing women's concerns on the disciplinary agenda, but I want to resist this temptation and urge my readers to do so as well. My intent is not evaluative: I have learned much from both authors, and my aim is to provide a reading of these texts that will highlight possibilities and problems in sociological writing about women's lives. I have chosen to discuss texts I know and admire, which I bring together here because they have provoked my thinking about writing sociology.

Constructions of Topic

Krieger's introduction to *The Mirror Dance* begins with a simple statement: "This book is about individual identity in a women's community." With this sentence, she has done two things: she has made a claim to speak about the general issue, "individual identity," but she has also revealed that she will discuss a women's community, and by the end of the first paragraph she specifies that this community is "composed primarily of lesbians." In the paragraphs that follow, she develops the idea of "loss of self," a problem in the women's community that seems related to its considerable intimacy and its separateness—to the point of stigmatization— from the rest of the town. Only after several pages of description quite specific to the women's community (and therefore built around the pronoun *she*) does Krieger return to a more general formulation of the issue of identity: "Now all social groups—communities, organizations, families—confront their members with this kind of conflict. In all groups there is a tension between the individual's desire to be part of a whole and the desire to be different" (p. xv). It is clear that Krieger believes the experiences of these lesbian women will be relevant to others; however, her attention is focused on the particular experiences of those she studied.

In the first chapter, where she sets the scene, Krieger repeats the rhetorical move that makes the community she will describe seem a special one, hidden from everyday view. She inverts the typical case-study introduction by beginning with a portrait of the ordinary and "representative" community, then moving on to a small, atypical part of that community. The chapter begins with four paragraphs that describe the town in terms that make it a kind of town the reader can imagine: "It was a medium-sized midwestern town. . . . It was a town in the middle of America. . . . It was a town where people had families. . . . It was a gray place beneath a gray sky" (pp. 3–4). The description gradually builds a picture of the very ordinary town. But with the fifth paragraph the reader learns that none of this is to be Krieger's topic. The topic will be something else that happens in this town, something that is not much seen, but that Krieger begins to show. Significantly, Krieger moves in this fifth paragraph from description of a place to a different kind of account that tells about things happening: "Once a month on a Friday night, a group of women would gather upstairs in a church not far from the center of town and meet and talk about what it was like to live here and to feel different—to feel part of a separate community" (p. 4). The separateness of this "separate community" is highlighted by this shift in language, seven paragraphs of moving process that describe how people got to this community and what they did once there.

Krieger's introductory material emphasizes separateness and particularity. This is an ordinary town, and the problems to be discussed are similar to other general problems of identity, but this book will focus on specific identity problems, the specific problems that seem likely to arise in lesbian communities. The effects of such an introduction will probably depend on the reader: lesbians, members of a group not often heard in and for itself, are placed at the center of the text and know immediately that this text—unlike most—is about people who share their experiences; readers who are not lesbians are placed in something of an outsider's position, perhaps unsure about the extent to which the problems to be discussed will be similar to their own.

Kanter's introduction to *Men and Women of the Corporation* begins differently, with epigraphs from Karl Marx, Adam Smith, and Peter Drucker. With her own first words, Kanter reinforces the authority of these theorists: "The most distinguished advocate and the most distinguished critic of modern capitalism were in agreement on one essential point: the job makes the person." In several paragraphs that describe how she will examine this process, Kanter draws on the mystique of commerce and the weightiness of the modern corporation to emphasize the significance of her topic and the particular firm she studied: "If jobs 'create' people, then the corporation is the quintessential contemporary people-producer. . . . Indsco is a good place to visit, not only because it is among the biggest and most powerful of the multinationals that dominate American industry but also because it is socially conscious" (p. 3). Kanter signals clearly her intent to deal with a site that is not only known to most readers but an important place, known because it is a significant location for the exercise of power.

Kanter's descriptive strategy in this introductory section is in one sense the opposite of Krieger's: she begins with the most generally applicable statement of her problem and only gradually develops its distinctive outlines for women. As she describes the modern corporation's work force she maintains a carefully gender-neutral language, even as she indicates that men and women are unevenly distributed among work categories. It is not until the eighteenth paragraph that she tells the reader that "the women's issue also appears as an important subtheme in this book" (p. 8). Even in this paragraph, she is careful to maintain a basis for considering women's and men's experiences in similar ways: it is important, she argues, to consider the "roles, positions and constraints affecting women in the public arena, *as well as* the men who have traditionally peopled organizational research." And she adds, "The fate of women is inextricably bound up with organizational structure and processes *in the same way* that men's life-at-work is shaped by them" (pp. 8–9, italics mine). These italicized phrases, joining women's fates with men's, have two kinds of effects. One is to point toward Kanter's argument (which she sets out explicitly in her preface) against theories that posit "special" female characteristics. The other, I think, is to provide for those readers who are not women a path toward interpreting "the women's issue" as a problem anyone might have.

In Kanter's first scene-setting chapters, she continues to emphasize the relevance of her topic to all kinds of "ordinary people." In the first chapter, for example, she begins: "Every day a large proportion of all Americans don their figurative white collars and go to work in offices, where they take their stations in the administrative machines that run large organizations" (p. 15). And she concludes the second chapter, a description of the corporation, by commenting that this particular firm is "neither a good nor a bad example . . . just ordinary people, reflecting the dilemmas created for them by the way they make their living" (p. 43). What Kanter does very skillfully with such framing is to include readers of all kinds in the scope of her discussion.

Kanter is even more explicit about such bases for comparison and connection in the final chapters, which summarize the implications of her study. "Feminists and men in dead-end jobs," she suggests, "both have a stake in seeing that organizations change" (p. 264). And in her final sentence, which urges efforts at reform in spite of imperfect knowledge, she extends the scope of her argument even further by explaining, "It is the people caught in such situations—and the people who cannot even find a job—women and men alike, that make me unwilling to wait" (p. 287).

When Krieger summarizes in her concluding chapter, she argues, like Kanter, that the experiences of women she has written about are relevant to others as well: "[The women] speak of experiences particular to lesbians. At the same time, they inform us about problems we all face. Like the women of this study in relation to their group, we are all to some extent outsiders in the communities to which we belong. Yet we need our communities to take us in when we are uncomfortable and ambivalent as much as we need them to welcome us when we seem to fit in, when we merge and conform" (p. 169). Here Krieger provides explicit instructions for readers who may be searching for a basis for comparing the dilemmas of these lesbian women to more typical dilemmas in the wider community. But once she has provided such instructions, she returns to the efforts of these particular women to build a community, and ends her book with a statement that honors those particular efforts: "There is perhaps no more worthy endeavor in social life than the struggle to build communities that might be truly accepting of their members. This study has recorded that in a midwestern town, in their own way, a small group of women attempted to create such a community" (p. 169).

Both Kanter and Krieger present their case studies as researches that illuminate issues extending beyond the groups they studied. This kind of presentation is central to any piece of sociological writing, which must aim at attaching the text to a body of scholarship. But the differences I have discussed point to different possibilities for positioning texts that deal with women's experience. By making "the women's issue" an instance of the issues of organizational power and mobility that have long preoccupied men and male theorists, Kanter produces a text accessible to male as well as female readers, a text whose relevance to the concerns of men is clear. Throughout the text, she provides instructions for applying her findings to men's situations as well as women's, and her language facilitates such application. In Krieger's *Mirror Dance,* this kind of framing is much less prominent. Ultimately, her desire to speak about general issues of identity and community is overshadowed by another purpose: to provide a portrait of a particular community not often depicted sympathetically, from the "inside." She makes a text that points toward application to more general issues, but does so subtly, leaving the details of such application to the reader.

To make a feminist issue an instance of some traditionally male concern, as Kanter does, is effective in some ways, risky in others. It probably eases the entrance of a text into the discourse of a discipline still largely built on an agenda shaped by privileged men. But it may also tend to submerge particularities of female experiences—the particularities so necessary to Krieger's kind of text, and to the feminist project of making previously neglected experience more visible. Krieger's strategy has characteristic strengths and risks as well. It provides a richly textured view of the lives of those she studied. But it may also tend to construct a topic that can be dismissed by readers not already interested in this community.

Some feminist issues are undoubtedly more amenable than others to placement on a traditional disciplinary agenda. The problems of women in managerial positions that Kanter deals with, for example, have emerged as more and more middle-class women have entered the paid labor force and have begun to share the experiences of men. They are problems of women (and some men) in a male world. By contrast, the problems of identity described by Krieger are problems that *might* emerge in any community, but that in fact are much discussed—that emerge as "problems"—in lesbian communities more often and more urgently than in most other communities. One can imagine other predominantly female experiences that might be even more difficult to study in terms of conceptual frameworks shaped by male concerns. It is possible, but probably misleading, for example, to study housework as a form of work like paid labor, rape as merely another kind of victimization, or pregnancy and childbirth as purely medical experiences. Thus, even if some feminist concerns can be framed quite effectively as instances of established topics, others will require a different sort of rhetorical treatment.

Method and Interpretation

Both Kanter and Krieger work with case-study methods that emerge from an established sociological tradition. Both speak about personal involvements in the settings they have studied, and both describe some of the personal interests that have shaped their researches. Both provide methodological appendices setting out the details of method that serve as warrant for their claims. Both reveal as well some of the false starts and troubles of their investigations. While they work with similar materials, however, Kanter and Krieger use the building blocks of the case-study method to construct very different texts. Case studies have traditionally occupied a somewhat ambiguous position relative to quantitative and interpretive branches of the discipline: case studies can be pointed, theoretically, in either direction. The two books I am concerned with represent the opposing impulses of case-study research. Kanter uses her field observations to build theory, producing a text that controls interpretation, while Krieger experiments with a method that displays patterns of voices, and leaves such interpretive work to her readers. In this sense, the texts represent two approaches to feminist research as well: Kanter takes up feminist concerns within a well-established, authoritative methodological tradition, while Krieger works in the style of a developing critical tradition (associated strongly, though not exclusively, with feminism).

Krieger's text is avowedly "unusual," "clearly an experiment." She is present as author only in the introduction, where she develops a statement about the problems of merger and separation, in a first chapter where she describes the setting, and in the postscript, where she provides a brief summary. The body of the text is made up entirely of her respondents' accounts of community life and events. Krieger guides the reader into her text: as she ends the description of the setting, she begins to introduce the voices that will constitute the text: "The community seemed to offer a promise: 'Here are women who can understand me, touch me the way I want to be touched,' Melissa felt. At the same time it provided an experience which was disconcerting: 'In the process of all that happened, all that mutual discovery of pleasure within our community, I think I lost a sense of my own development separate from other people'" (p. 6). In this paragraph Krieger uses quotation marks to present the voices of her respondents as evidence, framed by her own authorial voice. But with the next sentence, which begins the first substantive chapter, she leaves out the quotation marks, which would separate her own voice from those of others: "She saw several different lesbian communities in town, said Ruth, though she understood what people meant when they said 'the community'" (p. 7). With this sentence, Krieger has invented a convention, inviting the reader to listen in and to experience the very merger and separation she means to examine.

Krieger's text proceeds by way of this convention. A chapter titled "The Web of Talk," for example, begins: "There was this hotline that went around all the time, that kept the community together, felt Shelah. People were always talking about each other. It was not necessarily malicious, said Chip, but it was what traditionally was known as gossip. Things just went like wildfire, Leah observed" (p. 25). Some accounts are longer, providing stories about individuals and their relationships. Each chapter collects accounts about particular issues, events, or activities. The reader begins to recognize names and to connect individuals. The material that makes up this text is clearly talk, and the reader with sociological training sees that much if not all of it must have been produced in response to the kinds of questions Krieger has reported she asked in interviews. In spite of the absence of authorial voice, this material is talk that has been edited, sorted, collected, and combined in a variety of ways. Krieger argues in the introduction that her text's "analysis emerges through its ordering" (p. xvi). She indicates that the text is "composed of an interplay of voices that echo, again and again, themes of self and community, sameness and difference, merger and separation, loss and change" (p. xvii). The voices she presents "analyze and comment upon one another and guide the reader to an appreciation of the conflicts surrounding identity in the community" (p. xvii).

Kanter's text follows more conventional prescriptions for sociological writing. She includes examples and talk, but she subordinates these to her own voice, telling the reader in abstract language how to understand each piece of evidence. The core chapters of her book are organized around key processes that become the variables in her theoretical model: opportunity, power, and numbers. She comments in a concluding chapter that although she has discussed responses to particular situations in a specific organization, her intention has been to find "overarching dimensions of the person-organization relationship" (p. 245), and her rhetorical move is always to use the specific as an element in more general description. Kanter's concluding chapters, then, in a section of the book titled "Under-

standing and Action," represent her arrival at a coherent theoretical statement. Her introduction to this section suggests that the reader should
appreciate the distance between observation and theory, and the analytical
work through which she has imposed order on unruly realities:

> As I pulled together and looked for meaning in information from varied
> sources (objectified survey questions, official company forms, formal inter-
> views, group meetings, and idle comments made in passing in casual con-
> versations), I identified three variables as central explanatory dimensions:
> the structure of opportunity, the structure of power, and the proportional
> distribution of people of different kinds (the social composition of peer clus-
> ters). These variables contain the roots of an integrated structural model
> of human behavior in organizations, one that builds on but enlarges other
> frameworks, one that can point out dilemmas and guide change efforts.
> (pp. 245–246)

She encourages the reader, too, to understand the particular bits of information presented in the book in terms of these three major variables
and no others. She goes on to list general hypotheses related to each variable that can be derived from her study, and then to comment in some
detail on how her observations complement and extend several influential schools of thought on organizational processes. In many ways, Kanter
interprets more completely for her reader than Krieger does in *The Mirror Dance*. While Krieger allows the voices of her respondents simply to
"comment upon one another," Kanter's own authoritative voice is the
controlling one in her text.

Krieger's text also leads to a conclusion, but a conclusion of a somewhat different sort. After two sections dealing with the dilemmas and conflicts of insiders in the community, a third section considers contacts with
"the outside world" and circles back through respondents' comments to
a sense of the integrity of the community and the protection and privacy
it provides. Krieger, however, is a more cautious interpreter than Kanter.
Her summary indicates the tone of her presentation: "As the previous
chapters indicate, the web of personal entanglements in which identity is
formed in this lesbian community, or in any community, is exceedingly
complex. *The Mirror Dance* has attempted not to simplify that complexity, as social science ordinarily does, but rather to present it in something like its original form by depicting the community through the voices
of its members" (p. 169).

Krieger's text is both permissive and demanding; it allows readers to
participate in constructing its meaning, and therefore requires careful attention and a kind of active reading. In her introduction, Krieger calls for
a specific approach to reading: the text, she says, provides one interpreta-

tion but is also "open to other interpretations. It invites the reader to join, to take part, to overhear the gossip of women in one particular subcommunity . . . to muddle through their difficulties with them" (p. xvii). Where Kanter boasts of movement from the confusion of raw data to orderly theory, Krieger embraces the complexity of "gossip"; where Kanter speaks authoritatively, Krieger invites the reader to "muddle" along. Most readers of this chapter will probably have learned from professional training and the wider culture to read these descriptions evaluatively: speaking with authority is admirable, "muddling" a bit *outré*. Krieger practices a mode of presentation that may be unusual, but is disciplined nonetheless. Her account is "not intended to be objective; nor is it arbitrary." Instead of a set of hypotheses, she presents a "structured representation of a particular problem . . . in a particular setting" (p. xviii).

Krieger's text represents one approach to a method self-consciously different from conventional sociological representations. It can be seen as part of a developing tradition of fieldwork that emphasizes the representation of individual "voice." While this tradition is not exclusively feminist, the emphasis on voice has been central to much writing about women. Many feminist researchers aim at providing speech for women who have been left out of discourses, assuming the validity of each woman's experience and then subjecting it to analysis as women did in early feminist consciousness-raising groups. Learning from the tradition of oral history, and increasingly from experiments in anthropological writing, researchers in this tradition are cautious about defining the experiences of those they study, and search for unobtrusive ways to represent different realities. Often, they draw techniques from other disciplines, as Krieger draws from her understanding of fictional representation. *The Mirror Dance*, an experiment within this budding tradition, is interesting for its form as well as its substance. But like any text, it calls for a reader prepared to understand the aims and assumptions of its tradition.

The rhetorical strategies of these two authors call for very different kinds of reading. Kanter, in *Men and Women of the Corporation*, tells her reader explicitly how to interpret the evidence she presents and what to conclude from it. She draws out the implications of her findings in relation to other theoretical frames. She makes suggestions for action. The text is designed to lead to a single conclusion. This kind of presentation, conventional for social scientists, calls for a skeptical reader, one who either finds a basis on which to differ with Kanter's analysis or is compelled to accept it. The active work of reading, in this model, is critical work, aimed at possible flaws in the analysis. Krieger's text is quite different. Though it is "built on" her interpretation of her interviews, it is "open to other interpretations." It presents complexity without telling the reader how to sort through it. It refrains from spelling out theoretical implications. This kind of text calls for a devoted reader who will work at appreciating the patterns Krieger has displayed in the text. In this model, processes such as comparison, synthesis, and extension are central to the activity of reading. Most sociologists are taught to do "critical" rather than "devoted" reading. A text such as *The Mirror Dance* seems awkward and difficult at first. It does not supply an explicit argument, easily transported into a reader's own texts. Its innovative strategy brings with it the risks of dismissal by readers unwilling to read in a new way.

WRITERS AND AUDIENCES

Feminist texts have developed with the emergence of a feminist audience. That audience overlaps with a larger sociological community. Authors with feminist aims must position their texts with respect to these two audiences. Some aim more clearly toward sociological legitimacy, some toward a specifically or exclusively feminist readership. Many attempt to speak to both circles, on the reasonable assumption that feminists and other sociologists have much to learn from one another. Both of the issues I have considered in this chapter concern relations between rhetoric and audience. The question of topic is a question about who will be interested in a text. Writers construct topics with audiences in mind; feminist writers must make decisions about their overlapping but different constituencies. The question of method and how it is portrayed is a question of authority and its sources. Some feminists wish not to monopolize authority but to share interpretive power with their readers. They must experiment with new forms, for which audiences are only beginning to develop.

Judgment resides with the audiences for texts. Writers with dual allegiances, who write for two kinds of audiences, are often judged wanting by one or the other. Dominant groups, of course, have the power to make judgments stick. There is evidence, for example, that women (Showalter 1977) and Black novelists (McDowell 1986) who are part of distinctive traditions have been considered inferior in relation to dominant traditions of their times. Their distinctive forms and languages are too often seen only in terms of more widely accepted literary conventions. Rhetorical studies of scientific texts reveal that evaluative processes in these apparently objective disciplines also depend on the form and style of texts. And in sociology, as in literature, distinctively feminist traditions may be suppressed through routine evaluative practices. *Men and Women of the Corporation* is easily recognized as an important work, and on its way to becoming a sociological "classic." The fate of *The Mirror Dance* is less certain, though my hope is that sociologists will make room for such texts.

There is a growing audience in sociology for both feminist and experimental texts. My aim has been to highlight the importance of these innovative texts and to urge that as we continue to experiment with feminist writing, we attend as well to the interpretive and evaluative processes that surround and support new texts.

9 Metaphors of Silence and Voice in Feminist Thought

WITH CHRYS INGRAHAM

THIS TEXT grew out of a series of conversations we began a decade ago in the course of developing our separate, but related, lines of research. Each of us was engaged in work that dealt with the silencing of women. As soon as we began to talk together about these projects, we made the discovery that provided the impetus for this essay: that we were using the same words—or at least a single metaphor—to refer to an enormous field of related but often quite different phenomena. To discuss our projects, we had to explain to each other just what we meant by "silence" and "silencing"; thus, our conversations began to reveal the assumptions underlying our somewhat different notions. At the same time, we began to consider how our discussions were informed by a feminist discourse on silencing—as well as a sociological branch of that discourse—and to analyze work within that discourse, so as to build on its insights while also uncovering its assumptions and gaps. Our aim here is to share some of that conversation. We hope it might illuminate not only the potential and risks of metaphors of silence and voice, but also the more general ways that language and metaphor carry assumptions that shape research practices and texts.

In the text that follows, we tell readers the story of our conversation, sometimes together and sometimes, to reflect more individual contributions, in passages that foreground one or another of our contrapuntal voices.

Winter, 1988

I. Sources

In the local diner, over breakfast, we were perplexed to find that "silencing" held different meanings for us. Troubled, seeking to reestablish our sense of comradeship, we tried to clarify by pointing to specifics.

Marj: I'd been thinking mainly about things that didn't get said because of a variety of rather indirect mechanisms of control, and mainly about the everyday difficulties of talking in pairs and groups. My article on interviewing [chap. 4] was concerned with deficiencies of language and of sociological frameworks, both shaped by men's experiences, and the effects of "translating" women's life experiences and concerns in order to be heard within a dominant discourse. I was concerned with struggles toward speech and the difficulties of "bringing women in" to sociological discourse.

Chrys: I had been thinking about the kinds of punishment meted out to feminists who say things that those in power can't hear or accept, and about how feminist writings have been censored and suppressed. I was studying censorship in the late nineteenth century, as it affected feminist writers [Ingraham 1992]. The cases included theorists such as Matilda Josyln Gage, author of *Woman, Church and State;* Moses Harman, who published the freethought newspaper *Lucifer the Lightbearer,* dedicated to the campaign against sexual slavery within marriage; and Lois Waisbrooker, author of *A Sex Revolution.* All were prosecuted or threatened with prosecution under the Comstock Law, a federal anti-"obscenity" statute which grew out of the social purity crusade of the time. I wanted to show how this mechanism of suppression was related to the ideological interests of a ruling group and how these specific episodes of suppression developed.

We noticed, as we elaborated these differences, that we had experienced "silencing" in our early lives in two quite different ways and that, in some ways, our research interests paralleled these divergent experiences.

Chrys: I was the "mouthy" child, punished for talking back. I got hit hard for speaking up.

Marj: Yes, and I was the overly obedient child, learning early—and oh, so very well—to "control myself." I did that partly by suppressing what I felt.

Our early thinking led us to examine the umbrella metaphor of silence and silencing, and to consider its range. We began with the knowledge that feminist writers in many fields have relied on metaphors of "silence" and "silencing" to signify women's exclusion from the production of culture and the absence of female perspectives in dominant cultural and disciplinary traditions. Women have been silenced; feminism opposes the silencing of women. But this summary sentence now seemed too simple; we felt we needed to map in more detail the social processes that such talk refers to.

Concretely, the term "silence" refers to an absence—the absence of speech, or more generally, of sound. Some feminist uses of the term seem quite close to this most concrete meaning—as when linguistic researchers study the unequal participation of men and women in conversation. But feminist theorists have also used the concept of silence metaphorically, taking the concrete situation in which nothing is said as a model for understanding a variety of other phenomena. Thus, in addition to "not talking," being *silent* is taken to mean:

not being present
not participating
not writing
talking (or writing), but not being heard
talking (or writing), but being ignored, ridiculed, etc.
talking (or writing), but without confidence
talking (or writing), but without authority
talking (or writing), but inauthentically
talking (or writing), but only in limited ways: only on particular topics, or
    only in particular places, genres, times, situations
talking (or writing), but only ephemerally

Similarly, *silencing,* the more active form of the term, is taken to refer not just to quieting, but also to censorship, suppression, marginalization, trivialization, exclusion, ghettoization, and other forms of discounting.

In addition to collecting a variety of phenomena under a rubric built around the absence of speech, the metaphor of silence suggests its opposites: speech, voice, and noise. When feminists identify "silence" as a problem, they argue—directly or indirectly—for something else: speech, or more broadly, inclusion. Thus, we include as part of the metaphorical vocabulary of silence those feminist analyses that call upon ideas such as women's voices, giving women voice, talking back, making noise, and other visions of loud assertion.

Developing these thoughts, we also noticed that *feminist* talk about silence refers to a particular kind of silence, that of a powerless group. Feminist discourses of silencing do not usually consider the silences of the powerful, often used to maintain control. This observation suggests that silence is not always imposed or accepted. It can also be an act of rebellion. And it can include chosen silences, often cooperative and enabling.

II. Writings in the "Silencing" Tradition

With the brashness characteristic of a graduate student and new assistant professor (are women ever thought of as "young turks"?), we began by developing scathing critiques of two canonical feminist works. Both built analyses on metaphors of silence, used loosely, we felt, and with unfortunate consequences.

Marj: I went back to look at *Women's Ways of Knowing,* an account of women's intellectual development by a group of psychologists, recently published [in 1986] and widely read. It was a book I found both compelling and disturbing. It spoke to many women, it seemed, about deeply-felt experience. But how?

The authors of *Women's Ways of Knowing* organize their analysis around a metaphor of voice. As they conducted interviews, they found that women themselves drew on metaphors of silence and voice as they talked about themselves as knowers. They used phrases like "'speaking up,' 'being silenced,' 'not being heard,' 'really listening,' 'really talking,' 'words as weapons,' 'feeling deaf and dumb,' 'having no words,' 'saying what you mean,' 'listening to be heard,' and so on in an endless variety of connotations" (Belenky et al. 1986:18). Building from and on these metaphors found in the talk of their respondents, the authors construct an account of a general process of women's coming to voice. In this general account, however, they make a number of crucial assumptions about voice. They rely on unstated definitions, counting some kinds of speech as "voice" and others as "silence." They assume—without clearly stating the assumption—the desirability of particular kinds of speech. As a result, they highlight some kinds of speech and devalue others. And they obscure the mechanisms through which women are kept from speaking.

These problems are most noticeable in the first chapter on "silent women," the category invented by these authors to refer to the women they characterize as the least confident and developed knowers. "Silent women" are so named in spite of evidence presented in this chapter that refers not just to speech, but to assertively oppositional speech. The authors characterize these women with the phrase "deaf and dumb." Yet for examples of this state, they give us:

"I deserved to be hit, because I was always mouthing off." (p. 24)

"I don't like talking to my husband. If I were to say no, he might hit me." (p. 24)

"I had to get drunk so I could tell people off." (p. 25)

"I was a loudmouth. I didn't think nothing of telling someone where to go." (p. 25)

In fact, all of these women are talking about talk. If their words are read literally rather than metaphorically, it is clear that they have things to say and stories about saying those things. They also have a strong sense of the consequences of speaking up.

These authors make silence a trait, or characteristic, of individual women, but it looks here more like a strategy used in the face of coercive repression. This displacement of the source of silence also infects the account of causes. The authors argue that this pattern develops when women grow up in isolation, and especially when a parent is violent. Thus, they recognize the overt violence that appears in these quotations, but they make it a background variable, abstracting it and attaching it, again, to the women themselves rather than examining a process of active silencing.

Throughout this chapter, and the rest of the book as well, the authors sift and sort, rejecting some kinds of talk as insufficient and highlighting others as progress toward an ideal of fuller development. Constructing their account of a purportedly general process of "coming to voice," they give a distinctive shape to the "speech" that will count for them as the opposite of silence. In a summary of the deficiencies of the "silent women," for example, the authors characterize their ways of knowing as:

> limited to the present (not the past or the future); to the actual (not the imaginary and the metaphorical); to the concrete (not the deduced or the induced); to the specific (not the generalized or the contextualized); and to behaviors actually enacted (not values and motives entertained). (p. 27)

Ironically, these authors privilege here a kind of knowledge that much feminist work criticizes—an abstract, generalized knowing—and they devalue what we might call particular knowledge, which seems increasingly important in feminist formulations (e.g., Smith 1987, Harding 1986, Lugones and Spelman 1983). They argue that young women need environments where they can be "full participants in any ongoing dialogue" (p. 33). But their emphasis on the possibility of participation leaves the dialogue itself unquestioned. Their solution is based on a logic of inclusion: women's voices are to be developed so as to allow them to join an ongoing dialogue. How their speech might change the shape of that dialogue is left relatively unexplored.

Chrys: I wanted to talk about Tillie Olsen's well-known book *Silences* [1965]. It was a book that spoke powerfully to my interests in the feminist press movement. But I was also reading this text through the lenses of lesbian life and my knowledge of Native American sources for nineteenth-century feminism.

Olsen writes about a particular denial of access, and a particular kind of discounting or "eclipsing" to which women writers are subjected. She makes an important argument about opportunities to write and who has them, but she writes from a position that makes several assumptions about women, about writing, and about opportunity. She emphasizes women's family responsibilities in ways that seem to assume that women are heterosexual, married, and have children. She also writes from a position that privileges creativity and the written text, assuming an audience that, given the opportunity, would want to write. These assumptions form an attitude that one can recognize as distinctively associated with a Western, colonial point of view. They are assumptions that keep particular forms of knowledge production in place and help to legitimize the subordination of cultural groups who do not privilege written forms.

Making this kind of critique of Olsen's work produces a difficult political and strategic dilemma. It seems clear that access to education, time and support for intellectual work, and access to publication opportunities are critical for any subordinate group. Since writing is so central to public discourses in every society, and especially to the processes of ruling, one can hardly afford to ignore systematic exclusion from these forms. But one might also hope to avoid constructing these issues in terms of either-or choices, and instead to find ways to address systematic exclusion without privileging written forms in our own thinking. Such a strategy would require learning to use and interpret other forms (for example, the face-to-face communication of storytelling, singing, and teaching; art and craft forms; collective action), working to develop audiences for these forms, and challenging any monolithic model of authority. One would need to recognize and resist ways of thinking that devalue anything other than dominant versions of "fact," "science," and "truth." Placing Olsen's work in this context, then, might stimulate questions about what it is that writing gives access to.

III. Analyses of Silencing: A Sociological Tradition

Alongside these critiques, we began to identify a short list of sociological works that explored silencing as social process. These works also conceived of silence in ways that ranged from relatively literal to quite metaphorical conceptions of silence and speech. For example, feminist sociolinguists such as Robin Lakoff (1975), Dale Spender ([1980] 1985), and Paula Treichler and Cheris Kramarae (1983) were producing a body of research showing that women face obstacles to unfettered speech. In most settings, they suggested, women are interrupted more often than men, allowed less time to speak, and listened to less carefully. Barrie Thorne and Nancy Henley (1975) suggested that race and status differences produce similar effects. Pamela Fishman (1978) studied conversation between intimate partners, and found women doing what she called the "shit-work" of interaction—expressing interest and facilitating speech rather than speaking themselves. Dale Spender (1982) made a connection between these literal barriers to speech and the problems that women writers have faced gaining access to publication opportunities; Gaye Tuchman (1989) analyzed these kinds of processes in more detail, examining mechanisms of exclusion and occupational channeling in nineteenth-century publishing and their influence on the production of career and reputation for women novelists.

Sociologists were also considering the apparent "silence" of women in our discipline. Mary Jo Deegan (1981), for example, wrote about how and why the white men who shaped the early history of the field in the United States kept women out of the American Sociological Association, documenting systematic processes of exclusion and peripheralization that excluded not only women but also certain kinds of sociology. Shulamit Reinharz (1988b) also focused on women's exclusion from the sociological canon, and began to work on recovering the contributions of women sociologists. Her analysis of the life of Manya Shohat, creator of the kibbutz, provided a model for understanding how women's contributions are so often lost over time (Reinharz 1984).

Judy Long (1988, 1989) and Dorothy Smith (1987) provided more general analyses of how the production and organization of knowledge can produce such effects. Long's work on "telling women's lives" focused on the effects of genre: she argued that the historically constituted model for telling a life fits relatively well with many men's experience but often makes little room for the distinctive shapes of women's lives. These differences produce gendered processes of evaluation, which result in women's writing being eclipsed, appropriated, misattributed, or considered unintelligible or insignificant. Smith wrote about the material underpinnings of this "peculiar eclipsing" of women's thought, arguing that women's expression and authority have been systematically repressed through men's control of the institutions of knowledge production.

These, we realized, were the kinds of analyses that formed the basis for our metaphors of silence and silencing. They gave us pointers toward specific social processes and, considered together, identified an encompassing structure of social control. The metaphor of silence was powerful and compelling for us partly because of its range. But we could now see that, like any metaphor, it highlights some features of experience and obscures others. We turned next to an analysis of how this particular metaphor is located in common-sense cultural discourse, with a specific history and connections to prevailing relations of power and control.

IV. Analysis of the Metaphor and Its Problematic

Silencing is a concept that is readily available in contemporary Euro-American culture, and that is undoubtedly one of the reasons it has been so useful for feminist theorists. It may be differentially available, however—more comfortable perhaps for middle-class or white women, for example, who have some kinds of privilege, and many opportunities to observe intimate others who have authoritative voices. African American theorist bell hooks uses the metaphor very effectively in *Talking Back* (1989), and philosophers Maria Lugones and Elizabeth Spelman (1983) use it to discuss coalition between Latina and Anglo women. The authors of *Women's Ways* report that their respondents—drawn from different race and class groups—used metaphors of voice and speech when asked to describe their processes of developing as knowers. But interestingly, Wendy Luttrell's (1988, 1997) analysis of working-class women's ways of knowing is not built on this metaphor. Her respondents tend to frame knowing in terms of "having sense" and, especially, knowing how to do things. With this caveat, we would argue that a metaphor of silence fits well with prevailing "common sense." And the very availability of the metaphor makes it especially susceptible to simple, unexamined application and analysis that reproduces elements of a "common sense" that is always ideologically constructed (Belsey 1980). If this is so, one would want to analyze carefully what is at stake in deploying this vocabulary. What does one accomplish, and what sorts of concerns are obscured?

Talk about *silence,* in its various meanings, calls up aspects of the "feminine" rather than a critique of the patriarchal system that discounts women's words and texts. Silence has been central to the construction of traditional femininity. To claim that women have been silent is to make a claim that does not radically challenge the dominant ideology. It may be important for women to identify and name the facts of the exclusion, intimidation, and devaluation we have experienced. But once we have begun to identify and name these phenomena, it seems important to think analytically and strategically about where the metaphor of silencing will lead.

We see two different agendas that might arise from identifying a problem as one of "silence" or "silencing." The simplest relies on the notion that women have not had "voices," that "our stories" have simply not been told. The solution, then, seems to be increased participation: longer, louder, more confident speech, and access to knowledge-producing structures. But this kind of solution risks accepting the shape and terms of the larger discourse from which women have been excluded. The mere act of speaking—in this simple sense, without regard to what is said and how—is a limited solution to the problem. Conservative women speak, in defense of traditional gender distinctions. Revolutionary and battered women have spoken and paid for it, sometimes with their lives. And feminists of the first women's movement spoke, loudly and at length, but they disappeared from the historical record and feminists of the 1970s had to rediscover them.

There are also problems with "talk among women" as a solution to conflicts and divisions. For example, Maria Lugones (in Lugones and Spelman 1983:575) suggests that to talk of exclusion—apparently a kind of speech—actually produces a kind of silence for women of color. She writes:

> We (Hispanas) and you (white/Anglo women) do not talk the same language. When we talk to you we use your language. . . . But since your language and your theories are inadequate in expressing our experiences, we only succeed in communicating our experience of exclusion. We cannot talk to you in our language because you do not understand it . . . we either use your language and distort our experience . . . (or) we remain silent. Complaining about exclusion is a way of remaining silent.

These observations suggest that an adequate analysis of silence and speech should be concerned not only with expression but also with the content and consequences of speech.

A second kind of agenda developed around the problem of silences would consider how the social relations of speech, listening, and acknowledgment are embedded in a larger hegemonic discourse. As Lugones suggests, some things can be effectively said—that is, heard by particular others—while other messages intended by speakers are often misheard or unacknowledged. This observation suggests that the problem is not merely one of participation, but of how the "conversation"—through its organization, forms, and traditions—excludes the particular things that cannot easily be said and heard. A radical challenge to "silencing" would need to identify these forms and traditions, and actively seek some counter-hegemonic praxis with the potential to interrupt traditional relations of speech and authority. One might undertake this search by considering the kinds of speaking that seem more and less transgressive.

We have suggested that it is not necessarily "against the rules" of patriarchy to talk about women's silence; such a construction fits with dominant notions of femininity. Neither is it "against the rules" of capitalism; one can talk about silence in ways that ask for access to a hierarchy that already exists, legitimizing and perpetuating this hierarchical ruling apparatus with our spoken and unspoken desires. But some kinds of speech do stimulate social control, bringing repressive mechanisms of censorship into play. Speaking about those areas of womanly experience that are supposed to be "personal" and "private"—our intimate lives, menstruation, our own love for our bodies—typically produces embarrassment and ridicule. Speaking of our love for and connection with other women—of lesbianism and separatism in its varied manifestations (see Frye 1983)—often provokes charges of "man hating." Insisting on control of our own bodies is labeled "too extreme." In these and other ways, speaking strongly against male authority sets to work a system of control and censorship—whose mechanisms range from relatively mild forms of control like reminders about decorum to dismissive trivialization, social ostracism, and the dangerous violence of gay-bashing and rape. These mechanisms are also at work in attempts to discredit feminism by pointing to its connection with lesbian existence (Rich 1980).

These reflections provide clues to the social relations that are kept in place through the mechanisms of silencing, censorship, and suppression. Examining these areas of greatest resistance—naming them, theorizing them, and making them visible—helps to reveal the political stakes in talk about silencing, and thus to work toward more radical ways to challenge prevailing social arrangements. The simplest way to summarize, perhaps, is to say that analyses of "silencing"—if they are to be strong and radically challenging—must encompass the content as well as the act of speech. What matters is not only inclusion, but noticing which things can and cannot be said. A radical challenge to silencing is not only about having a say, but about talking back in the strongest sense—saying the very things that those in power resist hearing.

Postscript, 1998

Marj: Although parts of this essay are written in counterpoint, they represent only imagined "dialogue" with our readers—with my authorial voice ventriloquizing Chrys. It felt strange to write as Chrys, trying to assess and represent with sufficient delicacy what we share and where we differ. It's been several years now since we were local colleagues, who could visit frequently and easily share thoughts. This essay has languished and I have nearly abandoned it many times. But meeting face-to-face again—sharing another meal (dinner this time, at an Indian restaurant) and talking together again, literally—gave me the impetus to revisit this text and produce this version of our collaboration.

Each of us has moved on to other projects, pursuing separate paths. The metaphor of silence seems less compelling now, and this paper perhaps too dated to be worth a revision late in the 1990s. Feminist scholars are now more firmly "included"—Chrys and I, for example, both tenured—and they have spoken and written in a diverse and lively chorus. But upon reflection, I consider the possibility that there are reasons to return to the question of silence. I think of my mature professionalism, and all of the silences it requires. I realize that there are painful knots of silence around things I still fear to say—now, often, things I will not say to other feminists (or cannot hear from them)—

about sex, children, racism, affluence. I know that there are many more women to hear from, and though I often "forget," I realize that my "large and lively" feminist community can also be seen as a small, privileged enclave. And I consider the fate of the nineteenth-century women's movement and wonder: Will all of these voices fade away?

I find that I am still in many ways the overly obedient child, still envious and slightly fearful of Chrys's loud assertiveness, embarrassed at my fears and (too often) silences, still learning from her thought and example. And, as always, curious to know what she will write herself in a postscript to our collaboration.

Chrys: Look out, Edgar Bergen!

This chance to respond to our earlier work comes at an opportune moment, as I face, once again, a writing block in my current project. Reading our thoughts about women's lives and the power of silencing, I realize how well I have internalized messages about who is "authorized" to speak. Then I see how ironic it is to read Marj's words about being the "overly obedient child" in relation to my "loud"—read "bad"—child; and I know that these are her words rather than mine.

I know now how much I've learned from Marj's thoughtful, nuanced, quiet approaches to complex problems. What she calls "obedient" can manifest in cautionary forms that are frequently difficult to refute, formidable in their subtle complexity, and elegant in their delivery. Marj can be really "bad"!

Ten years later, metaphors of silence seem even more complex and powerful than I realized. Speaking loudly, for example, can cover tremendous fear. Some of us use the "blowfish" model for thwarting silencing practices—we puff ourselves up and hope we'll discourage such efforts. Meanwhile, obedient and disobedient children alike learn strategies for survival. Perhaps better than our oppressors, we discern what is acceptable and what's not, and find ways to get our needs met. I'm not sure Audre Lorde was right when she said, "Your silence will not protect you." Sometimes it is the only option, and we find ways to compensate.

As a professor at a women's college, I frequently see in bold relief the effects of gendered silencing practices. On standardized tests, our students score below the national average for "social self-confidence." First-year classes with entering students frequently become exorcisms, as we try to remove the silencing demons and encourage these young women to speak. Recently, we put in place a course called "Women of the World," now required for all incoming students. The texts are biographies of women from various parts of the globe—Rigoberta Menchu, Nobel Peace Prize winner; Roslind Franklin, scientist who discovered the structure of DNA; Rachel Calof, Jewish pioneer; Emma Mashinini, South African unionist; and Audre Lorde, African American lesbian feminist writer. Across the eight to ten sections of the course each year, we hear young women say, "This is a course in male-bashing," or "This is a 'femi-nazi' course"—simply because the focus is on women's lives. We seem to have come full circle, to a place where focusing on these prominent women's lives seems somehow disloyal to men. When I hear these reactions, I am struck by the similarity to 1970s efforts to embarrass women out of participating in feminist marches and activism by calling us lesbians. The degree to which this kind of resistance to feminism has become common in mainstream culture is a critical signal, suggesting that the moment we let our guard down, all that we have achieved can once again fall to the cutting room floor.

I'm fearful, too. Fearful that I will become more and more convinced that they were right, that I shouldn't speak. Fearful that the young people we teach will never appreciate the strength and courage of their predecessors, that they won't be able to learn from previous lives. And fearful that no one will publish essays like this one, or that we will stop writing them.

10   Speaking Up, Carefully

Authorship and Authority in Feminist Writing

WHEN I start a writing project, I sometimes agonize for days, feeling lost and hopeless, worrying as I go about my daily round of activities. Then, often suddenly, I think of a first sentence that feels right, like a way to enter a thicket of ideas and take hold of a branch that will lead to the heart of things. I am pleased when I find a sentence that feels both genuine and bold—I want it to be a statement that will open space, and claim attention, for my voice.

I became a sociologist because of my feminist interests and commitments; as I've built a career, I have been sustained by a sense that I was part of a movement, one of a group of outsiders struggling to gain a "voice" in the discipline. This construction of my purpose, however, has been tempered by my increasing awareness of the knowledge/power nexus in any scholarly work. One of the quandaries facing feminist researchers is how to incorporate such an awareness into our practices. If power is exercised through representation and interpretation, many ask, how can we justify writing about others? Should we continue? And if so, how?

Two views of ethnography—both held simultaneously by most ethnographers—suggest opposing arguments about the possibilities for ethnographic writing. On the one hand, fieldworkers proudly claim a method that calls for careful attention to local, everyday activity, and an attitude of respect for those encountered in the field. Ethnographers pride themselves on their ability to obtain a full and robust understanding of people's whole lives, and they often aim to "give voice" to those who do not usually speak publicly. Lila Abu-Lughod (1990), for example, identifies "the anthropologist in me" as a "professional recognizer of cultural difference," and suggests that her discipline prepares her to contextualize, noticing and pursuing differences in cultural expressions of gender. And Judith Stacey (1988) reports that she turned from more abstract sociological methods to ethnography in the hope that her practices would accord more respect and power than macrosociological techniques do to research "subjects," so that participants might become "full collaborators" in her projects.

These comforting elements of the ethnographic creed, however, are at odds with the other view, which emphasizes inequalities endemic to the fieldwork tradition. Both sociology and anthropology are disciplines that grew from the needs and curiosities of Western ruling and middle classes. Both rely on representational techniques developed to capture aspects of the lives of "natives," "the laboring classes," and the "socially malad-justed." In the classic traditions, investigators went into "the field" in or-der to collect material that they and their counterparts at home found useful and interesting. Their questions, and the answers they could see and hear, were shaped by the knowledges and ignorances of their classes and cultures: the exotic and different (for educated Western readers) were what counted as reportable knowledge. The practices of classical ethnog-raphy—modes of working in the field and reporting in textual form—assume for researchers the power to define and represent "others" without challenge from those subjects; researchers remain transparent themselves, ostensibly invisible. "Studying up"—the investigation of those more pow-erful than the researcher—is a more recent extension of this tradition, and one that is still underrepresented in the disciplines (and in feminist ethnog-raphy). Its relative neglect, and researchers' comments on the difficulties of studying up (Nader 1969, Hertz and Imber 1995), can be seen as indi-cations of the ways in which conventional ethnography depends on par-ticular relations of power between researchers and those they study.

This history has become more visible as older relations of power shift, in part because more of those previously defined as "other" have entered the discourses of social science in more active ways. For many feminist researchers, the question is whether the fieldwork approach is irremedi-ably marked by the classic, power-laden assumptions about "ethnogra-phers" and "others." Abu-Lughod notes with concern, for example, that anthropologists still assume "that there is an 'other,' with the corollary that there is a self which is unproblematically distinct from it" (1990:24). And Stacey, writing from a sociologist-ethnographer's point of view, con-cludes that ethnography can be only "partially feminist" because of inher-ent contradictions between the feminist goal of respectful collaboration among women and the intransigence of inequality in the enterprise. She wonders "whether the appearance of greater respect for and equality with research subjects in the ethnographic approach masks a deeper, more dan-gerous form of exploitation" (1988:22), arguing that the ethnographer's intense engagement with research subjects places them at greater risk of manipulation and betrayal than more distanced approaches.

Some writers, like Stacey, seem to reserve the label "feminist" for prac-tice that is fully collaborative, giving no special power to the researcher. And there are, among examples of feminist research efforts, a few projects that seem to me fully collaborative. One notable case is the work that produced a German study of women's "sexualization" (Haug et al. 1987). The project was undertaken by a group of fourteen socialist researchers who were all either students or professionals. Over a period of several years, working collectively, they analyzed their own histories through a process they call "memory work." They used childhood photographs and memory aids to stimulate vivid stories of their lives as young girls, and then refined and analyzed their stories through a consciousness-raising type of discussion. Their collaboration produced a fascinating text, and an important contribution to a feminist research tradition. But even this brief description points to the difficulties of organizing and sustaining such a project. The ideal of sharing authority will seldom be so fully met.

Stacey worries about feminist researchers' authorial power in the many cases when "collaboration" appears to fail—when researcher and informant have different interests and concerns, as they inevitably will. I share her concern, but I worry as well about a tendency in such discussion to construct moral standards that constitute "excessive demands" for feminist researchers (Reinharz 1993). Concerns about the ethics of representation, and attempts to equalize interpretive authority, are central to feminist methodological innovations. However, I wonder if they also reflect an unwitting collusion with ideological constructions of "woman" as especially moral or caring, or perhaps, a learned discomfort with authority that many women feel.

Another response to these questions of authority lies in attempts to mute or even remove researchers' own, interpretive voices. For example, feminists in several disciplines have taken up oral history approaches, in which the researcher appears to let others "tell their own stories." Of course, that appearance conceals a more complex reality, and the literature on oral history now includes increasingly sensitive discussions of the extent to which researchers themselves shape those others' stories (Personal Narratives Group 1989, Gluck and Patai 1991). Still, I wonder whether the attraction of oral history arises partly from the seductive comfort of speaking "softly," from the background—and from the traditionally womanly position of one who supports and encourages the talk of others.

Feminists have moved in another direction as well, by undertaking research on topics with personal significance. When I wrote about household caring work in *Feeding the Family* (DeVault 1991), I wrote strategically in a relatively standard academic voice, concerned with placing the analysis successfully within the professional world I hoped to join. But the writing felt intensely personal—it was an argument about experience that was central to my identity—and I often trembled at what I thought it revealed about me. I worried about misrepresenting the women I had interviewed, and I pored over transcripts trying to understand them, but I believe I felt authorized to interpret in part because I was writing about myself as well as others. However, this strategy provides no simple solution either. I did not want to write only about myself; the point of ethnography, after all, is to spend time in the world, in some other place, and to learn from other people. And while I shared some experiences and perspectives with the women I interviewed, there were profound differences as well. Like every researcher, then, I wrote about others through the lens of self—but a self that developed and changed as I met with those others.

All of these approaches represent only partial solutions to the problems of interpretive power. I would warn against delusions of ceding interpretive authority, and suggest instead that we work toward modes of writing that are strong without imposing a false unity. Though I am not always sure what it should look like on the page, I have in mind a voice that is thoughtful and self-reflective. I imagine a voice that is not imposingly authoritative, but clear and personal—the voice of an author who invites others to listen and respond, aiming more toward dialogue than debate. My aim is to write about others *carefully*, in both senses of the word—with rigor and with empathic concern.

As I search for opening sentences (and all those that follow), I am often reminded by intrusive anxieties that writing can be frightening. To write is to commit oneself to an interpretation; like any commitment, it closes off other possibilities. In addition, becoming an author means claiming attention—claiming that these words matter—and such assertion feels easier for some than for others. For many women, steeped in traditional lessons of "telling it slant" (Long 1989), a clear-sighted awareness of textual authority can be especially unnerving. In our concern for representing the voices of others, we sometimes fear to explore and develop our own voices. By highlighting these kinds of anxieties, I mean to address both intellectual and emotional aspects of writing and authority—and especially the point where these intersect. Our feelings about doing intellectual work will no doubt always be intertwined with our thinking about it, but sometimes they are twisted together more tightly than necessary. I would like to encourage engagement with the intellectual challenges of rethinking sociological authority, and also point to the ways that—for some of us, at least—fears about authority may interfere with constructive engagement.

Despite increasing interest in writing and lively experimentation with new forms among ethnographers, mainstream sociology continues along its own track, mostly in the traditional voice of authoritative science. Although I have written about these issues from within an ethnographic discourse—where they are perhaps easier to see—I mean to suggest that they have relevance for the discipline as a whole. Speaking up gently, with care, may seem contradictory or weak, too "womanly" a goal for social science. But new understandings suggest that acknowledging the limits of our authority will produce stronger forms of knowledge (Collins 1990). The "voice of science" attaches sociological work to a web of governing theory (Smith 1989, 1990a); whatever their methods, writers who wish to challenge prevailing arrangements will need to develop other voices.

VI. CRAFT KNOWLEDGE OF FEMINIST RESEARCH

Most teachers of research methods emphasize practice. We explain tools and techniques, but we also show how those tools work, devising practice exercises and giving students opportunities to work on supervised projects. We teach in this way because social research is a craft as well as a science—it is a practical, embodied activity whose practitioners share a store of seldom articulated, tacit knowledge. Through observation and practice, apprentice researchers learn vocabulary and the judgments associated with shared language: how to see some data as "rich," some lines of analysis as "fruitful" or "elegant." They learn what is practical or not, what kinds of techniques are likely to produce rich data (and how much is "enough"), how to deal with unexpected problems, and how to write in ways that conceal the "messier" realities of the process. Since these kinds of knowledge have a "hands-on" character, they are usually incompletely represented (if discussed at all) in formal accounts of research methodology.

The final chapter of this book is an attempt to convey some of the "craft knowledge" of feminist methodology I pass on to students. When I thought of writing such an essay,[1] I liked the idea of articulating knowledge I have gained from teaching—an activity that provides many opportunities to puzzle through research dilemmas and try out strategies, vicariously, by working through them with students. I also imagined that an essay of this sort might contribute to existing works on feminist research by addressing "practical" issues that arise in our inquiries. In the writing, I found that the questions I addressed were not practical in quite the way I expected: my answers certainly provide no step-by-step instructions. Instead, I have tried to articulate my approach to thinking through what it means to conduct research oppositionally. But I have written about questions my students are always eager to discuss, and I hope that my comments will at least have the practical benefit of extending discussions of such questions beyond our classrooms to more public arenas.

In writing this chapter, I have relied on recollections of my teaching experiences, discussions with others teaching in similar areas, and—most directly—on notes written to students in my seminar on feminist methodology. I have not tried to address every topic or issue that arises in such teaching; instead, I have emphasized questions that seem to me to deserve more extensive consideration than they have so far received. Still, I must stress that the ideas I present here are not mine alone. My teaching is in part an effort to represent perspectives developed across the range of writing on feminism and methodology, and what I present here is an interpretation of that body of literature.

11   From the Seminar Room
Practical Advice for Researchers

SINCE 1988, I have taught several versions of a graduate-level seminar on feminist methodologies. The seminar begins with readings that represent different strands of feminism and discussion of the meanings of feminism.[1] We move on to consider texts that focus more specifically on issues that arise in research practice, and the implications of feminist critique for the practices of empirical research. I try to include activist as well as academic feminist writings, so as to demonstrate and foster connections between these overlapping discourse communities. In addition to studying these writings, the seminar operates as a "workshop": each week, one or two students make a presentation based on their ongoing research, and the group responds.

When I reorganized the seminar in 1992, I devised a syllabus that foregrounds writings by feminists of color, in an attempt to keep issues of racism and other oppressions "on the table" throughout our discussions. I had learned from these writings to see how the hegemony of white scholarship is often held in place by an "exceptionalist" pattern of presentation, whereby writings by and about those in underrepresented groups are "added on" to the core material. In order to present to students a more adequate version of feminism, I resolved instead to make such writings part of our core. In an admittedly somewhat mechanical procedure, I chose three reading selections on each of our topics—one by a canonical white feminist, one by a U.S. feminist of color (usually African American), and one by a "third world" feminist. For example, our opening session, concerned with "feminism" and its meanings, focused one year on writings by white lesbian philosopher Marilyn Frye (1983), African American critic bell hooks (1984), and postcolonial theorist Chandra Talpede Mohanty (1991a); a later session, on critiques of "objectivity," included works by white Canadian sociologist Dorothy Smith (1987), African American sociologist Patricia Hill Collins (1990), and Vietnamese American filmmaker and theorist Trinh T. Minh-ha (1989). Sometimes it was easy to pull these selections from my library; on other topics, I became painfully aware of gaps in my knowledge. At these moments I felt anxious and inauthentic, scanning tables of contents for names that looked non-

European, embarrassed at the limits of my own networks and reading. Still, this artificial strategy for inclusion seemed better than none. In fact, this curricular reform has had powerful consequences—both for my own thinking and also for the character and content of class discussion and students' work in the seminar (though those effects have varied, depending in part on the racial/ethnic composition of the group).

As in most feminist classrooms, students approach these materials with widely varying expectations and very different kinds of background in feminist thought. Some are "curious" about feminism and read a great deal of new material in the seminar, experiencing the excitement of new insight; others have studied advanced feminist theory and come to the seminar ready to deploy sophisticated analytic and critical skills. Some students are longtime activists, without much exposure to academic writing; some introduce themselves as "natural" feminists, who have long shared the convictions of feminism without the support of formal education or organization. This variety of student backgrounds compounds the dilemma of finding workable shared meanings for "feminism" (and by extension, "feminist methodology"). It also provides a first lesson for the group, and one of the hardest to learn: that much of our energy, even in this space, will be devoted to addressing differences in the kinds of knowledge we bring to our work, seeking ways to foster everyone's full participation, and working to communicate honestly and effectively despite differences.

This range in students' experiences and commitments reflects a particular moment in the development of feminist scholarship. In the early days of second-wave activism, when words like "sexism" were being invented, there was a powerful sense of discovery at the heart of feminist scholarship. In the decades since, a considerable body of work has constituted those early discoveries as elements in relatively young but still increasingly institutionalized canons of feminist discourse. These key literatures are diverse and contentious, but canons nonetheless. The scholars who were present in those early days experience the resulting body of work as hard-fought but unfinished achievement; to some of those just encountering feminism, it seems already established, even rigid and unyielding. Passing on knowledge of feminism, then, requires negotiation of these different points of view. One of my first goals in the seminar—though one that is surprisingly difficult to realize fully for all participants—is to establish an appreciation for what feminists have already accomplished, while maintaining a sense of openness to critique and further development.

In recent years, drawing on Jane Mansbridge's (1995) notion of feminism as a discursive community, I have begun the seminar by suggesting that "feminism" must be defined broadly and open-endedly to encompass the range of the actual discursive communities that call themselves feminist—a position that some students resist as an insufficiently liberatory "anything goes" feminism. For some, the argument arises from an awareness of critiques of "white" and "bourgeois" feminisms; drawing on perspectives such as those of theorist bell hooks, they are willing to call "feminist" only a position that addresses all oppressions. Others bring to our discussion the idea that feminist scholarship is "personal" and "passionate," and wish to exclude any distanced, positivist approach. Still others point to the enormous elasticity of "feminism" as idea and rhetoric, and to the emergence of feminist rhetorics among conservative women with whom they have very fundamental disagreements. Each semester, we struggle over contending versions of feminist scholarship—defined through a focus on women, on oppression, or on some intellectual stance such as a critique of positivism.

My position in these discussions—that a broadly inclusive understanding of feminism is most useful—is in part a "teacherly" position: I wish to make space for all students to participate in our discussions, and to foster dialogue rather than adherence to an established position. But I believe that outside the classroom as well, feminist scholars are well advised to guard against rigid formulations of feminist principles, which too easily exclude potential participants in the scholarly community we wish to build. Even among academics, it is often quite difficult to speak constructively across disciplinary boundaries. In some fields, such as literary and cultural studies, feminist theory is highly developed and elaborated, and now incorporates extensive and pointed critiques of early perspectives. In other areas, such as the natural sciences and even some predominantly female fields such as nursing, feminist scholarship has been less accepted and is still developing slowly. It is also difficult to speak constructively across differences of class, race/ethnicity, sexuality, and ability. Those whose commitments develop out of other oppressions may have much to learn from longtime feminists, but they always have much to teach as well. Finally, it is often difficult for feminist scholars to speak constructively with feminist activists, who may be less schooled in formal theorizing but have a grounded, pragmatic knowledge of the actual conditions of women's lives and processes of making change. In my view, an open and inclusive definition of feminism signals a commitment to communication across these kinds of barriers. It reminds me to inquire, rather than to judge, when I encounter a feminist position that differs from my own—that seems to go "too far" or "not far enough."[2]

Dialogue of this sort does not have to mean that "anything goes." Rather, it should push me to articulate my own commitments more and more clearly. It should help me to see points of agreement and contention.

It should provide practical experience in formulating and receiving respectful critique. Dialogue of this sort is not easy. However, it seems to me essential to the development of alternatives to conventional, competitive models of learning and scholarship.

> *Therefore, a first piece of advice: It is crucial for any researcher to attend to and articulate the "version" of feminism underlying a project or argument, and to identify the commitments that a particular version of feminism entails. However, it does not seem to me so useful to expend energy policing the boundaries of feminism in order to exclude other perspectives.*

I. Topics

Making Space for Feminist Research

The first time I taught the seminar, in 1988, the group that came together felt fragile and needy (and I mean to include myself in this characterization). Sandra Harding's anthology, *Feminism and Methodology* (1987), had just appeared. There was a considerable body of feminist writing on research methods, across the social sciences, but it was only beginning to be seen as constituting a distinctive and coherent area of concern. I was a new assistant professor, and several students in that first group had been involved in the feminist organizing that led to my appointment. We thought of our engagement on the terrain of feminist methodology as a charged and significant collective event, and we agreed to tape-record our discussions. When we met in a small room at the beginning of the semester, we introduced ourselves quietly and somewhat tentatively. The one man who had registered asked if anyone "minded" that he was there, and one woman expressed concern about his participation. Her voice trembled as she said she wanted "our own space, for once."

He stayed, our voices strengthened, and we found multiple perspectives and more dissension than we expected within "our own space." But this opening moment gave me a keen sense of my students' sense of isolation, fear, and constraint in relation to their departments and the institution. In that first year, we heard stories about advisors who refused to consider projects dealing with women's lives: the experiences of women with breast cancer, one advisor had said, didn't seem likely to produce any strong theoretical contribution. Over time, these overtly misogynistic responses seem to have diminished; feminist work is now more widely accepted in our institution and in most disciplines. But students' sense of constraint remains strong, and rightly so. Often, our discussions of bold and innovative works bubble along, crest, and then crash on a shore of despair when someone sighs, "But they'd never let us do that, would they?"

Sometimes, now, I hear these comments with wry bemusement, and I want to tease my students with their unintended dismissal of my professional authority: "*I'm* one of 'them,' you know," I point out. But this response alone is too facile, too optimistic. Students do face hostility outside of feminist classrooms, and perhaps more often, they face ignorance of the cumulating body of innovative feminist work. Despite growing numbers of feminist faculty, feminist writing is incompletely integrated into so-called "core" literatures in the disciplines; students continue to have trouble finding knowledgeable advisors across a range of topic areas, and feminist advisors often find that they are not only overworked but stretched to the limits of their expertise.

Determining what "they" will let "us" do—and more importantly, what one will attempt and how—is a complex calculation, involving issues of intellectual empowerment and the social organization of knowledge. When students worry that "they won't let us do that," they reflect—in part—years of training in an educational "banking" model: the teacher has knowledge and the student learns to repeat what has been taught. Any scholar educated in this mode eventually faces the challenge of moving toward more independent, original scholarship. One layer of worry, then, is usually the fear that any writer faces starting out—a fear of self-exposure and, often, an impulse toward self-censorship even stronger than the criticism that might come from others. These are worries that perhaps dissipate only gradually, with experience and some success; as that begins to happen, however, it may be helpful to know that such anxieties are typical—a routine part of a creative, intellectual life.

For feminists and others pursuing activist scholarship, the challenge of pursuing original work is compounded by issues in the organization of knowledge. Feminist scholarship is still less integrated into the disciplines than feminists expected some years ago. The ghettoization of feminist research has been discussed by women's studies scholars since the early years of our field. It is also a serious, though less often acknowledged, problem for the adequacy of knowledge produced in the disciplines, and ought to be addressed as such. Most immediately, it creates a practical challenge for feminist researchers, who still must learn two literatures—the "standard" works in our topical areas and the gender-conscious writings that have developed from feminist thought—and negotiate some ground on which to stand between these often disjunctive discourses.

This layer of the problem raises questions of audience. Any scholar, but especially one aspiring to negotiate "mainstream" and oppositional literatures, makes decisions about where and how to present work; those decisions are based partly on what seems possible in different discursive spaces. A metaphor of scholarship as conversation can sometimes help to clarify and then to direct these decisions: in order to speak effectively, one must know and use the language of one's conversational partners. (Though of course, in a satisfying conversation, one relies on one's partner to listen and respond.) The metaphor also directs attention to the rhetorical, or performative, aspect of scholarly work. The various potential audiences for research appear as communities with distinctive customs and languages. The task for the researcher, then, is to negotiate membership in these different communities. The oppositional researcher must learn to be "bilingual"—that is, comfortable, or at least competent, in the kind of "world"-travelling that philosopher Maria Lugones (1987) identifies as the ordinary practice of Latinas in the United States, forced on them by demands for adaptation to Anglo "worlds." Lugones points to the effort and pain of this challenge, but she also suggests that those engaged in it construct it more positively, as an essential cultural skill and an opportunity for playful, creative agency. I borrow her metaphor here to point to the process of professional socialization—a process of learning assumptions, vocabulary, and customs—but with a twist. Oppositional researchers develop skills of "world"-travelling by cultivating an awareness of professional socialization, by noticing that the necessary badges of membership can be deployed strategically so as to facilitate movement among professional and activist "worlds."

The metaphors of conversation and bilingualism also highlight collective opportunities and responsibilities related to building more expansive and inclusive scholarly networks. No scholar works alone (though some are more conscious than others of the collective supports for individual work), and this observation implies that community building is a necessary part of the work of feminist scholarship. At the immediate, local level, oppositional scholars can benefit from building small, supportive personal networks. On a broader intellectual level, oppositional scholars build community and transform existing canons by reading widely and citing allies from neighboring literatures. And at the pragmatic level of disciplinary politics and gatekeeping, we build and shape fields through work as article and book reviewers and other kinds of professional service, undertaken reflexively, in ways that recognize both rules of the existing game and movement-inspired visions of alternative practice. I mean to suggest that this process of widening the range of speakers who are heard in our community is an essential part of a feminist method.

The preceding comments reflect the considerable successes of feminist research to date, and my fundamental (perhaps wishful) optimism. Finally, however, feminist scholars still encounter real, overt, and persistent hostility toward oppositional research, arising most often from the defensive reactions of privileged groups who feel their interests threatened. (Sometimes, the "threats" that produce such responses seem surprisingly "small": scholars established comfortably in the mainstream often seem oddly reluctant to consider new perspectives, despite the professed commitments of scientists to take account of competing arguments and all available data.) In addition, oppositional work is frequently mischaracterized; critics rely on other critics rather than reading the work thoroughly, so that their discussions reflect responses to increasingly parodic versions of "feminism." This kind of hostility has multiple consequences. It can stop or suppress innovative work, in directly coercive ways: faculty members refuse to approve dissertation work, funders turn away projects, editors reject articles. But hostile reactions often work in subtler ways, too: through dismissive, belittling, and puzzled responses to oppositional work that leave researchers uncertain and discouraged.

Feminist scholars need strategies for continuing to work in the face of hostility and for minimizing the psychic costs of such endurance. Collective organization provides one such strategy, the one most fundamental to feminist practice. A local network of supportive colleagues can provide a necessary personal context in which to discuss problems, brainstorm possibilities, and perhaps most important of all, to relax and laugh. Bernice Johnson Reagon (1983) points to this kind of space when she discusses the comforts of "home." Reagon wishes to urge feminists out of the safety of our most comfortable groups, toward necessary coalition work. But she begins with the need for home as a site of nurturance. The challenge she identifies is to balance struggles in hostile or difficult contexts with the ease and regeneration that come in more congenial settings. Scholars, like feminist activists, need to find spaces that will afford support as well as ones that challenge our work.

It is often helpful, as well, to reflect on hostility toward oppositional research as it arises and circulates within the academic context. Disciplines, and the institutions in which our work makes them manifest, are social formations that do not change easily. They are profoundly hierarchical arenas of professionalized work, with well-established mechanisms for reproducing themselves.[3] One can view these features of the scholarly world in various ways. Criticism and rigorous gatekeeping can be seen as truth-seeking mechanisms, for example, or more machiavellianly, as moves in a world of campaigning for power and advantage; both of these lenses are necessary, in my view. Recent social studies of science show in some detail how intellectual advances must be forwarded materially and politically as well. Scholars do not influence each other's work only through the brilliance of our analytic work and writing (though these help), but through gathering resources and building movements within our disciplines. Thus, critical work stimulates resistance. It is typically only partially heard and accepted; its less threatening aspects are often appropriated in adjustments of existing frameworks. Despite visions of scientific "revolution," change is nearly always slow and gradual. Work that challenges established knowledge is sometimes lost for years.

Early in the second wave, feminist artists and academics saw the outlines of these processes—in various fields of intellectual and artistic work—and their implications for representing women's achievements. Judy Chicago's (1979, 1980) "dinner party" installation, for example, brought women "written out of history" to attention by representing their lives through plates placed around a large triangular table; Dale Spender (1982) examined the lives and careers of women writers; Margaret Rossiter (1982, 1995) began her detailed history of the careers of women scientists in the United States; and Darlene Clark Hine (1989) wrote about the achievements of African American nurses. Such "reclamation" projects raised intriguing questions about the substantive significance of such exclusions. Feminist scholars, and those from other historically underrepresented groups, continue to refine these analyses. (In sociology, for instance, a recent book explores the thought of "women founders" of the field; see Lengermann and Niebrugge-Brantley 1998.) The stories uncovered are not stories of simple silence, raw coercion, or total exclusion. We have learned not only about absences, but also that women's and other oppositional perspectives have virtually always had some presence—everywhere. We have learned to search for these histories, using them for both warning and inspiration. They provide a context for evaluating hostility toward feminist work.

I do not mean to suggest that hostility toward one's ideas provides a simple proof of truth or radicalism. But these observations do suggest that oppositional scholars should expect resistance. To those working in established traditions, research that challenges those traditions will often appear "off-base," "trivial," and even "loony." Internalized, such judgments can produce doubts and depressions that stop a creative scholar. Considering the context that produces them can sometimes reduce these psychic consequences, as well as aid in the essential process of sifting the "wheat" and "chaff" of critical responses. This kind of perspective also helps to keep me modest about any successes I experience, which I see could mean that my critique simply has not yet gone as far as I would wish.

My advice on "making space":
Learn to navigate multiple intellectual "worlds"; practice multi-lingualism.

Build an intellectual "home" for nurturance and support.
Expect resistance, but don't overestimate it.
Use, and contribute to, gateways into scholarly communities.

Defining and Labeling Feminist Projects

Finding and refining a research topic is often a struggle, but those pursuing oppositional goals face distinctive problems. As a graduate student in the late 1970s—relatively early in the development of second-wave scholarship—I felt both an exhilarating sense of possibility and a frightening uncertainty about how to proceed with my work. I became aware, but only very gradually, of the power of disciplinary discourses that channel thought into established pathways. My feminist teachers were learning similar lessons, though our different positions gave us different views of the resulting challenges. Janet Abu-Lughod, for example, in an address to her faculty colleagues in 1981, wrote about the incipient "new discourse" emerging from women's feminist-inspired scholarship. Often, she commented, these scholars were required to "dig a rough trench, a foundation for a new structure that has not yet been built" (p. 15). I was moved when I found the following passage in her essay:

> I have seen some of my women graduate students struggle inchoately to formulate a problem given to them by prehension, rather than derived from an existing puzzle in the discipline. They turn to "received knowledge" and find little of relevance. They explore the topic with professors who, albeit gentle and sympathetic, cannot help but subtly rephrase the problematic into something they can see. The language the women need is not yet part of the discourse; it is their job to invent it. (Abu-Lughod 1981:15)

I know that I was only one of these women students, but the passage brings to mind vivid recollections: how inarticulate I could feel in such meetings with "gentle and sympathetic" professors; how difficult it felt to speak, despite their encouraging nods; my vague perception of their painful sense of inadequacy when we could not see how to proceed.

Now, feminist researchers benefit from a considerably stronger foundation; but all academic fields, at least in their mainstream versions, still revolve around fundamentals that do not easily accommodate feminist ideas. Thus, pursuing scholarship that is consciously feminist—consciously rooted in efforts to correct absences and overcome inequalities—still requires thinking beyond and often outside the established discourses of these fields. Acknowledging this situation, feminist teachers and students can notice and then consciously practice strategies of listening that nurture and refine research ideas that at first seem messy, muddled, and inchoate.

When students present initial research ideas, for example, I listen closely for moments of clarity and strength. Often, these are buried within more abstract and academic formulations. It seems helpful, when this is the case, to point to these specific moments of direct statement—literally quoting them back—which are typically moments of feeling as well. They are often the most productive starting points for discussion. For example, when a student-researcher reports that she is "frustrated" because women in a social change group were not discussing "larger issues," I want to know what counts for her as a "large" or "small" issue, as well as what the women were discussing. When another explains that her study will explore "how it feels" to work as a nurse's aide, I point out that she is using that phrase as shorthand for something she has not yet articulated. This kind of commenting combines evaluation and support: it points to areas of unclarity, but suggests that these are opportunities rather than problems.

I try to point out and analyze any suggestion that words are not quite right. One seminar member, quite near the beginning of a presentation on eating disorders, stumbled a bit with terminology: "that illness— if that's what you want to call it. . . ." It seemed a significant stumble; she seemed caught between medical discourses and other perspectives, and our discussion focused on strategies for seeing and making that position more explicit. We also found, in discussing several projects focused on various types of paid caregiving, that the term "occupation" seemed too narrow to capture fully the nature and organization of work in these areas. As an alternative formulation, we could talk easily about "women's work," but we began to push each other to explore the meanings of that phrase. Is "women's work" an idea that merely collects more specific instances, like "manual work"? Or does it point to a "caste"-like process that consigns a whole group to a certain status or activity? To what extent are these workers filling in for "women" in a general way?

Often, the language of social scientific discourses can evoke strong feelings, and it may be helpful to monitor those responses and put them on the table for discussion. I remember becoming acutely uncomfortable as we talked about research on family dynamics in the evolution of eating problems. Mothers whose daughters had problems were discussed in the literature as "over-concerned" with appearance, "over-involved" with their children, and so on—phrases that point clearly to the evaluative "tightrope" that women are made to walk, striving to achieve sufficient involvement or concern, but not too much. Similarly, I often become agitated listening to discussions of "social support" for family members with health problems, which tend to ignore the complex and often arduous concrete work of providing the help this concept names. In the seminar, reflecting on the realities we know from experience, we came to see that "support" points to only one end of a continuum of possible arrangements, and thus tends to obscure more complex situations. Discussing participants' studies of "spouse support," for example, the group heard about messy realities that called for additional labels: some women with breast cancer reported that their husbands, rather than simply providing support (as many researchers assumed) often needed considerable support themselves; and many women returning to school described interactions that looked more like active resistance than a lack of support.

In the early stages of defining a project, it may be especially important to hold on to knowledge the researcher brings to the topic, which is easily lost in the course of studying existing literature. Standard models for research design stress the importance of linking topics to existing theory, operationalizing concepts in standard ways, and simplifying data collection in the service of analytic clarity. Yet these routine practices have peculiar and alienating effects, since they often require that researchers set aside much of what they know from experience. It is important, then, to notice and cultivate "personal" sources for research projects—like the "agitation" I reported above and its roots in my painful experiences of providing "support" to an intimate partner. By "cultivate," however, I do not mean only to nurture these sources, but also to articulate them more clearly, analyze them, consider their implications, and especially, to notice their limitations. While personal knowledge is valuable, it is important to be disciplined about the uses of our own experiences, remembering that they provide starting points rather than fully-formed insights. It may seem obvious, but feminists must sometimes remind ourselves (and each other) that the reason for conducting an empirical investigation is not just to confirm personal experience. Even when such confirmation may be part of a project, one would want to explore that experience and identify its contexts—to find out how and where that kind of experience is produced, and what else is happening. This kind of goal calls for holding one's own experiences in view, but also searching for other experiences and perspectives, and analyzing how multiple locations and perspectives are related to one another.

The desire to label a project "feminist" sometimes brings additional worries to the process of defining a research topic. Each time I have offered my seminar, one or more men have enrolled, and they have usually expressed concern about whether it is possible or appropriate for them to do feminist research. These questions echo debates about whether men can be feminists: one line of argument constructs feminism as an ideological perspective that anyone can hold, while another emphasizes women's direct experience of gender oppression and suggests that men can at best be allies and supporters of feminists. My own view is that it is perhaps more difficult but certainly possible for men to do feminist research; however, this is only a simple answer to an artificial question. Most of the men in my classes—and some of the women as well—take up projects that they worry do not seem unambiguously or only "feminist." Examples have included projects dealing with economic restructuring, the place of "outsiders" in civic discourse, community inclusion issues, and the exercise of privilege. Such projects may be informed by feminist ideas or focus on issues with which feminists are concerned. They may be treated in ways that place women at the center of analysis. They may open possibilities for focusing on gender and also developing the kind of multilayered analysis that could include less privileged men as well. Whether these kinds of projects can (or should) be labeled feminist is therefore a question that might be answered in multiple ways. I do not believe that being a feminist so pervades one's being that any research conducted by someone who identifies as such will necessarily be a project that should be called "feminist." And by the same token, I do not think that either men or women should assume that only feminist projects are good and valuable.

To ask whether such projects can be "really feminist," then—especially in the preliminary stages of planning research—seems wasted effort. Instead, I would urge researchers asking this kind of question to consider more nuanced and "strategic" issues of labeling: Why does one want to call one's project "feminist"? How would that label advance this particular project? How would it contribute to feminist discourse? How might calling it feminist create problems for the researcher? Could it create problems for feminists? I also advise that the problem—both at these early stages and later, in the presentation of findings—is not simply to label a project feminist or not, but to discuss in some detail how it is related to feminist research. Such discussion provides opportunities to acknowledge (though I really mean something stronger, like insist upon) how feminist research has informed the conceptualization and analysis of a study, to explain how the analysis is different because of sources in feminism, and to stress the need for researchers concerned with topics that may not be "obviously" feminist to take into account the ideas and methods that feminists are developing. This kind of fuller presentational strategy, it seems to me, allows researchers to avoid fights about what one "can" and "cannot" do, and also highlights contributions to both feminist and mainstream traditions. The point is not to draw lines of exclusion, but to use the label cautiously enough that it retains a strong and compelling meaning.

Strategies for defining topics:
Learn to listen sympathetically to unformed thoughts.
Try out new vocabularies.
Set aside (at the beginning) worries about what "counts" as feminist; pursue what the topic or setting offers.

Planning Inclusive Research

Feminist theorizing has grown enormously during the 1980s and 1990s. Theorists have attended more explicitly to the contributions of lesbian feminists. They have insisted on the centrality of African American, Latina, Asian American, Native American, and international perspectives. White, heterosexual feminists have more carefully considered the racism and heterosexism of some feminist theory. And some writers have paid more careful attention to issues of class, disability, and age (though these dimensions of inequality seem less prominent than others in recent theorizing). Most feminists would now agree—at least in principle—that feminist theory must be theorizing about multiple simultaneous oppressions, or what Patricia Hill Collins (1990) calls a matrix of domination. But these ideas, which have been so central in feminist theorizing of the past decade, have entered discussions of feminist methodologies more slowly and unevenly. Working with students in this area, I have come to feel that the development of feminist theory has outpaced our methodological innovations, so that there is often a serious mismatch between the goals of feminist researchers and what we know how to do in our empirical projects. Often, my seminar groups engage in extended abstract conversations about multiple oppressions, but lose these concerns when our talk turns to their developing projects and the challenge of designing a "doable" dissertation. These practical anxieties are important and ought not to be ignored, but observing this slippage has stimulated my interest in devising a variety of strategies for attending to issues of differential location and cross-cutting dimensions of inequality—strategies that can be deployed in any project in order to maintain the visibility of "differences" that are socially significant.

An obvious place to start thinking about this issue is in decisions about "sampling"—who will be included in a study. A 1988 *Gender and Society* article by Lynn Weber Cannon, Elizabeth Higginbotham, and Marianne L. A. Leung suggests that the qualitative studies favored by feminist researchers are especially likely to include relatively homogeneous samples, as a consequence of techniques like "snowball" sampling and the use of personal networks to recruit volunteer participants. They argue that it is critical to develop fully stratified samples with adequate representation across categories such as race and class. And they acknowledge that this demand calls for special attention to recruitment, and usually, more labor-intensive recruitment strategies.

These authors present one strategy for designing inclusive research projects, using as an illustration their in-depth study of Black and white professional, managerial, and administrative women's well-being. Their relatively large interview study—with two hundred participants—allowed them to build a sample structured by three dimensions of inequality (race and class background of the respondent and the gender composition of her occupation), producing eight cells with twenty-five interviewees in each cell. This approach to sampling allowed them to examine the separate and intersecting effects of race and class, and they point out that had they not done so, class-related differences might have been erroneously identified as racial effects, fueling a "cultural deficit" interpretation of the findings. Their article raises important issues for feminist researchers, and their research design might be taken as a kind of ideal model for attention to multiple inequalities. But it is a strategy that requires a large sample and relies on a logic of variables that may not be so appropriate for ethnographic investigation (or for secondary analysis of survey data, already collected). Reading their article pushed me to consider several additional strategies that may be more practically applied in the conduct of smaller interview studies, ethnographies, and—with appropriate modifications—other kinds of social research.

(1) As one begins to develop any topic, one ought to be acutely conscious of the composition of the group or setting to be studied. Many naturally-occurring groups are relatively homogeneous in terms of race, class, gender, sexuality, and so on; when that is the case, these features of the group ought to be part of the analysis—from the beginning. Researchers can notice the composition of the group they're concerned with and consider why it forms in the communities it does or attracts these members, and whether this group or setting has counterparts in other communities or with differing memberships. The answer to this latter question provides a basis for considering whether it is practical or desirable to seek additional subjects and sites. Are there other settings where it's different?

A key strategy—central to feminist thought—involves attention to what is missing: Where are those we don't see in this group? If they are not in similar sites elsewhere, why not? How does it happen that this group includes these people and not others? In some cases, I believe that this kind of reflection may suggest expanding one's view. Instead of content analysis using only *New York Times* articles, one might look for ethnic newspapers as well; instead of seeking participants only through private physicians, one might make contacts at public clinics as well; and so on. In other cases, exploring such options may suggest that homogeneity is a feature of this type of setting and, therefore, not so much a matter of sampling as a topic for analysis as the study proceeds. One might discover, for example, that formal support groups for family caregivers are rare in African American communities. This kind of discovery mitigates the need to fill a sampling "cell," but it brings other demands: to consider why one finds this kind of ethnic distribution of the activity under study and what kinds of counterparts to the activity one would find in other communities.

(2) Whether one decides to sample varied or homogeneous groups or settings, it seems important to identify carefully, in some detail, who is included. Such identification should take into account the social organization of "marked" and "unmarked" positions. In the routine practice of social research, studies of subordinated groups are nearly always labeled as such, while those of dominant groups are not. Feminists, and others concerned with inequalities, suggest that this practice reproduces dominance. It takes dominance for granted—normalizes and naturalizes it—and sustains a notion of subordination as exceptional and of subordinate identities as "other." By contrast, a more adequate empirically-grounded description assumes that dominance and subordination are always in play, part of the seen-but-(often)-unnoticed ground for human interaction. At the very least, it seems to me that any empirical study ought to give some substantial attention to identifying the group under consideration and locating it within a national, or even global context. That is, one ought to make readers aware—at least briefly—of how the membership of a particular site compares with the composition of surrounding communities, a wider regional population, and so on. If it accomplishes nothing else, even a minimal discussion of this sort could serve the purpose of highlighting the partiality of the analysis. One objection to this suggestion takes it as a mandate for "politically correct" labeling, and I would agree that a merely mechanical deployment of "identities" such as "white middle-class heterosexual" can simply reify such categories without providing any useful context. Even that is perhaps better than saying nothing, but I do have in mind a more nuanced and thoughtful description.

One relatively straightforward descriptive strategy that moves some distance in this direction is simply to elaborate the most typical identity categories. For example, in describing a group of U.S. "whites," one might say more about their ethnic ancestry and whether and how it is meaningful for them. Rather than simply labeling a neighborhood "middle class," one might say more about its location, history, employment base, and so on. Another strategy for making these descriptions more meaningful would involve keeping them in play as an analysis unfolds. Too often, such identificatory notes appear briefly in remarks that introduce a study and then fall away, so that the analysis appears as generic or universalized.

(3) These strategies of elaborated description lead to a third possibility for improving studies of homogeneous and relatively privileged groups: making privilege itself a topic for analysis. We see some of the possibilities in an emerging group of studies dealing with "whiteness," heterosexuality, and masculinity (e.g., Frankenberg 1993, Ingraham 1994, Messner 1992, Connell 1995, Kimmel and Messner 1998).

(4) Another strategy for making research more "identity-conscious"— a strategy that may or may not show up in the research product—involves reflexive autobiographical work. My assumption here is that learning more about how and why we see things as we do will allow us to understand more about the meanings others make of their (and our) lives, and to locate ourselves (and others) in more complex and meaningful ways rather than only through simplistic identity categories. In the seminar, we read *Yours in Struggle* (Bulkin, Pratt, and Smith 1984), a collection of three variously autobiographical essays that deal with racism and antisemitism among feminists. Each author tells personal stories, searching her own background for clues to the dynamics of oppression that she encounters, resists, and sometimes inadvertently helps to sustain at different moments in her feminist activism. The fact that all three writers are lesbian-feminists deepens their analyses and adds a layered significance to their accounts that is quite useful in the seminar context. For lesbian students, their stories make visible identities more typically obscured in the classroom; for straight students, the stories teach about lesbian lives and resistance to homophobia as well as racism. The essays provide provocative models for reflexive analysis, and they have often inspired seminar participants to undertake autobiographical writing as one of their projects in the course.

Again, I do not mean to suggest that our own realities should be an endpoint in our investigations. The reason for autobiographical investigation and analysis is to understand better where we fit into a larger system and in relation to others. I understand the feminist call for attention to the personal, or for unabashedly partial and located standpoints, as a struggle against the positivist ideal of a neutral, "value-free" stance toward the field of inquiry. This movement has begun to make it possible for researchers to include themselves as part of the picture, and to treat our own realities as one kind of touchstone by which to evaluate our analyses. But this view also suggests that the most illuminating investigations will always be setting a partial reality in a larger context, and considering how others' views would change the picture.

(5) All of these research strategies depend on knowing something about the operation of the major systems of social inequality that structure people's interactions. Thus, they suggest that social researchers, regardless

of specialization, have a responsibility for "continuing education" in this arena (especially about groups historically or typically excluded from our accounts of society and about the processes/mechanisms of exclusion). I would also suggest that the project of inclusive scholarship can be moved forward through thoughtful use of existing scholarship and a concern for using related studies to draw out the ways that particular groups are shaped by the wider social processes that produce inequality. Any researcher studying a homogeneous group or setting, it seems to me, ought to be searching for related studies conducted in other groups and communities. Explicit comparison with other work can highlight the operation of processes that might otherwise go unnoticed or unremarked.

Setting Standards of Inclusion

As empirical researchers understand these challenges better, it seems not uncommon—especially for relatively privileged researchers—to feel guilty, "overwhelmed," and defensive about the choices one inevitably makes. One unfortunate response to such feelings is to become too paralyzed to do any investigation; another is to stop hearing the challenge; another might be to pay lip service to "all oppressions" in a rather mechanical way. All these pitfalls seem to me to argue for noticing the kind of attitude we will need in order to keep on trying: a recognition that we won't succeed absolutely (at least as individuals), but that it is crucial to keep the challenge on the agenda.

I focus here on a psychic or emotional part of the research process that isn't usually taken up as an aspect of methodology. Noticing that emotional element, in order to take it into account, seems to me a feminist move in itself—underlining that research is done by actual people, living complex everyday lives suffused with emotion. The issues are not only or primarily psychic, however, but also structural: how to build feminist groups, spaces, actions, and habits of thought that struggle against racism rather than reproducing it. (And I would underline that there are four questions here, not just one. Again, my intention in making that distinction is to focus on dimensions of the research process as lived experience, and the material underpinnings of that experience—aspects of research that are often left out of abstract and idealized accounts.)

My argument for attention to feelings is not meant to deflect us from questions about standards. These questions arise, in a graduate seminar, in a raw and somewhat panicky form: What do I have to do? In this setting, they are driven, understandably, by the hurdles of dissertating, mediated by that small and very particular intellectual community—the "dissertation committee." But I urge participants in my seminar to begin thinking beyond these immediate concerns toward wider intellectual com-

munities, recognizing that scholars always choose where and how to locate ourselves, and that by choosing and entering intellectual communities
we not only become responsible to them but also shape the standards of
work within them. In this context, questions about standards are broader
and more broadly consequential: What do we expect from our own work?
from work by other feminists? What responsibilities do we have for constructing better standards (and how does that happen)? How do we select
the audiences to whom we will make ourselves accountable? When and
how do we call others to be accountable?

During the 1990s, it has become increasingly likely that feminists who
present unidimensional, universalized gender analysis could expect critique from many other feminists (though not all). Still, the likelihood of
encountering this kind of critique varies considerably, depending on the
type of setting (conference, dissertation hearing, journal submission) and
the identities and politics of those involved in a particular site. Even when
these critiques are made—and especially in face-to-face settings—there
is a strong norm of "politeness" in professional settings that I have very
mixed feelings about; I appreciate its "usefulness" (e.g., in saving people
enough face to avert tears and fisticuffs), but I also know that the practice
of "politeness" can blunt or deflate strong challenges to racism in our
scholarship. It certainly contributes to the maintenance of relatively isolated intellectual "clubs" (as opposed to communities[4]) that rarely communicate across boundaries of identity, interest, and concern.

I suggest that one major contribution feminist methodologies can make
to social science research is the idea that general standards for a complete
and adequate social analysis should include continuing attention to the
structuring effects of major systems of social inequality. How much attention? What kind? Those are questions we are only beginning to address.
But we will develop satisfactory answers only if these questions are introduced routinely into our discussions and evaluations of any empirical investigation. One thing I have learned from my seminar is that inclusion
depends on making space for these concerns, and then keeping them on
the table. These goals, in turn, raise questions about intellectual connections and networks, what we read and attend to, how we listen to others,
and the risks of appropriating works that arise from others' interests and
positions.

Those who do empirical research will always be doing limited investigations; no one study can include everything, and doing empirical investigation well often means doing it deeply rather than broadly. But the call
for inclusive scholarship, as I understand it, is not to do "everything" at
once. Rather, it seems to me that every study ought to be conducted and

written with an acute consciousness of what's being left out and the implications of omissions for the claims that can be made. That will help readers to see and understand a particular study as one useful piece of a much larger picture, a piece that must be connected with, and interpreted against, studies that explore other experiences and processes.

Advice:
Plan for inclusion, from the beginning of every study.
Recognize that doing "everything" is impossible, but also that one can almost always do much more than immediately comes to mind.

II. Process

Emotion

Once underway, most researchers experience alternating moments of intensely pleasurable engagement and almost paralyzing doubt and depression. Or perhaps I should say, in the interest of accuracy, that this roller-coaster image captures my typical experience. Observation of others, and of the fits and starts through which student projects develop, lead me to believe that I am not alone. I suspect, as well, that these emotions are heightened for oppositional researchers. The conduct of research is, for this group, meant to be more than just a job or an intellectual puzzle, more than a quest for individual success. Research and writing are supposed to contribute to liberation projects, to benefit oppressed communities and lead to change. When these goals seem in reach, our elation is intensified; when we fear failure, we fear the shame of failing our communities; when we suspect that we are only doing a job, or see that we might be rewarded for our achievements, we often feel guiltily hypocritical.

Some may scoff at this seeming excess of emotion, dismissing such feelings as products of unrealistic expectations. But dismissing feelings is usually shortsighted, since they typically persist as muted but powerful barriers to productive work. Recent writing on feminist research has perhaps exacerbated these emotional challenges, by heightening expectations and honing our critical tools to a razor-sharp edge. As an alternative to "dry and distant" objectivist research, the idea of feminist methodology has accumulated an increasingly "rosy glow," with high expectations for cooperation, intimacy, and authenticity. In addition, as feminists (and others) examine the research encounter more and more closely, we understand with ever greater precision the barriers to cooperation and the risks of exploiting those who participate in our research. Shulamit Reinharz (1993) suggests that these developments have produced "excessive demands" for feminist researchers. She worries that discussions calling for intense rapport and strong personal involvement will have the paradoxical effect of inhibiting feminist investigation by setting unattainable goals.

Jane Mansbridge (1995) provides a related structural analysis that illuminates the challenge facing the oppositional researcher and the context that produces such demands. She points out that virtually all feminists work within organizations designed to serve purposes other than feminist ones. They bring feminist commitments into workplaces, voluntary groups, and their encounters in other institutions, and they struggle to find ways of reconciling those commitments with the often conflicting demands of those organizations. Many join with other feminists and develop collective strategies. Sometimes, they find ample room for feminist practice; sometimes, only the tiniest openings for resistant efforts. In either case, it would be unrealistic to assume that feminists in these settings can freely choose and shape their own practices. Their actions are better understood as strategic compromises, worked out day by day as part of the ongoing business of the organization. Feminist teachers may work to diminish hierarchies of authority, for example, but they are required to give grades at the end of the semester; feminist nurses may hold conceptions of care that diverge from those of physicians, but they are also bound by institutional structures of authority; feminist waitresses may resist patrons' objectifying gestures, but in many establishments they must accept sexist treatment in order to hold a job and make a living wage. The pragmatism of these choices does not "spoil" these workers' feminism; rather, it reveals the inevitably rocky terrain of feminism in practice.

The academic disciplines and the settings where oppositional researchers work—colleges and universities, policy organizations, and so on—shape their practices in similar ways. Often, these settings provide considerable autonomy—so much, in fact, that feminist students and academics may lose sight of the real constraints on our work. Our distinctive challenge is to make accurate assessments of the kinds and degrees of freedom we do have—often, more than we might think, but generally not so much that we can expect to achieve an unimpeachable feminist practice. "Realism," then, seems necessary—and yet potentially dangerous, if it means that the oppositional researcher aims for less than she might reasonably accomplish. As a study goes forward, the challenge of finding ambitions that are both worthy and reasonable may produce inflated desires and feelings of intense anxiety, guilt, and despair. Painful as these feelings can be, they are most usefully treated as inevitable and informative aspects of the process of oppositional research.

Expect strong feelings; pay attention, but try not to wallow.

Privilege, in Theory and Practice

Many of the worries that beset oppositional researchers revolve around issues of domination. Researchers exercise particular kinds of interpretive and representational power: they define topics, set the boundaries of their investigations, choose participants and control their participation, interpret data, and of course, craft the text that will be taken as authorized "knowledge." Some critics, then, argue that systematic study of others is an objectifying process inimical to liberation and that analytic writing is inevitably a project of mastery (e.g., Clough 1992). Feminist researchers who take such critiques to heart often come to fear that, rather than dismantling systems of domination, we can only add stones to an edifice of power.

The moral dimension of the critique of empirical research gives it an edge that stimulates confession and apology. While these kinds of responses are sometimes informative, they often leave writers stuck in a moment of guilty paralysis. One pitfall is that researchers may spend so much of their analytic energy on possible problems that their solutions to these problems remain underdeveloped (and therefore perpetuate the flaws of standard practice). My hope is that feminist methodologists will continue to study these critiques of empirical research, but also maintain the sense of possibility that allows us to explore opportunities for better practical strategies.

"Practical," here, means more than just "pragmatic" (though my approach does involve a considerable dose of pragmatism, for better or worse). It points to the fact that empirical research is a practice, unfolding in time, in particular places and in concrete interactions. The point may seem too obvious to mention; it is important because it underlines distinctively methodological imperatives and constraints. The tendency to value theory over method appears to lead some researchers to look to theoretical writing as if it could provide fully developed answers to methodological questions. But intriguing and fruitful ideas—Sandra Harding's (1991) suggestion that we "start thought" from lesbian life, for example, or bell hooks' (1984) notion of bringing marginal perspectives to the center of feminism—do not tell researchers, in practical terms, how to proceed. Thus, it may be useful to acknowledge more explicitly a division of labor among feminist thinkers. Theory and method—"sister" elements in empirical investigation—should always intertwine and inform each other. But when I work with students, I encourage them to see, alongside the critiques of feminist theorists, a space for specifically methodological innovation.

In addition, the injunction to examine the researcher's privilege may sometimes have paradoxical effects. The analysis of privilege is an important corrective to a long history of scientific study conducted by the powerful, and it seems extremely useful for researchers to look critically at the actual relations of inequality that precede such research encounters—often, the relations that make them possible—and that persist beyond these encounters. But what does it mean to "examine" privilege? It might usefully mean examining one's daily life, discovering and cataloging unearned advantage (as Peggy McIntosh [1988] does). It might mean reviewing one's biography, following threads of privilege through a personal history (as Minnie Bruce Pratt does [Bulkin, Pratt, and Smith 1984]). It might mean that one would use the knowledge thus gained as a lens toward a clearer-sighted view of daily interactions. And sometimes, one might want to find a way to acknowledge one's privilege explicitly. Unfortunately, in my view, the last response seems most common, both among students and in feminist writing. It is relatively easy to announce that "I am inordinately privileged" and to elaborate this theme; it is considerably more difficult to know how to move productively beyond the announcement. My worry concerns the border where "examination" becomes the arrogant assertion of privilege. When a man faces a woman classmate and states, "Of course, it's easier for me to get my views heard," he intends to unmask but perhaps inadvertently perpetuates male privilege. Similarly, when straight women use seminar time for elaborate confessions of heterosexual privilege, they intend to correct their dominance but may miss opportunities to learn about lives that are different. These kinds of assertive confessions can reproduce relations of dominance in that they define a situation from a single (privileged) point of view and leave little room for mutual conversation.

In face-to-face research relations (as in the small intellectual community of the seminar), disciplines of courtesy and restraint go farther than one might think in constructing more mutual, less exploitative relations across lines of difference and inequality. While it is true that the researcher writes up the study and thereby defines the interaction, research participants will exercise agency, too, if we let them; they decide whether to talk with us, what to say and how, when to withdraw, and so on. Watching carefully for those decisions and respecting them are large steps toward leveling the power relations of the research encounter.

A discipline of restraint might mean recognizing refusal, avoidance, and withdrawal as meaningful responses to privilege and representing these somehow as meaningful data. It might mean accounting for the life circumstances that make participation in research difficult—bringing along to interviews with parents a research assistant to care for participants' children, for instance. It might mean offering opportunities for collaboration in the research, but without insisting on a formal equality of effort that imposes unmanageable burdens on participants. Finally, restraint should imply extremely careful listening to the words and actions of participants and an openness to unexpected meanings. In studies that bridge cultures, researchers sometimes make assumptions about difference and miss subtle responses that challenge those assumptions. (I have noticed in the seminar, for instance, that white students just beginning to explore issues of oppression and privilege can take from the writings of African American feminists a somewhat reductive view of "an African American perspective," and they sometimes seem nonplused when the comments of African American classmates move in different directions.)

It is also worth mentioning that critical writing on empirical research (and my discussion thus far) focuses almost entirely on the situation of research in communities considered less powerful than the researcher's. The idea of "studying up"—focusing on those who are more powerful—has a venerable but somewhat muted presence in oppositional discourses, and has been quite underdeveloped in feminist methodology. Strategies for studying up would presumably call for a different set of virtues—bold assertion rather than restraint, for example—and these virtues are perhaps less comfortable for many women than solicitous restraint.

Finally, however, neither of these alternatives—studying "up" or "down"—can be adequate by itself. Focusing primarily on oppressed communities risks ignoring the dynamics of power; focusing on the powerful may obscure dynamics of resistance that fall outside the orbit of dominant institutions and ideologies. It seems important in every project, therefore, to attend to connections, aiming for an analysis that shows in some way both the consequences of power and how it is exercised. Working in this way will not eliminate the power and privilege of the analyst, but it can make that power more visible and deploy it in ways that chart systems of privilege and inequality, offering road maps to change in those systems for those working from various locations within them.

> *Privilege cannot be talked away. Therefore, my suggestion for researchers conscious of their unearned advantages: Resist impulses toward elaborate confession; work instead toward projects that demonstrate an awareness of privilege by advancing understandings of its mechanisms and consequences.*

Acknowledgment and Appropriation

I have been arguing that feminist method is necessarily collective and cumulative—that its creativity and strategic distinctiveness come from a continuing conversation that always seeks to extend itself. This collective aspect of the approach means that situating one's investigation in relation to other work is quite important—not only as a matter of presentation, but as a technique for seeing further into the significance of one's own material. In the seminar, we work on such issues through discussion (and disputation) over how to read and use the texts of other feminists. Three kinds of issues that arise with some regularity illustrate characteristic challenges and opportunities in using scholarly and activist literatures in oppositional research.[5]

The burgeoning feminist writing of the past two decades, and its increasing sophistication and specialization, produce a generational issue. I include on our syllabus several works by relatively early second-wave feminists, partly in order to give students a sense of feminist history, and partly because these works have been especially meaningful for me and introduce ideas I know I will want to develop in the seminar. Often, the tone of these works is fresh and urgent—a tone of ideas newly discovered by their authors; some also seem dated and relatively undeveloped, and students steeped in more recent feminist work often complain that they lack the nuance and specificity of later theorizing.

As one example, we read several chapters from *Man Made Language* (originally published in 1980) by Australian feminist Dale Spender. Spender's book addresses several topics, including gender bias in language, gendered differences in speech and listening, and gendered aspects of writing and publishing. I like its range, as well as the fact that much of her data comes from feminist meetings and conferences: one can see that she has used her own local activities creatively, as settings for empirically grounded, low-budget research. Spender's analysis examines sexism as a form of oppression; she compares it to other forms, such as racism, but her focus is on gender, with little attention to cross-cutting inequalities.

In recent years, students have responded quite differently to this material. Some—usually those relatively new to feminism—find Spender's approach fresh and illuminating; others, accustomed to the more densely differentiated theorizing that has gained prominence in the United States, read her as insufficiently attentive to differences among women. We have argued, sometimes bitterly, over whether and how to use or acknowledge Spender's work. Some favor dismissing authors such as Spender, arguing that such "unidimensional" gender analysis is irrelevant now and harmful because it obscures differences in ways that severely limit feminist solidarity. Those who have learned from reading Spender (who have typically come to class with excitement, eager to explore the implications of that new knowledge) are sometimes stung by the strong words of these critics, feeling suddenly as if they have erred by reading enthusiastically.

As facilitator of these discussions, working toward a feminist style of reading and critique, my aim is to stake out a productive middle ground. I want students to work toward ways of making strong critiques when they seem necessary—and I agree with the critics that Spender's relatively unidimensional analysis needs extension. But I also feel that such critiques should include an acknowledgment of the contributions made by early feminists like Spender. The point is not to construct feminist heroines, but to recognize the founders of a field. And that much said, these discussions have also made me keenly aware of the risks of recognizing privileged "founders" while losing sight of others. That awareness can in turn lead to fruitful research and reflection on our history and attempts to write about it more inclusively (some of my efforts in this direction show up, I hope, in chap. 2).

These discussions have intensified, and become more complex, since I revised the syllabus for inclusion. Writings by feminists of color in the early weeks of the semester provide the background that supports students' critiques of Spender's work. And for our discussion of language, I assign, in addition to Spender, June Jordan's (1985) extraordinary essay on teaching Black English, "Nobody Mean More to Me Than You And the Future Life of Willie Jordan." Discussing *The Color Purple,* Jordan notices that her New York City students reject Celie's Black English as "wrong," despite its similarity to their own everyday talk, and she resolves to offer a course in Black English. Working from their own sense of the language, she and her students gradually develop its rules. They derive much pleasure from the experience, until a classmate disappears and they discover that his brother has been shot by the police. Then, they confront a tragic dilemma: Will they express their rage in a "standard" English letter to the editor, or in their own tongue?

My hope is that people will read Spender with and against June Jordan. I do not have a clear sense of where this kind of "with and against" reading will lead; my goal in making the juxtaposition is to help students notice both parallels and differences. For example, both writers deal with the languages of oppressed groups, issues of "translation," and what can be said and understood in different languages or registers. Both authors suggest that these "muted" forms of speech are devalued, even by their "native" speakers. And both suggest that the situation of such groups poses serious questions of how to speak and to what end. Yet their essays also give a sense of the different communities and contexts associated with gendered and raced languages: Spender draws material from some of the myriad gatherings of relatively privileged Western women involved in feminist activism, while Jordan discusses a single moment, the first time that she or her students had taken Black English seriously. Spender discusses a range of gendered constraints and oppressions related to speaking and writing, some quite subtle; Jordan's essay focuses on a violent death at the hands of police, and her students' rage, frustration, and ultimate impotence to protest a friend's loss. Neither essay makes a clear place for African American women as "women," and one might ask, reading them together, why this is so. Students often have trouble reading these essays "together"—we talk about one, then the other. At the least, however, I hope they will see that issues of language and speech appear in multiple sites, manifest in different ways, and deserve deeper exploration than a single view provides.

A second kind of issue, of "appropriation," sometimes arises in white readings of feminist texts by women of color. Here, there are questions of interpretation and emphasis. For example, for a seminar session on "self and subjectivity," we read an essay by Latina philosopher Maria Lugones, "Playfulness, 'World'-Travelling, and Loving Perception" (1987). She describes the skills Latina women develop as they struggle to survive in Anglo contexts: double-edged skills that involve modifying the self so as to operate successfully in both native and dominating cultures. In one discussion of the essay, I began (mistakenly, perhaps) by asking the class (all white that semester) whether they had recognized aspects of their own experiences in Lugones's discussion. Some had, and we shared thoughts along that line for some time; I became increasingly concerned that no one had mentioned racism as an aspect of the piece, and I finally suggested that something was missing from our discussion. Even then, the group seemed reluctant to name race as key to the essay, and this reluctance became a matter for debate among the seminar members over the next few weeks, with some arguing that we had revealed a blind and debilitating racism.

Since I teach in a predominantly white institution (and perhaps also because feminist courses in many universities have too often been inattentive to racial/ethnic diversity), the members of my seminar are often mostly white. But this statement obscures significant difference. As the group involved in this discussion fought over questions of guilt and responsible action, members began to assert invisible differences of ethnicity, sexuality, and class. Still, we eventually recognized and could agree that our diverse backgrounds did not negate the white-skin privilege that gave us all unearned advantages. The questions became: How might such a group usefully read works about race? What pitfalls might we encounter in the attempt? It seemed to me that Lugones's essay has to be "about race" in some sense, but I was not convinced that it had to be about only race. (Indeed, I would resist the notion of a "correct" reading of any such text—though some readings certainly seem closer to an author's intentions than others.) Lugones seems to use the term "'world'-travelling" to

refer to at least two different kinds of experiences: one that is about relations with white feminists and one about her mother. Her discussion of
"travelling" in Anglo worlds points relatively directly toward some quite
specific complaints about the willful blindness of white feminists, but the
discussion of her mother's "world" seemed more open and ambiguous in
its implications. (I wasn't so sure I understood about her mother; perhaps I was limited as a reader whose ancestors have long been part of the
dominant white culture of the United States.) Thus, it seems to me that
Lugones's text itself suggests that "world"-travelling occurs in various
forms. Considering whether others besides women of color sometimes
do "world"-travelling, then, would not have to be taken to mean that
these experiences are all "the same." Instead, considering various forms of
"world"-travelling might be helpful in articulating differences. The risks,
however, are that some readers will miss the particular experience that
Lugones wants to convey, and that some readers who emphasize com-
parisons may never reach the point of considering differences.

As we wrestled with these issues, I began to understand them in relation to the composition of our scholarly networks. Borrowing from other
scholars, taking up existing writings and using them for our own purposes, extending ideas in original ways—these are practices at the heart
of scholarship. Within a network of scholars who interact in various
ways—reading each other's work, attending the same lectures and conferences, working together in programs and organizations, and spending
social time together—such practices produce fruitful intellectual community. In such contexts, it seems relatively easy for colleagues to use each
other's work in ways that honor its intentions and nuances, because there
are so many avenues for sharing understandings and so much history of
shared work and discussion. Using work produced in other locations—
where one does not participate in such dense interchange—is more risky,
because of the greater likelihood of misunderstanding or superficial adoption of appealing ideas (and the risk of "forgetting" more challenging
ones). In this situation, one needs to read more carefully, to educate oneself in the contexts that produce analyses, and to proceed with some
caution.

I do not mean to suggest that we cannot learn from scholars outside
our immediate networks—we must. But attention to these structural issues can serve as a reminder, revealing the depth of the challenge of inclusion. It helps to explain, for example, why white feminists cannot solve
problems of racism in scholarship by collecting a few "women-of-color"
texts and using them to "decorate" our work. Instead, we need to take
seriously the work of educating ourselves about the networks that have
produced multicultural feminisms. This kind of analysis also suggests that

risks of appropriation will be heightened if our networks remain isolated and unconnected to those groups of scholars doing antiracist work.

Finally, I have sometimes felt that seminar members miss opportunities to learn more about inclusion, because they are limited by their expectations. For example, our university is the home for an extraordinary research center devoted to advocacy work for people with disabilities,[6] and nearly every year the seminar includes one or more members who are experts in the disability field and passionately committed to bringing disability issues into view. Over the years, I have gained important insights from work with these students, whose lens captures views of lives rarely seen in standard sociological writing. I knew from my own research (DeVault 1991), for example, that women work hard at producing family sociability. But Rannveig Traustadottir's dissertation (1992; see also 1991, 1995) on the work of mothers whose children have disabilities showed me how strongly this work is oriented toward producing "normality." It also provides a frighteningly compelling view of how easily a woman's autonomy can disappear when her life is engulfed by the responsibility of caring for a child with problems—a kind of appropriation of women's labor that is not so strikingly visible in families whose problems are more manageable.

My sense is that other seminar participants are often unprepared to take advantage of the opportunity to learn from such studies. Too often, they see these projects only in relatively narrow ways, as "specialized" topics that lack general interest. One student from the disabilities studies program, for example, prepared a presentation on her ethnographic study of a community women's group that included one member with a disability. The seminar group that semester had engaged in extensive discussion of racism in feminist scholarship and included several "out" lesbian students who had pushed us to consider the heterosexism that kept surfacing in our discussions. Given that history, I looked forward to hearing about another dimension of inclusion and hoped that we might glean some useful strategies from efforts in this relatively unfamiliar arena. Our presenter, no doubt also conscious of the group's history and shared concerns, mentioned in her introductory comments that the group she had studied was racially homogeneous (all white) and that she now saw that it would be useful to pursue questions of racial/ethnic inclusion. To my consternation (and despite my attempts to redirect the discussion), seminar participants could talk only about race. They asked questions about race, made suggestions about race, and recommended readings about race. But hardly anyone seemed able to be interested in the question of including a member with a disability, or even the more general question of how a nearly homogeneous group dealt with one member they perceived as "different."

I felt the discussion we'd had was useful, but only half finished, and even now, as I write, I feel impatient with the group for approaching their colleague's project in this programmatic way (a feeling that surprises me, lingering so long). Examining that feeling, I realize that my general point is both moral and intellectual: it involves listening carefully and respectfully, and remaining open to unexpected points of view. Good listening, in my view, is a moral value. Remaining open to unexpected points of view is a strategy for avoiding the dangers of narrow adherence to a theoretical program. I would not dismiss the essential (and inevitable, even if unacknowledged) role of theory in empirical work; but it is helpful to remember that sometimes, in addition to usefully directing attention, theoretical commitments can serve as blinders, and thus diminish the value of empirical investigation.

The class discussions I have described always feel quite challenging for me as facilitator, and I often leave our sessions thinking deeply about what has gone on. My challenge is to support students' useful critiques, of readings and each other's ideas, and still keep lines of discussion open. All of us experience strong feelings at times—desire, hope, anger, shame, and more—and we need to allow such feelings without letting them overpower us. It is also important to recognize the play of identities in the classroom, without forcing students into reductive positions that make them unwilling representatives of some social location. Students who speak from experience about particular oppressions can provide powerful lessons for others, but if they do so, they may also bear the brunt of other students' nervous defensiveness. Teachers sensitive to these dynamics have learned not to require students to teach the class about oppression, and, if such students do choose to speak up, to support those choices in various ways. We learn these lessons both from reading (e.g., Moraga and Anzaldúa 1981) and from painful experience. I am indebted, for example, to a lesbian undergraduate student from a dozen years ago who frequently challenged my too-casual remarks about women's family lives, asking, "But it's different for lesbians, isn't it?" With chagrin and respect, I watched her stubbornly endure the other students' hostile stares and I resolved that I would try to remember her lessons; I have tried since then to speak the words that will make space for a consideration of sexual and other differences. I still need and rely on students' assistance, but I believe that my teacherly responsibility includes opening the floor for such conversations. As group dynamics unfold over the semester, I hope that clusters of students may begin to support each other's comments and testimonies: small groups of lesbian and gay students, students of color, or students from working-class backgrounds, for example, may learn to support each other's interventions, joining together in order to remind the class about the circumstances of lives we risk forgetting too easily.

In order to organize my facilitation of these discussions, I think of the seminar as a laboratory for pursuing issues of inclusion and transformation: I watch our interactions, follow the consequences of various readings and lines of critique, and try to intervene in ways that invite all participants not only to express views but also to think through their implications. Sometimes, I call attention to the importance of listening to one another in ways that seek full expression before moving to a defense or critique. I try to model a stance in this kind of discussion—an attitude that genuinely seeks to hear what might be left out of my analysis. Airing and understanding multiple perspectives then becomes a procedure for building knowledge together, rather than a morally charged contest for truth and correctness.

Some might contend that the matters I have discussed in this section are issues of "content" rather than "method," but I want to challenge this distinction. I have tried to identify a technique for thinking through multiple perspectives. In all of the cases I have discussed, it seems useful to hold competing readings side by side, to resist a resolution that comes too easily, and to explore the tensions that arise from different interpretations. I have also tried to identify some elements of respectful reading and listening, pointing to (though without spelling out) practices of close reading of texts that honor authors' intentions and recognize contexts as well as exploring critiques and extensions. Finally, I have suggested that oppositional researchers can reap intellectual benefits from the conscious formation of scholarly networks designed to promote productive and wide-ranging discussion.

Reading and listening widely can be tools for acknowledging forerunners, constructing intellectual community, and developing more open, expansive, and nuanced interpretations. Reading and listening choices mark the products of investigation far more deeply than the conventional literature review suggests. Therefore, choose wisely and, above all, consciously.

And a corollary: Citation—of forerunners and contemporaries—signals alliance and coalition, and contributes to a canon of authoritative feminist scholarship. Thus, it should not be dismissed as a mere exercise of convention but treated creatively as an arena for conscious, collective self-production.

III. Presentation

Research and Social Change

Oppositional research is meant to promote social change. We choose projects and design studies in the hope that they will make a difference. However, when I wrote the survey of feminist methodology included here as chapter 2 ("Talking Back to Sociology"), I was struck by a disjuncture in this literature: nearly every feminist researcher mentions social change as an important goal, but few of us examine closely how our writing might actually bring about change. In a way, this lacuna is unsurprising—the question is formidable—but still, it seems important to move beyond vaguely optimistic references to social transformation, toward a closer consideration of the more modest and specific kinds of changes that oppositional research is more likely to foster.

Observation and analysis of the structures of research activity can produce a deep skepticism about the possibility of contributing to change: powerfully conservative forces organize our approaches to research and the ways in which any research results are used (or ignored). For example, researchers' questions most often come from the specialized discourses of established disciplines; we learn specialized vocabularies and, most importantly, to "think as researchers" rather than as activists. As graduate students and later, for those who become academics, efforts are driven by incentive structures of the university: rewards come for writing a dissertation rather than for making change; for contributing to the established academic journals rather than the newsletters of activist groups; for securing large grants, usually tied to policy interests of the powerful, rather than serving those with few resources. There are always some openings, of course, to bend these structures in other directions, but there are also many daily responsibilities and finite stores of time and energy. Despite the best intentions, it is difficult to swim against this tide. Outside the university, "applied research" sometimes offers intriguing possibilities, but it is also usually driven by economic pressures as well as legislative and policy mandates.

For all of these reasons, I resist privileging the academy as a leading site for activism and change. Observation of past struggles suggests that the most significant sources of change are those driven from below, by grassroots activism. When such movements arise, however, they are connected to changes in every part of society. Researchers can certainly change their own institutions—the shape and composition of university departments, the canons of social scientific knowledge, the standards by which research efforts are judged, and so on—making them more hospitable and more useful to broader activist movements. Often, researchers have opportunities to oppose conservative forces within their institutions, both in everyday practice and through intellectual production. And sometimes, we may be able to negotiate relationships with activist groups that enable us to conduct research they can use in specific programs of social change. These relatively modest goals seem to me the ones that are most realistically attainable for feminist researchers, and therefore the ones worth striving for.

The students in my seminar are typically just beginning to think about projects; their work has not advanced to a point where we can evaluate its effects, but we often consider the ways that various types of projects might contribute to feminist change efforts. Some projects, for example, are primarily descriptive but approach description in ways that seem relevant for social action. Some students study feminist or other activist groups with the purpose of adding their stories to an archive of change efforts; one woman who planned to study feminist teaching explained, "I don't want what we're doing to get lost." Sometimes, these projects focus on particular problems of such groups: failures of cooperation, conflicts that stand in the way of action, barriers to including participants from a range of racial/ethnic and other communities, and so on. Others have focused directly on making change in their immediate academic contexts, especially in fields relatively untouched by feminism, by undertaking critiques of disciplinary literature or surveys that explore perceptions of feminism and feminist scholarship in the field. These kinds of projects can help to build feminist scholarship; their authors can bring feminist ideas from one discipline to another, explain emerging feminist work to nonfeminists, and also provide resources and support for their feminist colleagues. And some of these critical and evaluative projects aim at changing feminist discourses, by insisting on attention to diversity among women. In all of these kinds of projects, there is a balance to be struck: it is useful to acknowledge past success, but a project that is only celebratory cannot move emergent understandings forward.

Some projects aim to change the literature of a field—and associated constructions of social problems and policy questions—by insisting on the inclusion of women (or others typically left out). For example, students working on studies of economic restructuring in our region have found that these issues are often construed primarily as problems for those men who held secure industrial jobs in the past. Considering the experiences of such men's partners or of displaced women workers can bring relatively neglected dimensions of these changes to attention. Or, researchers might examine the programs put in place to assist displaced workers for unacknowledged gender and racial/ethnic biases.

As my students begin to formulate research questions, we examine the possibilities for different kinds of projects that might operate differently as elements of change efforts. For students working on "women's status" projects—in a campus organization, a religious order, or a field of work, for example—I might point out that such studies can be conceived in either of two ways. The "mapping contours" project documents and analyzes patterns, while the "asking why" project attempts a more specifically organizational analysis of "how it happens" (see chap. 3). It is necessary, and often easiest, to show the consequences of gender domination; but an analysis of how such patterns have been orchestrated would seem more useful for those aiming to change them.

I try to emphasize the importance of thinking through how these kinds of inquiries would connect to change efforts. When a researcher shows that school settings are organized so as to reinforce a heterosexual dating "regime," for example, it seems important to consider how that insight might be conveyed to audiences outside of a circle of theorists—an audience that might include students, teachers, parents, and school administrators—those in a position to act on such findings.

Some of my students develop projects from already-existing relationships with social change and advocacy groups, and these offer especially promising prospects for analysis that might be useful outside an academic world. Some of these projects are meant to produce findings that such groups can deploy (often, proving for other audiences things that activists already know from experience); in other cases, research questions come from the puzzles and problems of these groups, so that the group itself is conceived as the main audience for the work. These projects also bring distinctive challenges. Researchers in these situations often wish to be directed in their investigations by group or community assessments of the benefits of research. But determining such views is no simple matter, since it means collecting and synthesizing diverse perspectives from within the group. Sometimes, too, the questions that result may seem unimportant (or "merely applied") in an academic context, so that researchers must negotiate competing demands. Should they decide to pursue parallel agendas (producing both an academic dissertation and also a change-oriented report for a community group, for example), they must evaluate the costs and difficulties of such decisions and develop strategies for balancing competing demands. One valuable but difficult approach to this kind of problem might involve efforts at making space within academic discourses for this kind of change-oriented work. The approach labeled "participatory action research" (Hall 1975, Maguire 1987) has laid important groundwork in this direction—especially in international research efforts—

and those pursuing institutional ethnographies (D. Smith 1987, G. Smith 1990, Campbell and Manicom 1995) have also worked explicitly at making intellectual space within the disciplines for research that originates in the concerns of grass-roots groups.

I believe that my students are sometimes surprised and disappointed by my pessimism about the prospects for making change through academic research. I try to convince them that a realistic and thoughtful pessimism seems more useful than unrealistically optimistic sloganeering. I point out that my pessimism has not dissuaded me from the effort to undertake research that will change at least small parts of the world. And I urge them to think in very specific terms about how investigation and analysis might be connected to activity outside of academic discourses. I mean to suggest that critical researchers might usefully attend more closely to a final stage of work, in which we try more assiduously to identify and address audiences who might use our findings in ways that will complete our intentions.

> *Researchers cannot bring change by proclamation. Therefore, oppositional researchers must realistically assess the kinds of change their projects might bring, and if they direct efforts toward change outside the academy, devote particular and sustained attention to cultivating audiences who can use research in practical ways.*

Writing

Usually, students in the seminar are most immediately concerned with writing in a particular genre: they must prepare a dissertation proposal. For some, the moment of producing this "official" text—with such significance for their careers—is a critical turning point. I am often surprised when students who have been articulate, funny, and passionate in the seminar turn in first proposal drafts that are dull and dead—they seem to have lost their voices! I have learned that most often, they are in thrall to some image of the properly "scientific" text, parroting a voice of imagined authority that they hope will sound "important" (as Becker [1986b] reports in his book on teaching writing). I have also learned that even quite simple questions can be helpful in loosening these constraints and encouraging a new start: "But what did you *want* to say? And why didn't you just say *that*?" The point is to encourage students to sit comfortably with their own writing: "You don't have to copy someone else," I might say. "This is your text."

As a teacher and advisor, I often instruct students in the proper use of standard forms, and in many contexts I insist on the rules, quibbling over grammar and footnote form along with the most curmudgeonly of my colleagues. But I try to make the seminar a space for looking beyond rules and indulging in experimentation. I include in our collective reading several texts that are "unusual" in social science—because they are "personal" (Bulkin, Pratt, and Smith 1984), "evocative" (Trinh T. Minh-ha 1989), or "experimental" (Orr 1990). Students often have mixed reactions, and as we discuss these pieces, we talk about both benefits and risks of adopting such writing strategies in social scientific texts.

Sometimes I tell stories of my own writing practices. For example, I sometimes talk about my meditations on words that are especially important and the discoveries that have come from adopting new usages. For several years, I have been experimenting with using the word "family" as an adjective rather than a noun, since the noun form seems only to contribute to a reified and falsely monolithic conceptualization. And I have become extremely interested in the consequences of writing as "I" or as part of a "we" (see DeVault 1997b). I tell about my writing anxieties and the strategies I have developed for managing my inevitable mood swings. And I tell the story of making room for my anger while writing (see the introduction to Part V). These accounts are meant to encourage students to be more conscious of their writing and to prepare them to follow Laurel Richardson's (1994) advice—to treat writing as an "exercise," using it not just to present a finished piece of work, but also to discover and develop new lines of thought.

Following Richardson's lead, I encourage students to use their course papers to try things out rather than to prepare a final and definitive argument. I often propose that students prepare "sampler" papers—practicing different modes of presentation in the same way that embroiderers combine a variety of stitches in a practice piece of work. In addition to longer papers based on their empirical work, I encourage students to undertake shorter autobiographical essays. These projects provide an opportunity to reflect on our discussions about identity and knowledge, and also to try out an unaccustomed mode of writing that still has a scholarly purpose. My own effort at autobiographical writing (chap. 1) was written by trial and error, drawing from the examples of other authors. When I began to advise students undertaking the task, I tried to articulate what I had learned. Usually, I emphasize the one guideline that seems to me most important for social scientists: remember that you are telling this story for some intellectual reason; figure out what you want to accomplish and craft your story toward that end (see also DeVault 1997a).

Above all, my aim is to show students a range of possibilities for taking charge of their own writing. If they worry about how readers will respond to a text, I encourage them to be more explicit about how they would like readers to respond, incorporating these instructions for readers into the text. If they wish to adopt some unusual voice or format, I encourage them to explain why as fully as possible, since more conservative readers will need convincing; in addition, the effort helps to ensure that the innovation is motivated by more than fashion alone.

These writing issues also provide opportunities to discuss "professionalism" and changing expectations for academic work. I am always aware of the two contradictory layers of our work in the seminar: we are preparing students for places in their chosen fields and also preparing them for struggles to change those fields. Their research texts are tickets of admission. Students must learn what it means to write a "proper" text, but they need not always do so slavishly. Instead, I try to hone their ability to assess the kinds of professionalism they value, the kinds that are necessary in particular contexts, and the kinds they may decide to resist. I work with them to devise strategies for "performing" professionalism when it seems useful and crafting sound explanations for the moments when they depart from established practice. And I try to help them "see" professionalism, so as not to take it for granted. As the discourses of feminist methodology grow, they are inevitably marked by the dynamics of research as professional activity. Such changes cannot be wished away, but instead must become part of the continuing challenge of oppositional practice.

Write often, thoughtfully, carefully; learn to write flexibly and adapt textual practices to the demands of different occasions.

CONCLUDING THOUGHTS

I have tried to adopt a voice in this writing that conveys my thinking clearly without slipping into a tone of judgment or complacency. I do not mean to resolve questions of feminist research practice, but rather to share the ongoing thinking I have done with several groups of students—often about goals not yet realized rather than settled accomplishments. Such writing has been frightening at times, since I am not only a teacher but also a researcher who struggles with these issues myself. In this writing, as in teaching generally, I find myself urging, "Do as I say," without the confident knowledge that I can always live up to my own demands. One of the joys of setting difficult problems for students, however, is that they sometimes find elegant solutions; so I have learned the value of posing problems without seeing solutions in advance.

At some moments in this writing, I have been haunted by fantasized questions from mainstream social scientists: Isn't this just "good practice"? Shouldn't good researchers always work in these ways? My answer is "yes," but it must always be a qualified yes—a yes that refuses to set aside these concerns. Even if researchers should always attend to difference and power in their varied manifestations, too often we do not. The hallmark of feminist and other liberatory methodologies is that they aim explicitly at these goals. The concerns, aspirations, and strategies I have discussed here certainly could be thought of as aspects of "good science"; but in fact, they have not been treated in a sustained manner in more standard methodological discourses (where they are typically judged "political" and therefore outside the terrain of appropriate concern). Thus, labeling these strategies "feminist" or "liberatory" serves two important purposes: it announces that these concerns are still too often absent in the production of knowledge, and it points toward the history of activism and liberatory scholarship that has brought them to attention.

At other moments, I have worried about complaints from more activist scholars—that I am too firmly and comfortably situated in the academy—and the risk that my talk of opposition might ring hollow for those facing more difficult struggles (or waging them with fewer resources) than I. As a woman privileged in many ways, living a life so full of possibility, I have sometimes felt suspended in my own location—fearing almost equally to own or to disown words like "resistance" and "liberation." In the end, speaking such words seems worth the risk. I will be pleased if readers judge that I have been bold enough to encourage and support other researchers opposed to routinely oppressive practices in the production of knowledge.

APPENDIX A
List of Data for Sources in Chapter 6: Commentary on *The Late Bourgeois World*

Reviews at the time of publication:

(a) Anderson, Patrick. "Day on the Rand." *Spectator* July 1, 1966:20.
(b) Beichman, Arnold. "Responsibility can have no end." *Christian Science Monitor* June 30, 1966:13.
(c) Elson, Brigid. Review. *Commonweal* November 4, 1966:149–150.
(d) Fuller, Hoyt W. Review. *Negro Digest* December, 1966:51–52.
(e) Hamilton, Ian. "Sunsets." *New Statesman* July 1, 1966:22.
(f) McCabe, Bernard. "A code for the pale." *Saturday Review* August 20, 1966:32.
(g) Mitchell, Adrian. "Climate of fear." *New York Times Book Review* September 11, 1966:54.
(h) *National Observer.* "Novels of today: Masquerading in many forms." August 8, 1966:21.
(i) *Newsweek.* Review. July 4, 1966:90.
(j) Shrapnel, Norman. "Dead and dying worlds." *Manchester Guardian Weekly* June 30, 1966:11.
(k) Shuttleworth, Martin. "New novels." *Punch* July 6, 1966:32.
(l) *Times Literary Supplement.* "On the brink." July 7, 1966:589.
(m) Toynbee, Philip. "Disillusioned heroine." *New Republic* September 10, 1966:24–25.
(n) Weeks, Edward. "The peripatetic reviewer." *Atlantic Monthly* August, 1966:116.

Later critical works:

(o) Gerver, Elisabeth. 1978. "Women revolutionaries in the novels of Nadine Gordimer and Doris Lessing." *World Literature Written in English* 17:38–50.
(p) Haugh, Robert F. 1974. *Nadine Gordimer.* New York: Twayne.
(q) JanMohamed, Abdul R. 1983. *Manichean Aesthetics: The Politics of Literature in Colonial Africa.* Amherst: University of Massachusetts Press.
(r) Parker, Kenneth. 1978. "Nadine Gordimer and the pitfalls of liberalism." In *The South African Novel in English.* Edited by K. Parker, pp. 114–130. London: Macmillan.
(s) Wade, Michael. 1978. *Nadine Gordimer.* London: Evans Brothers.

APPENDIX B
Readings for a Seminar on "Feminist Methodologies"

This outline lists readings used in the course discussed in chapter 11, "From the Seminar Room." I have combined readings and topic areas from several iterations of the seminar, offered at Syracuse University between 1991 and 1997.

1. First meeting—introductions.

Marge Piercy, "Unlearning to Not Speak." From *To Be Of Use*. Garden City, NY: Doubleday, 1973.

Donna Kate Rushin, "The Bridge Poem." In Cherríe Moraga and Gloria Anzaldúa (eds.), *This Bridge Called My Back: Writings by Radical Women of Color*. Watertown, MA: Persephone Press, 1981.

2. Groundwork: Some readings in feminism and women's studies.

bell hooks, *From Margin to Center*: preface, chs. 1–3, 6–8.

Marilyn Frye, *Politics of Reality*: "Introduction," "Oppression," "A Note on Anger," "To Be and Be Seen."

Jane Mansbridge, "What is the Feminist Movement?" From Ferree and Martin, *Feminist Organizations: Harvest of the New Women's Movement*.

Marilyn J. Boxer, "For and About Women: The Theory and Practice of Women's Studies in the United States." From Minnich *et al.*, *Reconstructing the Academy: Women's Education and Women's Studies*.

Gloria T. Hull and Barbara Smith, "Introduction: The Politics of Black Women's Studies." From Hull et al., *All the Women are White, All the Blacks are Men, But Some of Us are Brave*.

Chandra T. Mohanty, "Cartographies of Struggle: Third World Women and the Politics of Feminism." From Mohanty et al., *Third World Women and the Politics of Feminism*.

3. A circle of speakers: "On the right to say 'we.'"

Elly Bulkin, Minnie Bruce Pratt and Barbara Smith, *Yours in Struggle: Three Feminist Perspectives on Anti-Semitism and Racism*.

Shulamit Reinharz, "Feminist Research Methodology Groups: Origins, Forms, Functions." From Patraka and Tilly, *Feminist Re-Visions*.

Bernice Johnson Reagon, "Coalition Politics: Turning the Century." From Smith, *Home Girls*.

4. Epistemology: Objectivity myths and exclusions.

Dorothy E. Smith, *The Everyday World as Problematic*, ch. 2.

Patricia Hill Collins, "Toward an Afrocentric Feminist Epistemology" and

"Knowledge, Consciousness, and the Politics of Empowerment." From *Black Feminist Thought*.

Trinh T. Minh-ha, *Woman, Native, Other*, chs. 2–3.

5. What is "feminist methodology"?

Shulamit Reinharz, *Feminist Methods in Social Research*, Introduction, conclusion, and at least 3 additional chapters (choose those that seem most appropriate for you).

Marjorie DeVault, "Talking Back to Sociology: Distinctive Contributions of Feminist Methodology." *Annual Review of Sociology*, Vol. 22, 1996.

6. Nonsexist research methods/Approaches to quantitative and policy research.

Margrit Eichler, *Nonsexist Research Methods: A Practical Guide*.

Christine Oppong, "Family Structure and Women's Reproductive and Productive Roles: Some Conceptual and Methodological Issues." From Anker, Buvinic, and Youssef, *Women's Roles and Population Trends in the Third World*.

Roberta Spalter-Roth and Heidi Hartmann, "Small Happinesses: The Feminist Struggle to Integrate Social Research with Social Activism." From Gottfried, *Feminism and Social Change*.

7. Moral/ethical issues.

Nebraska Feminist Collective, "A Feminist Ethic." *Women's Studies International Forum*, 1983, 6:535–543.

Judith Stacey, "Can There Be a Feminist Ethnography?" From Gluck and Patai, *Women's Words*.

Daphne Patai, "U.S. Academics and Third World Women: Is Ethical Research Possible?" From Gluck and Patai, *Women's Words*.

RECOMMENDED: Elizabeth E. Wheatley, "How Can We Engender Ethnography with a Feminist Imagination?" *Women's Studies International Forum*, 1994, 17:403–416. (And exchange with Stacey, pp. 417–423.)

8. "Women's voices": Issues of representation.

Kathryn Anderson, Susan Armitage, Dana Jack, and Judith Wittner, "Beginning Where We Are: Feminist Methodology in Oral History." From Nielsen, *Feminist Research Methods*.

Joan W. Scott, "The Evidence of Experience." *Critical Inquiry* 1991, 17:773–797.

Marjorie Mbilinyi, "'I'd Have Been a Man': Politics and the Labor Process in Producing Personal Narratives." From Personal Narratives Group, *Interpreting Women's Lives: Feminist Theory and Personal Narratives*.

9. Self and subjectivity.

Susan Krieger, chs. 1, 4, 5 from *Social Science and the Self: Personal Essays on an Art Form.*

Alison M. Jaggar, "Love and Knowledge: Emotion in Feminist Epistemology." In Jaggar and Bordo, *Gender/Body/Knowledge: Feminist Reconstructions of Being and Knowing.*

Maria Lugones, "Playfulness, 'world'-travelling, and loving perception." In Anzaldúa, *Making Face, Making Soul/Haciendo Caras: Creative and Critical Perspectives by Feminists of Color.*

RECOMMENDED: Frigga Haug and others, *Female Sexualization: A Collective Work of Memory.*

10. Language.

Dale Spender, "The Dominant and the Muted" and "Woman Talk: The Legitimate Fear." From *Man Made Language.*

June Jordan, "Nobody Mean More to Me than You And the Future Life of Willie Jordan." From *On Call: Political Essays.*

Trinh T. Minh-ha, *Woman, Native, Other,* ch. 1.

RECOMMENDED: Marjorie DeVault, "Talking and Listening from Women's Standpoint: Feminist Strategies for Interviewing and Analysis. *Social Problems* 37(1):96–116, February, 1990; and "Ethnicity and Expertise: Racial-Ethnic Knowledge in Sociological Research." *Gender and Society* 9(5):612–631, October, 1995.

11. Analyzing social relations.

Smith, *The Everyday World as Problematic,* ch. 4–5.

Roxana Ng, "Immigrant Women: The Construction of a Labour Market Category." *Canadian Journal of Women and the Law* 1990, 4:96–112.

Adele Mueller, "Beginning in the Standpoint of Women: An Investigation of the Gap between *cholas* and 'Women of Peru.'" In Campbell and Manicom, *Knowledge, Experience, and Ruling Relations: Studies in the Social Organization of Knowledge.*

Liza McCoy, "Activating the Photographic Text." Also in Campbell and Manicom.

12. Research and activism/Social change.

Maria Mies, "Towards a Methodology for Feminist Research." From Bowles and Duelli Klein, *Theories of Women's Studies.*

Deborah A. Gordon, "Worlds of Consequences: Feminist Ethnography as Social Action." *Critique of Anthropology* 1993, 13:429–443.

George Smith, "Political Activist as Ethnographer." *Social Problems* 1990, 37:629–648.

Julie Park, "Research Partnerships: A Discussion Paper Based on Case Studies From 'The Place of Alcohol in the Lives of New Zealand Women' Project." *Women's Studies International Forum* 1992, 15: 581–591.

Ronnie J. Steinberg, "Advocacy Research for Feminist Policy Objectives: Experiences with Comparable Worth." From Gottfried, *Feminism and Social Change.*

Fiona Poland, "The History of a 'Failed' Research Topic: The Case of the Childminders." From Stanley, *Feminist Praxis.*

Anne Pugh, "My Statistics and Feminism—A True Story." From Stanley, *Feminist Praxis.*

13. Pushing boundaries: Postmodernist approaches.

Patti Lather, "Deconstructing/Deconstructive Inquiry" and "Reinscribing Otherwise." From *Getting Smart: Feminist Research and Pedagogy With/In the Postmodern.*

Trinh T. Minh-ha, *Woman, Native, Other*, ch. 4, "Grandma's Story."

Jackie Orr, "Theory on the Market: Panic, Incorporating." *Social Problems* 1990, 37: 460–484.

Notes

1. Becoming a Feminist: A Second-Generation Story

Acknowledgments: Some of the material in this chapter first appeared in my remarks at a panel discussion I organized jointly with Ruth Linden ("Works/ Disciplines/Lives: Locating Ourselves as Feminists in Sociology," Annual Stone Symposium of the Society for the Study of Symbolic Interaction, University of California, San Francisco, February, 1991); our discussions then shaped some of these reflections.

1. I have borrowed the phrase "cultural contradictions" from Mirra Komarovsky (1946), who describes aspects of the situation I mean to evoke in this section, even though her analysis is based on data from an earlier generation.

2. What I remember, actually, is an extended argument about the logistics of a dual-career marriage; as I recall it, I was the only one willing to argue that a woman shouldn't necessarily follow her husband wherever he might go. Now, as my partner and I struggle through our tenth year of a 300-mile separation, this memory has an uncomfortably ironic edge.

3. Her first article on the topic was Fennema (1974). She went on to collaborate with Julia Sherman on a series of studies sponsored by the National Science Foundation that examined differential participation and attitudes and were widely quoted as interest in gender and mathematics grew. Her most recent thinking on the topic is summarized in Fennema (1996). Other Wisconsin faculty who were important for my developing outlook were Jack Kean, in whose language arts class I read *Dick and Jane as Victims* (Women on Words and Images 1972), and my advisor Thomas Popkewitz, who introduced me to sociology via *The Social Construction of Reality* (Berger and Luckmann 1966).

4. This course, which provided the foundation for my understanding of women's studies as an academic field, was taught by literary scholars Susan Stanford Friedman and Susan Snaider Lanser.

5. Abu-Lughod was probably chosen to deliver this prestigious annual lecture because she had just published a book on North African cities. She surprised the faculty selection committee, she believes, when she used the occasion to address issues of women's status in the academy, which were being discussed by a newly-formed Organization of Women Faculty at Northwestern. The group still exists there, and Arlene Daniels's decision to use the 1993–94 lectureship to provide an update to Abu-Lughod's lecture illustrates the kind of collaborative activism I learned from them.

6. I relied heavily on Oakley (1974); Berheide, Fenstermaker Berk, and Berk (1976); Berk and Fenstermaker Berk (1979). There was also an earlier study

(Lopata 1971), which took "housewives" (rather than "housework") as the topic, but also took their activity seriously as work. And there was an emerging marxist literature on domestic labor.

7. Eventually the dissertation became a book (DeVault 1991).

8. I use the term "acceptable" with Sara Ruddick's analysis of "maternal thinking" in mind (Ruddick 1980, 1989). She points out that one of the demands of mothering is to produce a child "acceptable" to society—a demand that sometimes conflicts with mothers' own values.

9. For an account of her cancer experience in light of her writing on medical error, see Paget (1993). On women sociologists, see Reinharz (1988b, 1989) and the historical material in Reinharz (1992).

2. Talking Back to Sociology: Distinctive Contributions of Feminist Methodology

Acknowledgments: My title for this chapter is inspired by hooks (1989). The bibliography prepared by Nancy Naples and participants in the Sex and Gender Section's pre-conference workshop at the 1994 Annual Meeting of the American Sociological Association provided a valuable resource in my literature search. In addition, I'm grateful for comments on an earlier draft from Susan Borker, Robert Chibka, Julia Loughlin, Dorothy Smith, Barrie Thorne, and Judith Wittner, though I have not done justice to all their suggestions.

1. Scholars refer to the women's movement of the 1960s as the "second wave," to distinguish it from the earlier period of feminist organizing in the nineteenth century. The earlier wave also brought women into the universities and produced a significant body of work by feminist scholars; Reinharz's (1992) survey of feminist research includes these forerunners in order to emphasize the continuity of feminist concerns and strategies.

2. For reference to a similar history in Britain, see Stanley and Wise 1983/93; for the different story of Australian "femocrats," see Eisenstein 1995.

3. Institutional Ethnography: A Strategy for Feminist Inquiry

Acknowledgments: Portions of this chapter are based on my remarks in a presentation, prepared jointly with Alison I. Griffith, for the 1997 American Sociological Association Sex and Gender Section's pre-conference workshop on institutional ethnography. I am grateful to Alison not only for helpful discussion at that time, but for a decade of useful exchange. I have also incorporated material from a presentation at an American Sociological Association panel organized by Jaber Gubrium and James Holstein, "What Makes Qualitative Method Critical?" (1995 Annual Meeting, Washington, D.C.).

1. For example, Burawoy et al. 1991, whose extended case method shares ethnographic and marxist commitments with the approach discussed here, but ties inquiry much more closely to disciplinary theoretical development.

4. Talking and Listening from Women's Standpoint:
Feminist Strategies for Interviewing and Analysis

Acknowledgments: The earliest version of this chapter was presented at the annual meeting of the Society for the Study of Symbolic Interaction, New York, August 1986, and portions of that talk were excerpted in *Women and Language,* 1987, 10:33–36. I am indebted to Arlene Kaplan Daniels and Howard S. Becker for teaching me about interviewing and for helpful comments on this paper; to the late Marianne Paget, Dorothy E. Smith, Darlene Douglas-Steele, and Judith Wittner for many discussions of these issues; to the Stone Center for Developmental Services and Studies at Wellesley College, where I began to write this paper; and to Syracuse University, whose assistance enabled me to complete the work.

1. Compare Paget (1983) and Mishler (1986b). Mishler, though without making gender the issue, comments perceptively on the difference between Paget's case and an example from his own interviewing. He notes that their different practices produced quite different results.

2. Carol Gilligan's analysis of women's moral reasoning relies in part on a similar "hearing" of hesitation in women's speech. See Gilligan (1982:28–29, 31).

3. As an example, he cites the frequent use of "crutch words" such as "you know," though he warns that this kind of repetitiveness should not be confused with "controlled and conscious repetition for rhetorical effect" (Blauner 1987: 51). My discussion of the phrase "you know," above, suggests that such material can be analytically useful precisely because it is not used consciously by respondents toward some end, but rather points toward issues they cannot fully articulate.

4. Another solution to the problem—developing new vocabulary—has produced several experiments with the idea of a feminist dictionary (e.g., Daly and Caputi 1987, Kramarae and Treichler 1986). These books are resources that should encourage feminist sociologists to think about words in new ways. But, while feminists have successfully coined some new words ("sexism," for example), the usefulness of this kind of invention is limited by most of our audiences' impatience with such experimentation.

5. Ethnicity and Expertise:
Racial-Ethnic Knowledge in Sociological Research

Acknowledgments: This research was facilitated by an Appleby-Moser research grant from the Maxwell School of Citizenship and Public Affairs, Syracuse University; two research leaves granted by Syracuse University; and an appointment during 1993–94 as Visiting Scholar in the Women's Studies Program at Brandeis University. Rosanna Hertz, Catherine Kohler Riessman, Nancy Jurik, and Margaret L. Andersen made helpful comments on an early draft. And I am most grateful to all the dietitians and nutritionists who have spoken with me about their work.

1. I rely on a view of race-ethnicity that sees both as socially constructed, though materially consequential, categories of social differentiation (cf. Omi and Winant 1986, Nagel 1994, Frankenberg 1993). While there are clearly good rea-

sons to distinguish differences labeled "ethnic" and "racial" for some purposes, I want to avoid drawing a sharp distinction here. While I mean to work primarily with a notion of "race-ethnicity" (cf. Glenn 1987, Amott and Matthaei 1991), I prefer "ethnicity" as the umbrella term since it suggests sociocultural rather than fixed and essential differences.

2. Actually, this feature of the early discussions may be largely an effect of an older research tradition that follows positivist natural science models more closely. Such models construe issues of method as quite separate from findings; therefore, access and rapport are matters usually disposed of in introductory comments and kept out of the analysis.

3. These informants range in occupational status from a few paraprofessional workers in community clinics to a few university nutrition faculty. Because of my interest in activism and policy work within the profession, I emphasized, and oversampled, practitioners in the community nutrition area. About a quarter of the interviewees worked in hospital settings, by far the most common place of work for dietitians. Slightly less than half worked in community health settings, including WIC programs, programs providing food for elderly citizens, and county and community clinics. The remainder worked as private consultants, in corporations or food industry organizations, or in universities. Although none of the interviewees worked in food service management (another typical work site) at the time of the interviews, many had done this work earlier in their careers. Almost all had undergraduate, some graduate, degrees in nutrition, and most were certified by the American Dietetic Association as Registered Dietitians. Ethnically, all but four interviewees were white, and the white women who identified ethnically were of European descent (German, Irish, Italian). In addition to the three women of African descent who are discussed in this paper, there was one Asian American interviewee who had come to the United States as a college student. All but one of the informants were women.

4. The names used here are pseudonyms.

5. The WIC program (Special Supplemental Food Program for Women, Infants, and Children) is a major U.S. government nutrition program that provides food subsidies and nutrition education for low-income women who are pregnant and for their infants and children.

6. At the other end of the spectrum, in what is admittedly an unusual case, one white woman reported that she had dropped out of her degree program, in order to make a "political statement," just before she was certified. Within a year, one of her teachers sought her out at the hospital where she was working as a diet technician (the hospital equivalent of a nutrition assistant) and asked her quite sternly: "What *are* you *doing*?" After "a couple uncomfortable conversations," they worked out an informal arrangement that allowed her to complete the work necessary for certification.

7. Her "storytelling" approach to making meaning in this situation is similar to the narrative strategy adopted by "Marta," the Puerto Rican narrator in Riessman's (1987) study. My discussion suggests that this kind of strategy may not be tied to a speaker's ethnicity, but motivated by a context that makes communication difficult.

8. All of the community nutritionists I talked to shared with Janetta Thompson some awareness of the cultural dimension of their work. At a minimum, they spoke of the ethnic composition of their client groups, and the need to tailor services. Many spoke of the importance of bilingualism and a knowledge of different cultures. A few talked, much as Thompson did, about the politics of working as white, Euro-American professionals in African American and immigrant communities.

9. One might also suggest that, as in nutrition work, researchers in privileged groups have often relied on those from other racial-ethnic groups to bring such insights into the research community, a strategy that exploits the racial-ethnic knowledge of others rather than seeking such knowledge for oneself.

10. See Collins (1990:208) on knowledge and wisdom.

6. Novel Readings: The Social Organization of Interpretation

Acknowledgments: Work on this essay was carried out as part of the project on Modes of Representing Knowledge about Society, Center for Urban Affairs and Policy Research, Northwestern University, supported by a grant from the System Development Foundation. I am indebted to Howard S. Becker, the project director, for providing the opportunity to do this work and for helping to develop the analysis, and to the other members of our research group (Bernard Beck, James Bennett, Samuel Gilmore, Andrew Gordon, Robert K. LeBailly, Robin Leidner, Michal McCall, Lawrence McGill, and Lori Morris). I also wish to thank Robert Chibka for detailed comments on several drafts of the paper; Marianne Paget, Kathryn Addelson, Dorothy E. Smith, George V. Zito, Sam Kaplan, and several anonymous reviewers for thoughtful responses; and my sister Ileen DeVault for suggesting that I read Gordimer.

1. Examples of both arguments can be found in Burns and Burns (1973) and Routh and Wolff (1977).

2. Consider, e.g., the examples provided by Schutz (1962) or Garfinkel (1967).

3. Other examples can be culled from everyday observation; e.g., students read novels in sociology classes, social theorists refer to fictional anecdotes as if to actual events, citizens read novels and are moved to participate in social movements.

4. This distinction must be a heuristic rather than an absolute one; indeed, some theorists are interested in examining "society as text" in order to reveal cultural meanings associated with any kind of object.

5. Griswold (1987:1080–1081) provides a concise summary of "institutional" and "interpretive" approaches in the sociology of literature.

6. This social-organizational approach is related to research in the "production of culture," which treats cultural objects as products of the concerted work activities of artists, producers, and distributors (Peterson 1976, Coser 1978, Becker 1982), though studies in this tradition have rarely focused on processes of interpretation. For sociological approaches to textual interpretation, see Smith (1990a, especially chap. 6; 1990b, especially chap. 5), Chua (1979), McHoul (1982), and the articles by Iser and Fish in Tompkins (1980).

7. In taking statements as objects of analysis, my approach follows the logic of Scott and Lyman's (1968) discussion of excuses and justifications as "accounts."

8. My aim was to examine published readings available to a "literary world" in the United States as completely as possible. I searched for reviews of *The Late Bourgeois World* in *Book Review Digest* and *Book Review Index*. Of twenty-three listings, I analyzed fourteen; eight were excluded because they were in library trade journals whose reviews were typically only a paragraph or two, and one was in a British newspaper I was unable to obtain. I located critical articles about the novel through *MLA Bibliography* listings between 1966 and 1984. Although there were thirty-six references to Nadine Gordimer or her work, most of these dealt with other novels, with Gordimer's career, or with the censorship of Gordimer's writings. I located five sources that included some extended discussion of *The Late Bourgeois World;* these included three books (two devoted entirely to discussion of Gordimer's work) and two critical articles.

9. This convention works less well, however, for those literary scholars who have recently begun to attend to previously neglected texts, texts outside of traditional literary genres, and the politics of canon formation in general.

10. Wolff (1977) discusses this kind of problem in the sociology of literature in terms of Hans-Georg Gadamer's notion of a "hermeneutic circle."

11. This statement, and the comments that follow, represent the reading I constructed retrospectively on the basis of my remembered, rather amorphous responses during the initial *act* of reading. I take up the question of my two readings—initial and later versions—toward the end of the chapter.

12. This reviewer's plot summary mentions Max, Liz, and Graham and then identifies Bobo as "his son" in a sentence that gives Liz's child rather ambiguously to one of the men, apparently Graham. This grammatical imprecision seems to me a further indication of the reviewer's overpowering focus on Max and his situation.

13. Since three of the reviews are unattributed, there is no way to know the authors' genders.

14. The processes involved are similar to the processes of "inscription" (Latour and Woolgar 1979) or "re-representation" (Gerson and Star 1984) that constitute the textual basis of scientific work.

15. Differences between professional and amateur readings are more difficult to summarize. In both historical periods, amateur readings are certainly more difficult to study than published accounts produced by reviewers and critics, and I have included only my own lay account in this analysis. One of the requirements for further development of this kind of study will be methods for examining the activities of "ordinary" rather than "literary" reading. See Holland (1975) for one approach to experimental investigation and Radway (1984) for an approach to studying reading in a more natural setting.

16. As noted above, there is no perfect fit between being and reading as a woman. This observation raises the possibility that men too can read "as women," which seems to me feasible, and not necessarily undesirable, but probably quite difficult and relatively unlikely, both because women's experiences are "muted" in

the larger culture (E. Ardener 1975a,b), and because a structure of incentives and rewards encourages the telling of "male" stories (Long, 1988).

17. This observation, especially in the context of this analysis, calls to mind the phenomenon of the "feminist novel" and the ways that many women have used novels during the past two decades as part of the process of feminist consciousness raising. Such reading seems similar to that discussed by Brownstein (1982), who argues that girls and women read novels about heroines in a way that makes the stories both reflections of and patterns for their lives.

7. Whose Science of Food and Health? Narratives of Profession and Activism in Public Health Nutrition

Acknowledgments: Julia Loughlin, Linda Shaw, and Arlene Kaplan Daniels provided useful comments on an early draft of this chapter. I am also grateful to Adele Clarke, Virginia Olesen, and other participants in the "Re/visioning Women, Health and Healing" conference for helpful responses to my work and the inspiration of theirs. The question in my title alludes to the work of philosopher Sandra Harding (1991), who has been a leader in recent thinking about how feminists and other liberatory thinkers might transform science for their purposes.

1. Recent work in social studies of science, however, has revealed that this claim obscures a considerably "messier" and more complex practice and product (see, e.g., Latour and Woolgar 1979, Haraway 1989).

2. There are several ways in which existing feminist work on the professions has accomplished this kind of revision. Simply calling attention to the differences between historically "male" and "female" professions puts one kind of heterogeneity on the agenda (see, e.g., Stromberg 1988). Analyses of segregation and stratification within professions have also shown the differentiating effects of gender (Rossiter 1982) and race (Hine 1989). And studies that emphasize the struggle and contentiousness that always mark the process of professionalization (e.g., for nursing, see Melosh 1982, Reverby 1987, Fisher 1995) work against monolithic accounts of any professional field.

3. For exceptions to this pattern, however, see Griffith (1995) and Biklen (1995) on connections between teachers and mothers.

4. All names are pseudonyms. I have provided individual identification for the three women whose stories I analyze closely here; there are also occasional references to others included in the study, who are not identified by name.

5. See chap. 5, n. 5.

6. I have borrowed this characterization from Rupp and Taylor's (1987) account of U.S. feminism during its relatively quiescent period from World War II until the 1960s.

VI. Craft Knowledge of Feminist Research

1. I was nearly finished by the time I realized that my idea no doubt came in part from the example of my teacher, Howard S. Becker, who was himself working on a text about craft knowledge of research (Becker 1998).

11. From the Seminar Room: Practical Advice for Researchers

1. Appendix B lists specific readings I have used in the seminar.

2. Such judgments always remind me of Robin Morgan's (1977) book of essays, whose title, *Going Too Far,* suggests that feminist positions will almost always be seen by some as "extreme."

3. My discussion here emphasizes dynamics of knowledge production; but the disciplines as "professions" can present problems for women whether feminists or not, simply because some still feel that we are not "supposed" to belong.

4. My thanks to seminar member Robin Riley for providing this metaphorical contrast, in a moment of inspired exasperation.

5. These examples come from the Spring 1996 semester, when the seminar group carried on a series of sustained and often difficult debates, both in class sessions and on an email discussion list. The members of that group deserve special mention for pursuing issues of inclusion with courage and determination.

6. The Center on Human Policy, School of Education, Syracuse University, Syracuse, New York 13244.

References

Abu-Lughod, Janet L. 1981. "Engendering knowledge: Women and the university," College of Arts and Sciences Annual Faculty Lecture for 1980–81, Northwestern University, Evanston, Illinois.

Abu-Lughod, Lila. 1990. "Can there be a feminist ethnography?" *Women and Performance: A Journal of Feminist Theory* 5(1):7–27.

Acker, Joan, Kathleen Barry, and Joke Esseveld. 1983. "Objectivity and truth: Problems in doing feminist research." *Women's Studies International Forum* 6(4):423–435.

Allen, Pamela. 1973. "Free space." In *Radical Feminism*. Edited by Anne Koedt, Ellen Levine, and Anita Rapone, pp. 271–279. New York: Quadrangle. (Reprinted from *Free Space,* by Pam Allen, Times Change Press, 1970.)

American Dietetic Association. 1991. Selected Information from the 1990 Membership Database of The American Dietetic Association. Chicago: The American Dietetic Association.

Amott, Teresa, and Julie A. Matthaei. 1991. *Race, Gender, and Work: A Multicultural Economic History of Women in the United States.* Boston: South End Press.

Anderson, Elijah. 1978. *A Place on the Corner.* Chicago: University of Chicago Press.

Anderson, Kathryn, Susan Armitage, Dana Jack, and Judith Wittner. 1990. "Beginning where we are: Feminist methodology in oral history." In *Feminist Research Methods: Exemplary Readings in the Social Sciences.* Edited by Joyce McCarl Nielsen, pp. 94–112. Boulder: Westview.

Anzaldúa, Gloria. 1990a. *Making Face, Making Soul, Haciendo Caras: Creative and Critical Perspectives by Feminists of Color.* San Francisco: Aunt Lute Books.

———. 1990b. "La conciencia de la mestiza: Towards a new consciousness." In *Making Face, Making Soul, Haciendo Caras: Creative and Critical Perspectives by Feminists of Color.* Edited by Gloria Anzaldúa, pp. 377–389. San Francisco: Aunt Lute Books.

Ardener, Edwin. 1975a. "Belief and the problem of women." In *Perceiving Women.* Edited by Shirley Ardener, pp. 1–17. New York: John Wiley and Sons.

———. 1975b. "The 'problem' revisited." In *Perceiving Women.* Edited by Shirley Ardener, pp. 19–27. New York: John Wiley and Sons.

Ardener, Shirley, ed. 1975. *Perceiving Women.* New York: John Wiley and Sons.

Atkinson, J. Maxwell, and John Heritage. 1984. *Structures of Social Action: Studies in Conversation Analysis.* Cambridge: Cambridge University Press.

Baca Zinn, Maxine. 1979. "Field research in minority communities: Ethical, methodological and political observations by an insider." *Social Problems* 27: 209–219.

Baca Zinn, Maxine, Lynn Weber Cannon, Elizabeth Higginbotham, and Bonnie Thornton Dill. 1986. "The costs of exclusionary practices in women's studies." *Signs* 11(2):290–303.

Bannerji, Himani. 1995. *Thinking Through: Essays on Feminism, Marxism, and Anti-Racism*. Toronto: Women's Press.

Bauer, J. 1993. "Ma'ssoum's tale: The personal and political transformations of a young Iranian 'feminist' and her ethnographer." *Feminist Studies* 19(3): 519–548.

Becker, Howard S. 1982. *Art Worlds*. Berkeley: University of California Press.

———. 1986a. "Telling about society." In *Doing Things Together: Selected Papers*, 121–235. Evanston, Ill.: Northwestern University Press.

———. 1986b. *Writing for Social Scientists: How to Start and Finish Your Thesis, Book, or Article*. Chicago: University of Chicago Press.

———. 1998. *Tricks of the Trade: How to Think about Your Research While You're Doing It*. Chicago: University of Chicago Press.

Belenky, Mary Field, Blythe McVicker Clinchy, Nancy Rule Goldberger, and Jill Mattuck Tarrule. 1986. *Women's Ways of Knowing: The Development of Self, Voice, and Mind*. New York: Basic.

Belsey, Catherine. 1980. *Critical Practice*. London: Methuen.

Beoku-Betts, Josephine. 1994. "When Black is not enough: Doing field research among Gullah women." *NWSA Journal* 6(3):413–433.

Berger, Peter L., and Thomas Luckmann. 1966. *The Social Construction of Reality*. Garden City, N.J.: Doubleday.

Berheide, Catherine White, Sarah Fenstermaker Berk, and Richard A. Berk. 1976. "Household work in the suburbs: The job and its participants." *Pacific Sociological Review* 19:491–517.

Berk, Richard A., and Sarah Fenstermaker Berk. 1979. *Labor and Leisure at Home: Content and Organization of the Household Day*. Beverly Hills: Sage Publications.

Bhavnani, Kum-Kum. 1993. "Tracing the contours: Feminist research and feminist objectivity." *Women's Studies International Forum* 16(2):95–104.

Biklen, Sari Knopp. 1995. *School Work: Gender and the Cultural Construction of Teaching*. New York: Teachers College Press.

Billson, Janet Mancini. 1991. "The progressive verification method: Toward a feminist methodology for studying women cross-culturally." *Women's Studies International Forum* 14(3):201–215.

Blauner, Bob. 1987. "Problems of editing 'first-person' sociology." *Qualitative Sociology* 10:46–64.

Bleich, David. 1977. "The logic of interpretation." *Genre* 10:363–394.

Boden, Deirdre. 1990. "People are talking: Conversation analysis and symbolic interaction." In *Symbolic Interaction and Cultural Studies*. Edited by Howard S. Becker and Michal M. McCall, p. 244–274. Chicago: University of Chicago Press.

Boden, Deirdre, and Denise D. Bielby. 1986. "The way it was: Topical organization in elderly conversation." *Language and Communication* 6:73–89.

Bogdan, Robert, and Steven J. Taylor. 1975. *Introduction to Qualitative Research
Methods: A Phenomenological Approach to the Social Sciences.* New York:
John Wiley and Sons.

Bolles, A. Lynn. 1993. "Doing it for themselves: Women's research and action in
the commonwealth Caribbean." In *Researching Women in Latin America and
the Caribbean.* Edited by Edna Acosta-Belen and Christine E. Bose, pp. 153–
174. Boulder: Westview.

Bowles, Gloria, and Renate Duelli Klein, eds. 1983. *Theories of Women's Studies.*
London: Routledge and Kegan Paul.

Brown, Richard H. 1977. *A Poetic for Sociology.* Cambridge: Harvard University
Press.

Brownstein, Rachel M. 1982. *Becoming a Heroine: Reading about Women in
Novels.* New York: Viking Press.

Bulkin, Elly, Minnie Bruce Pratt, and Barbara Smith. 1984. *Yours in Struggle:
Three Feminist Perspectives on Anti-Semitism and Racism.* New York: Long
Haul Press.

Burawoy, Michael, et al. 1991. *Ethnography Unbound: Power and Resistance in
the Modern Metropolis.* Berkeley: University of California Press.

Burns, Elizabeth, and Tom Burns, eds. 1973. *Sociology of Literature and Drama.*
Harmondsworth: Penguin.

Campbell, Marie L. 1998. "Institutional ethnography and experience as data."
Qualitative Sociology 21(1):55–73.

Campbell, Marie, and Ann Manicom. 1995. *Knowledge, Experience, and Ruling
Relations: Studies in the Social Organization of Knowledge.* Toronto: University of Toronto Press.

Cancian, Francesca M. 1992. "Feminist science: Methodologies that challenge inequality." *Gender and Society* 6(4):623–642.

———. 1993. "Reply to Risman, Sprague and Howard." *Gender and Society*
7(4):610–611.

Cannon, Lynn Weber, Elizabeth Higginbotham, and Marianne L. A. Leung. 1988.
"Race and class bias in qualitative research on women." *Gender and Society*
2:449–462.

Chase, Susan E. 1995. *Ambiguous Empowerment: The Work Narratives of
Women School Superintendents.* Amherst: University of Massachusetts Press.

Chicago, Judy. 1975. *Through the Flower: My Struggle as a Woman Artist.* Garden City, N.Y.: Doubleday.

———. 1979. *The Dinner Party: A Symbol of Our Heritage.* Garden City, N.Y.:
Anchor Doubleday.

———. 1980. *Embroidering Our Heritage: The Dinner Party Needlework.* Garden City, N.Y.: Anchor Doubleday.

Chua, Beng-Hut. 1979. "Democracy as textual accomplishment." *Sociological
Quarterly* 20:541–549.

Clifford, James, and George E. Marcus, eds. 1986. *Writing Culture: The Poetics
and Politics of Ethnography.* Berkeley: University of California.

Clough, Patricia Ticineto. 1992. *The End(s) of Ethnography: From Realism to Social Criticism.* Newbury Park, Calif.: Sage.

———. 1993a. "On the brink of deconstructing sociology: Critical reading of Dorothy Smith's standpoint epistemology." *Sociological Quarterly* 34(1): 169–182.

———. 1993b. "Response to Smith's response." *Sociological Quarterly* 34(1): 193–194.

Cockburn C. 1992. "Technological change in a changing Europe: Does it mean the same for women as for men?" *Women's Studies International Forum* 15(1): 85–90.

Collins, Patricia Hill. 1990. *Black Feminist Thought: Knowledge, Consciousness, and the Politics of Empowerment.* Boston: Unwin Hyman.

———. 1992. "Transforming the inner circle: Dorothy Smith's challenge to sociological theory." *Sociological Theory* 10(1):73–80.

Combahee River Collective. 1982. "A black feminist statement." In *All the Women are White, All the Blacks are Men, But Some of Us are Brave.* Edited by Gloria T. Hull, Patricia Bell Scott, and Barbara Smith, pp. 13–22. Old Westbury, N.Y.: Feminist Press.

Connell, R. W. 1995. *Masculinities: Knowledge, Power, and Social Change.* Berkeley: University of California Press.

Cook, Judith A., and Mary Margaret Fonow. 1986. "Knowledge and women's interests: Issues of epistemology and methodology in feminist sociological research." *Sociological Inquiry* 56(1):2–29.

Coser, Lewis A., ed. 1978. Special issue. "The Production of Culture." *Social Research* 45.

Coser, Lewis A., Charles Kadushin, and Walter W. Powell. 1982. *Books: The Culture and Commerce of Publishing.* New York: Basic.

Cotterill, Pamela. 1992. "Interviewing women: Issues of friendship, vulnerability, and power." *Women's Studies International Forum* 15(5/6):593–606.

Culler, Jonathan. 1980. "Literary competence." In *Reader-Response Criticism from Formalism to Post-Structuralism.* Edited by Jane P. Tompkins, pp. 101–117. Baltimore: Johns Hopkins University Press.

———. 1982. *On Deconstruction: Theory and Criticism After Structuralism.* Ithaca: Cornell University Press.

Daly, Mary, and Jane Caputi. 1987. *Websters' First New Intergalactic Wickedary of the English Language.* Boston: Beacon Press.

Daniels, Arlene Kaplan. 1987. "Invisible work." *Social Problems* 34:403–415.

———. 1988. *Invisible Careers: Women Civic Leaders from the Volunteer World.* Chicago: University of Chicago Press.

———. 1994. "When we were all boys together: Graduate school in the fifties and beyond." In *Gender and the Academic Experience: Berkeley Women Sociologists.* Edited by Kathryn P. Meadow Orlans and Ruth A. Wallace, pp. 27–43. Lincoln: University of Nebraska Press.

Darroch, Vivian, and Ronald J. Silvers, eds. 1983. *Interpretive Human Studies: An Introduction to Phenomenological Research.* Lanham, Md.: University Press of America.

Deegan, Mary Jo. 1981. "Early women sociologists and the American Sociological Society: The patterns of exclusion and participation." *American Sociologist* 16:14–24.

———. 1988. *Jane Addams and the Men of the Chicago School, 1892–1918.* New Brunswick, N.J.: Transaction Books.

de Montigny, Gerald A. J. 1995. *Social Working: An Ethnography of Front-Line Practice.* Toronto: University of Toronto Press.

DeVault, Ileen. 1990. *Sons and Daughters of Labor: Class and Clerical Work in Turn-of-the-Century Pittsburgh.* Ithaca: Cornell University Press.

DeVault, Marj, Lisa Jones, and Patty Passuth. 1983. "Gender differences in graduate students' experiences." Unpublished paper prepared as a project of the Graduate Student Association, 1982–83. Evanston, Ill.: Department of Sociology, Northwestern University.

DeVault, Marjorie L. 1991. *Feeding the Family: The Social Organization of Caring as Gendered Work.* Chicago: University of Chicago Press.

———. 1995. "Between science and food: Nutrition professionals in the health-care hierarchy." In *Research on the Sociology of Health Care,* vol. 12. Edited by Jennie J. Kronenfeld, pp. 287–312. Greenwich: JAI Press.

———. 1997a. "Personal writing in social research." In *Voice and Reflexivity.* Edited by Rosanna Hertz, pp. 216–228. Thousand Oaks, Calif.: Sage.

———. 1997b. "'Are we alone?'" *Qualitative Sociology* 20(4):499–506.

DeVault, Marjorie L., and James P. Pitts. 1984. "Surplus and scarcity: Hunger and the origins of the food stamp program." *Social Problems* 31:545–557.

Diamond, Arlyn, and Lee R. Edwards, eds. 1977. *The Authority of Experience: Essays in Feminist Criticism.* Amherst: University of Massachusetts Press.

Dill, Bonnie Thornton. 1979. "The dialectics of black womanhood." *Signs* 4(3): 543–555.

Dixon-Mueller, Ruth. 1991. "Women in agriculture: Counting the labor force in developing countries." In *Beyond Methodology: Feminist Scholarship as Lived Research.* Edited by Mary Margaret Fonow and Judith A. Cook, pp. 226–247. Bloomington: Indiana University Press.

Echols, Alice. 1989. *Daring to Be Bad: Radical Feminism in America, 1967–1975.* Minneapolis: University of Minnesota Press.

Edwards, Rosalind. 1990. "Connecting method and epistemology: A white woman interviewing black women." *Women's Studies International Forum* 13:477–490.

Eichler, Margrit. 1988. *Nonsexist Research Methods: A Practical Guide.* Boston: Unwin Hyman.

Eisenstein, Hester. 1995. "The Australian femocratic experiment: A feminist case for bureaucracy." In *Feminist Organizations: Harvest of the New Women's Movement.* Edited by Myra Marx Ferree and Patricia Yancey Martin, pp. 69–83. Philadelphia: Temple University Press.

Ellis, Carolyn. 1993. "'There are survivors': Telling a story of sudden death." *Sociological Quarterly* 34(4):711–730.

Evans, Sara. 1979. *Personal Politics: The Roots of Women's Liberation in the Civil Rights Movement and the New Left.* New York: Random House.

Farran, Denise. 1990. "'Seeking Susan': Producing statistical information on young people's leisure." In *Feminist Praxis: Research, Theory and Epistemology in Feminist Sociology.* Edited by Liz Stanley, pp. 91–102. New York: Routledge.

Fausto-Sterling, Anne, and Lydia L. English. 1987. "Women and minorities in science: An interdisciplinary course." *Radical Teacher* 30:16–20.

Fennema, Elizabeth. 1974. "Mathematics learning and the sexes: A review." *Journal for Research in Mathematics Education,* 5:126–139.

———. 1996. "Mathematics, gender, and research." In *Towards Gender Equity in Mathematics Education.* Edited by Gila Hanna, pp. 9–26. Dordrecht: Kluwer.

Ferree, Myra Marx, and Patricia Yancey Martin. 1995. *Feminist Organizations: Harvest of the New Women's Movement.* Philadelphia: Temple University Press.

Fetterley, Judith. 1978. *The Resisting Reader: A Feminist Approach to American Fiction.* Bloomington: Indiana University Press.

Fish, Stanley E. 1980. *Is There a Text in This Class?* Cambridge: Harvard University Press.

Fisher, Berenice. 1990. "Alice in the human services: A feminist analysis of women in the caring professions." In *Circles of Care: Work and Identity in Women's Lives.* Edited by Emily K. Abel and Margaret K. Nelson, pp. 108–131. Albany: State University of New York Press.

Fisher, Sue. 1995. *Nursing Wounds: Nurse Practitioners, Doctors, Women Patients, and the Negotiation of Meaning.* New Brunswick, N.J.: Rutgers University Press.

Fisher, Sue, and Alexandra Dundas Todd. 1983. *The Social Organization of Doctor-Patient Communication.* Washington, D.C.: Center for Applied Linguistics.

Fishman, Pamela M. 1978. "Interaction: The work women do." *Social Problems* 25:397–406.

Fonow, Mary Margaret, and Judith A. Cook. 1991. *Beyond Methodology: Feminist Scholarship as Lived Research.* Bloomington: Indiana University Press.

Foucault, Michel. 1972. *The Archaeology of Knowledge.* New York: Pantheon.

Frankenberg, Ruth. 1993. *White Women, Race Matters: The Social Construction of Whiteness.* Minneapolis: University of Minnesota Press.

Freeman, Jo. 1973. "The tyranny of structurelessness." In *Radical Feminism.* Edited by Anne Koedt, Ellen Levine, and Anita Rapone, pp. 271–279. New York: Quadrangle. Reprinted from *The Second Wave* 2(1): 20, 1972.

———. 1975. *The Politics of Women's Liberation: A Case Study of an Emerging Social Movement and Its Relation to the Policy Process.* New York: David McKay.

Friedan, Betty. 1963. *The Feminine Mystique.* New York: Norton.

Frontiers. 1993. Special issue. "Feminist Dilemmas in Fieldwork." Vol. 13, no. 3.

Frye, Marilyn. 1983. *The Politics of Reality: Essays in Feminist Theory.* Trumansburg, N.Y.: The Crossing Press.

Game, Ann. 1991. *Undoing the Social: Towards a Deconstructive Sociology*. Toronto: University of Toronto Press.

Garfinkel, Harold. 1967. *Studies in Ethnomethodology*. Englewood Cliffs, N.J.: Prentice-Hall.

Gelsthorpe, Loraine. 1992. "Response to Martyn Hammersley's paper 'On feminist methodology.'" *Sociology* 26(2):213–218.

Gerson, Elihu M., and Susan Leigh Star. 1984. "Representation and re-representation in scientific work." Unpublished working paper. San Francisco: Tremont Research Institute.

Gilkes, Cheryl Townsend. 1982. "Successful rebellious professionals: The Black woman's professional identity and community commitment." *Psychology of Women Quarterly* 6:289–311.

———. 1983. "Going up for the oppressed: The career mobility of Black women community workers." *Journal of Social Issues* 39:115–139.

Gilligan, Carol. 1982. *In a Different Voice*. Boston: Harvard University Press.

Glazer, Nona Y. 1991. "Between a rock and a hard place: Women's professional organizations in nursing." *Gender and Society* 5:351–372.

Glazer-Malbin, Nona, and H. Y. Waehrer. 1971. *Woman in a Man-Made World*. Chicago: Rand McNally.

Glenn, Evelyn Nakano. 1987. "Racial ethnic women's labor: The intersection of race, gender, and class oppression." In *Hidden Aspects of Women's Work*. Edited by Christine Bose, Roslyn Feldberg, and Natalie Sokoloff, with the Women and Work Research Group, pp. 46–73. New York: Praeger.

Gluck, Sherna Berger, and Daphne Patai. 1991. *Women's Words: The Feminist Practice of Oral History*. New York: Routledge.

Goetting, Ann, and Sarah Fenstermaker. 1995. *Individual Voices, Collective Visions: Fifty Years of Women in Sociology*. Philadelphia: Temple University Press.

Goodwin, Charles. 1979. "The interactive construction of a sentence in natural conversation." In *Everyday Language: Studies in Ethnomethodology*. Edited by George Psathas, pp. 97–121. New York: Irvington.

Goodwin, Charles, and Marjorie H. Goodwin. 1989. "Conflicting participation frameworks." Paper presented at the annual meetings of the American Sociological Association, San Francisco.

Gordimer, Nadine. 1966. *The Late Bourgeois World*. New York: Penguin.

Gordon, Deborah A. 1988. "Writing culture, writing feminism: The poetics and politics of experimental ethnography." *Inscriptions* 3/4:7–24.

———. 1993. "Worlds of consequences: Feminist ethnography as social action." *Critique of Anthropology* 13(4):429–443.

Gordon, Margaret T., and Stephanie Riger. 1989. *The Female Fear*. New York: Free Press.

Gorelick, Sherry. 1989. "The changer and the changed: Methodological reflections on studying Jewish feminists." In *Gender/Body/Knowledge: Feminist Reconstructions of Being and Knowing*. Edited by Alison M. Jaggar and Susan R. Bordo, pp. 336–358. New Brunswick, N.J.: Rutgers University Press.

————. 1991. "Contradictions of feminist methodology." *Gender and Society* 5(4):459–477.

Gould, Stephen Jay. 1981. *The Mismeasure of Man.* New York: Norton.

Grahame, Peter. 1998. "Ethnography, institutions, and the problematic of the everyday world." *Human Studies* 21:347–360.

Greenhalgh, Susan, and Jiali Li. 1995. "Engendering reproductive policy and practice in peasant China: For a feminist demography of reproduction." *Signs* 20(3):601–641.

Griffith, Alison I. 1995. "Mothering, schooling, and children's development." In *Knowledge, Experience, and Ruling Relations: Studies in the Social Organization of Knowledge.* Edited by Marie Campbell and Ann Manicom, pp. 108–121. Toronto: University of Toronto Press.

Griffith, Alison I., and Dorothy E. Smith. 1987. "Constructing cultural knowledge: Mothering as discourse." In *Women and Education: A Canadian Perspective.* Edited by Jane Gaskell and Arlene McLaren, pp. 87–103. Calgary, Alberta: Detselig.

Griswold, Wendy. 1987. "The fabrication of meaning: Literary interpretation in the United States, Great Britain, and the West Indies." *American Journal of Sociology* 92:1077–1117.

Hall, Budd L. 1975. "Participatory research: An approach for change." *Convergence* 8(2):24–31.

Hanmer, Jalna, and Sheila Saunders. 1984. *Well-Founded Fear: A Community Study of Violence to Women.* London: Hutchinson.

Haraway, Donna. 1985. "A manifesto for cyborgs: Science, technology, and socialist feminism in the 1980s." *Socialist Review* 15(2):65–107.

————. 1988. "Situated knowledges: The science question in feminism and the privilege of partial perspective." *Feminist Studies* 14(3):575–599.

————. 1989. *Primate Visions: Gender, Race, and Nature in the World of Modern Science.* New York: Routledge.

Harding, Sandra. 1986. *The Science Question in Feminism.* Ithaca: Cornell University Press.

————, ed. 1987. *Feminism and Methodology: Social Science Issues.* Bloomington: Indiana University Press.

————. 1991. *Whose Science? Whose Knowledge?: Thinking from Women's Lives.* Ithaca: Cornell University Press.

————. 1992. "Rethinking standpoint epistemology: What is 'strong objectivity'?" *Centennial Review* 36(3):437–470.

Hartsock, Nancy M. 1981. "The feminist standpoint: Developing the ground for a specifically feminist historical materialism." In *Discovering Reality: Feminist Perspectives on Epistemology, Metaphysics, Methodology, and Philosophy of Science.* Edited by Sandra Harding and Merrill Hintikka, pp. 283–310. Boston: Reidel.

Haug, Frigga, et al. 1987. *Female Sexualization: A Collective Work of Memory.* London: Verso.

Heritage, John. 1984. *Garfinkel and Ethnomethodology.* Cambridge, U.K.: Polity Press.

Hertz, Rosanna, and Jonathan B. Imber, eds. 1995. *Studying Elites Using Qualitative Methods*. Thousand Oaks, Calif.: Sage.

Hill, Bridget. 1993. "Women, work and the census: A problem for historians of women." *History Workshop Journal* 35:78–94.

Hine, Darlene Clark. 1989. *Black Women in White: Racial Conflict and Cooperation in the Nursing Profession, 1890–1950*. Bloomington: Indiana University Press.

Holland, Norman N. 1975. *Five Readers Reading*. New Haven: Yale University Press.

hooks, bell. 1981. *Ain't I a Woman: Black Women and Feminism*. Boston: South End Press.

———. 1984. *Feminist Theory: From Margin to Center*. Boston: South End Press.

———. 1989. *Talking Back: Thinking Feminist, Thinking Black*. Boston: South End Press.

Howell, Mary. 1979. "Can we be feminists and professionals?" *Women's Studies International Quarterly* 2:1–7.

Hughes, Everett. 1984. "The place of field work in social science." In *The Sociological Eye: Selected Papers*. New Brunswick, N.J.: Transaction Books.

Hull, Gloria T., Patricia Bell Scott, and Barbara Smith, eds. 1982. *All the Women are White, All the Blacks are Men, But Some of Us are Brave*. Old Westbury, N.Y.: Feminist Press.

Hunter, Albert, ed. 1990. *The Rhetoric of Sociology*. New Brunswick, N.J.: Rutgers University Press.

Ingraham, Chrys. 1992. "Out of Print, Out of Mind: Toward a Materialist Feminist Theory of Censorship and Suppression." Ph.D. dissertation, Syracuse University.

———. 1994. "The heterosexual imaginary: Feminist sociology and theories of gender." *Sociological Theory* 12(2):203–219.

Inscriptions. 1988. Special issue. "Feminism and the Critique of Colonial Discourse." Nos. 3/4.

Iser, Wolfgang. 1978. *The Act of Reading: A Theory of Aesthetic Response*. Baltimore: Johns Hopkins University Press.

Jackson, Jacquelyn Johnson. 1973. "Black women in a racist society." In *Racism and Mental Health*. Edited by Charles V. Willie, Bernard M. Kramer, and Bertrand S. Brown, pp. 185–268. Pittsburgh: University of Pittsburgh Press.

Jaggar, Alison M. 1989. "Love and knowledge: Emotion in feminist epistemology." In *Gender/Body/Knowledge: Feminist Reconstructions of Being and Knowing*. Edited by Alison M. Jaggar and Susan R. Bordo, pp. 145–171. New Brunswick, N.J.: Rutgers University Press.

Jaggar, Alison M., and Susan R. Bordo, eds. 1989. *Gender/Body/Knowledge: Feminist Reconstructions of Being and Knowing*. New Brunswick, N.J.: Rutgers University Press.

Jauss, Hans Robert. 1970. "Literary history as a challenge to literary theory." *New Literary History* 2:7–37.

Jordan, June. 1985. *On Call: Political Essays*. Boston: South End Press.

Joseph, Gloria I., and Jill Lewis. 1981. *Common Differences: Conflicts in Black and White Feminist Perspectives.* New York: Anchor Doubleday.

Kanter, Rosabeth Moss. 1977. *Men and Women of the Corporation.* New York: Basic Books.

Kasper, Anne. 1994. "A feminist, qualitative methodology: A study of women with breast cancer." *Qualitative Sociology* 17(3):263–281.

Katz, Jack. 1983. "A theory of qualitative methodology: The social system of analytic fieldwork." In *Contemporary Field Research.* Edited by Robert M. Emerson, pp. 127–148. Boston: Little Brown.

Keller, Evelyn Fox. 1985. *Reflections on Gender and Science.* New Haven: Yale University Press.

Kelly, Liz, Sheila Burton, and Linda Regan. 1994. "Researching women's lives or studying women's oppression: What constitutes feminist research?" In *Researching Women's Lives from a Feminist Perspective.* Edited by Mary Maynard and June Purvis, pp. 27–48. London: Taylor and Francis.

Kimmel, Michael S., and Michael A. Messner. 1998. *Men's Lives* (4th ed.). Boston: Allyn and Bacon.

Kolodny, Annette. 1981. "Dancing through the mine-field: Some observations on the theory, practice, and politics of a feminist literary criticism." In *Men's Studies Modified.* Edited by Dale Spender, pp. 23–42. New York: Pergamon Press.

Komarovsky, Mirra. 1946. "Cultural contradictions and sex roles." *American Journal of Sociology* 52:184–189.

Kondo, Dorinne K. 1990. *Crafting Selves: Power, Gender, and Discourses of Identity in a Japanese Workplace.* Chicago: University of Chicago Press.

Kramarae, Cheris, and Dale Spender, eds. 1992. *The Knowledge Explosion: Generations of Feminist Scholarship.* New York: Teachers College Press.

Kramarae, Cheris, and Paula A. Treichler. 1986. *A Feminist Dictionary.* New York: Routledge, Chapman, and Hall.

Kremer, Belinda. 1990. "Learning to say no: Keeping feminist research for ourselves." *Women's Studies International Forum* 13:463–467.

Krieger, Susan. 1983. *The Mirror Dance: Identity in a Women's Community.* Philadelphia: Temple University Press.

———. 1991. *Social Science and the Self: Personal Essays on an Art Form.* New Brunswick, N.J.: Rutgers University Press.

———. 1996. *The Family Silver: Essays on Relationships among Women.* Berkeley: University of California Press.

Ladner, Joyce A. 1971. *Tomorrow's Tomorrow: The Black Woman.* Garden City, N.Y.: Doubleday.

———, ed. 1973. *The Death of White Sociology.* New York: Random House.

Lakoff, Robin. 1975. *Language and Women's Place.* New York: Harper and Row.

Lather, Patti. 1991. *Getting Smart: Feminist Research and Pedagogy With/In the Postmodern.* London: Routledge.

———. 1993. "Fertile obsession: Validity after poststructuralism. *Sociological Quarterly* 34(4):673–693.

Latour, Bruno. 1984. Unpublished manuscript. (Some of the same ideas are discussed in Latour, Bruno, and Francoise Bastide. 1983. "Essai de science-fabrication." *Etudes Francaises* 19:111–133.)

Latour, Bruno, and Steve Woolgar. 1979. *Laboratory Life: The Social Construction of Scientific Facts.* Beverly Hills: Sage.

Leidner, Robin. 1991. "Stretching the boundaries of liberalism: Democratic innovation in a feminist organization." *Signs* 16:263–289.

Lengermann, Patricia Madoo, and Jill Niebrugge-Brantley. 1998. *The Women Founders: Sociology and Social Theory, 1830–1930.* Boston: McGraw-Hill.

Lessing, Doris. [1962] 1973. *The Golden Notebook,* with a new introduction by the author. New York: Bantam Books.

Levenstein, Harvey A. 1988. *Revolution at the Table: The Transformation of the American Diet.* New York: Oxford University Press.

Leveque-Lopman, Louise. 1988. *Claiming Reality: Phenomenology and Women's Experience.* Totowa, N.J.: Rowan and Littlefield.

Liebow, Elliott. 1967. *Tally's Corner.* Boston: Little Brown.

Linden, R. Ruth. 1993. *Making Stories, Making Selves: Feminist Reflections on the Holocaust.* Columbus: Ohio State University Press.

Liquori, Toni. 1995. "Food Matters: The Influence of Gender on Science and Practice in the Nutrition Profession: An Institutional Ethnography." Ed.D. dissertation, Teacher's College, Columbia University.

Long, Judy. 1988. "Telling Women's Lives." Unpublished manuscript.

———. 1989. "Telling women's lives: 'Slant,' 'straight,' and 'messy.'" *Current Perspectives on Aging and the Life Cycle* 3:191–223.

Lopata, Helena Z. 1971. *Occupation: Housewife.* New York: Oxford University Press.

Lorde, Audre. 1981. "The master's tools will never dismantle the master's house." In *This Bridge Called My Back: Writings by Radical Women of Color.* Edited by Cherríe Moraga and Gloria Anzaldúa, pp. 98–101. Watertown, Mass.: Persephone Press.

Lugones, Maria. 1987. "Playfulness, 'world'-travelling, and loving perception." *Hypatia* 2(2):3–19.

Lugones, Maria C., and Elizabeth V. Spelman. 1983. "Have we got a theory for you! Feminist theory, cultural imperialism and the demand for 'the woman's voice.'" *Women's Studies International Forum* 6:573–581.

Luttrell, Wendy. 1988. "Working-class women's ways of knowing: Effects of gender, race, and class." Paper presented at the American Sociological Association Annual Meeting. Atlanta.

———. 1997. *Schoolsmart and Motherwise: Working-Class Women's Identity and Schooling.* New York: Routledge.

MacKinnon, Catharine. 1983. "Feminism, marxism, method, and the state: An agenda for theory." In *The Signs Reader.* Edited by Elizabeth Abel and Emily K. Abel, pp. 227–256. Chicago: University of Chicago Press.

Maguire, Patricia. 1987. *Doing Participatory Research: A Feminist Approach.* Amherst, Mass.: Center for International Education, University of Massachusetts.

Mansbridge, Jane. 1995. "What is the feminist movement?" In *Feminist Organizations: Harvest of the New Women's Movement.* Edited by Myra Marx Ferree and Patricia Yancey Martin, pp. 27–34. Philadelphia: Temple University Press.

Marshall, Annecka. 1994. "Sensuous Sapphires: A study of the social construction of Black female sexuality." In *Researching Women's Lives from a Feminist Perspective.* Edited by Mary Maynard and June Purvis, pp. 106–124. London: Taylor and Francis.

Mascia-Lees, Frances E., Patricia Sharpe, and Colleen Ballerino Cohen. 1989. "The postmodernist turn in anthropology: Cautions from a feminist perspective." *Signs* 15:7–33.

Maynard, Douglas W., and Don H. Zimmerman. 1984. "Topical talk, ritual and the social organization of relationships." *Social Psychology Quarterly* 47: 301–316.

Maynard, Mary, and June Purvis, eds. 1994. *Researching Women's Lives from a Feminist Perspective.* London: Taylor and Francis.

McCoy, Liza. 1995. "Activating the photographic text." In *Knowledge, Experience, and Ruling Relations: Studies in the Social Organization of Knowledge.* Edited by Marie Campbell and Ann Manicom, pp. 181–192. Toronto: University of Toronto Press.

McDermott, Patrice. 1994. *Politics and Scholarship: Feminist Academic Journals and the Production of Knowledge.* Urbana: University of Illinois Press.

McDowell, Deborah E. 1986. "'The changing same': Generational connections and Black women novelists." *New Literary History* 18:281–302.

McHoul, A. W. 1982. *Telling How Texts Talk: Essays on Reading and Ethnomethodology.* London: Routledge and Kegan Paul.

McIntosh, Peggy. 1988. "White privilege and male privilege: A personal account of coming to see correspondences through work in women's studies." No. 189. Wellesley College Center for Research on Women. Wellesley, Mass.

Melosh, Barbara. 1982. *"The Physician's Hand": Work Culture and Conflict in American Nursing.* Philadelphia: Temple University Press.

Merton, Robert K. 1972. "Insiders and outsiders: A chapter in the sociology of knowledge." *American Journal of Sociology* 78:9–48.

Messner, Michael A. 1992. *Power at Play: Sports and the Problem of Masculinity.* Boston: Beacon.

Mies, Maria. 1983. "Towards a methodology for feminist research." In *Theories of Women's Studies.* Edited by Gloria Bowles and Renate Duelli Klein, pp. 117–139. London: Routledge and Kegan Paul.

———. 1991. "Women's research or feminist research? The debate surrounding feminist science and methodology." In *Beyond Methodology: Feminist Scholarship as Lived Research.* Edited by Judith A. Cook and Mary Margaret Fonow, pp. 60–84. Bloomington: Indiana University Press.

Millar, Jane. 1992. "Cross-national research on women in the European Community: The case of solo women." *Women's Studies International Forum* 15(1): 77–84.

Miller, Casey, and Kate Swift. 1977. *Words and Women.* Garden City, N.Y.: Anchor Doubleday.

Miller, Jean Baker. 1976. *Toward a New Psychology of Women.* Boston: Beacon.
———. 1986. "What do we mean by relationships?" Working paper no. 22, Stone Center for Developmental Services and Studies, Wellesley College, Wellesley, Mass.

Millman, Marcia, and Rosabeth Moss Kanter. 1975. *Another Voice: Feminist Perspectives on Social Life and Social Science.* Garden City, N.Y.: Anchor Doubleday.

Mills, C. Wright. 1959. *The Sociological Imagination.* New York: Oxford University Press.

Mishler, Elliot G. 1984. *The Discourse of Medicine: Dialectics of Medical Interviews.* Norwood, N.J.: Ablex.
———. 1986a. *Research Interviewing: Context and Narrative.* Cambridge: Harvard University Press.
———. 1986b. "The analysis of interview-narratives." In *Narrative Psychology: The Storied Nature of Human Conduct.* Edited by T. R. Sarbin, pp. 233–255. New York: Praeger.

Moerman, Michael. 1988. *Talking Culture: Ethnography and Conversation Analysis.* Philadelphia: University of Pennsylvania Press.

Mohanty, Chandra Talpede. 1991a. "Cartographies of struggle: Third world women and the politics of feminism." In *Third World Women and the Politics of Feminism.* Edited by Chandra Talpede Mohanty, Ann Russo, and Lourdes Torres, pp. 1–47. Bloomington: Indiana University Press.
———. 1991b. "Under Western eyes: Feminist scholarship and colonial discourses." In *Third World Women and the Politics of Feminism.* Edited by Chandra Talpede Mohanty, Ann Russo, and Lourdes Torres, pp. 51–80. Bloomington: Indiana University Press.

Mohanty, Chandra Talpede, Ann Russo, and Lourdes Torres, eds. 1991. *Third World Women and the Politics of Feminism.* Bloomington: Indiana University Press.

Moraga, Cherríe, and Gloria Anzaldúa, eds. 1981. *This Bridge Called My Back: Writings by Radical Women of Color.* Watertown, Mass.: Persephone (2d ed. 1983. New York: Kitchen Table Women of Color Press).

Morgan, Robin. 1977. *Going Too Far: The Personal Chronicle of a Feminist.* New York: Random House.

Nader, Laura. 1969. "Up the anthropologist: Perspectives gained from studying up." In *Reinventing Anthropology.* Edited by Dell Hymes, pp. 284–311. New York: Vintage.

Nagel, Joane. 1994. "Constructing ethnicity: Creating and recreating ethnic identity and culture." *Social Problems* 41:152–176.

Narayan, Uma. 1989. "The project of feminist epistemology: Perspectives from a nonwestern feminist." In *Gender/Body/Knowledge: Feminist Reconstructions of Being and Knowing.* Edited by Alison M. Jaggar and Susan R. Bordo, pp. 256–269. New Brunswick, N.J.: Rutgers University Press.

Nebraska Feminist Collective. 1983. "A feminist ethic for social science research." *Women's Studies International Forum* 6(5):535–543.

Nebraska Sociological Feminist Collective, ed. 1988. *A Feminist Ethic for Social Science Research*. Lewiston, N.Y.: Edwin Mellen.

Nielsen, Joyce McCarl. 1990. *Feminist Research Methods: Exemplary Readings in the Social Sciences*. Boulder: Westview.

Oakley, Ann. 1974. *The Sociology of Housework*. New York: Pantheon Books.

———. 1981. "Interviewing women: A contradiction in terms." In *Doing Feminist Research*. Edited by Helen Roberts, pp. 30–61. London: Routledge and Kegan Paul.

Ochs, Elinor. 1979. "Transcription as theory." In *Developmental Pragmatics*. Edited by Elinor Ochs and Bambi B. Schieffelin, pp. 43–72. New York: Academic Press.

Olesen, Virginia L., and Elvi W. Whittaker. 1968. *The Silent Dialogue: A Study in the Social Psychology of Professional Socialization*. San Francisco: Jossey-Bass.

Olsen, Tillie. [1965] 1978. *Silences*. New York: Dell.

Omi, Michael, and Howard Winant. 1986. *Racial Formation in the United States: From the 1960s to the 1980s*. New York: Routledge and Kegan Paul.

Opie, Anne. 1992. "Qualitative research, appropriation of the 'other' and empowerment." *Feminist Review* 40:52–69.

Oppong, Christine. 1982. "Family structure and women's reproductive and productive roles: Some conceptual and methodological issues." In *Women's Roles and Population Trends in the Third World*. Edited by Richard Anker, Mayra Buvinic, and Nadia H. Youssef, pp. 133–150. London: Croon Helm.

Orlans, Kathryn P. Meadow, and Ruth A. Wallace. 1994. *Gender and the Academic Experience: Berkeley Women Sociologists*. Lincoln: University of Nebraska Press.

Orr, Jackie. 1990. "Theory on the market: Panic, incorporating." *Social Problems* 37(4):460–484.

Ortega y Gasset, Jose. 1968. *The Dehumanization of Art and Other Essays on Art, Culture and Literature*. Princeton: Princeton University Press.

Paget, Marianne A. 1981. "The ontological anguish of women artists." *The New England Sociologist* 3:65–79.

———. 1983. "Experience and knowledge." *Human Studies* 6:67–90.

———. 1990. "'Unlearning to not speak.'" *Human Studies* 13:147–161.

———. 1993. *A Complex Sorrow: Reflections on Cancer and an Abbreviated Life*. Edited by Marjorie L. DeVault. Philadelphia: Temple University Press.

Park, Julie. 1992. "Research partnerships: A discussion paper based on case studies from 'The place of alcohol in the lives of New Zealand women' project." *Women's Studies International Forum* 15(5/6):581–591.

Patai, Daphne. 1991. "U.S. academics and third world women: Is ethical research possible?" In *Women's Words: The Feminist Practice of Oral History*. Edited by Sherna Berger Gluck and Daphne Patai, pp. 137–153. New York: Routledge.

Personal Narratives Group. 1989. *Interpreting Women's Lives: Feminist Theory and Personal Narratives*. Bloomington: Indiana University Press.

Peters, Suzanne. 1985. "Reflections on studying mothering, motherwork, and mothers' work." Paper presented at The Motherwork Workshop, Institut Simone de Beauvoir, Concordia University, Montreal.

Peterson, Richard, ed. 1976. *The Production of Culture*. Beverly Hills: Sage.

Phoenix, Ann. 1994. "Practising feminist research: The intersection of gender and 'race' in the research process." In *Researching Women's Lives from a Feminist Perspective*. Edited by Mary Maynard and June Purvis, pp. 49–71. London: Taylor and Francis.

Piercy, Marge. 1973. *To Be Of Use*. Garden City, N.Y.: Doubleday.

Psathas, George. 1973. *Phenomenological Sociology: Issues and Applications*. New York: Wiley and Sons.

———. 1995. *Conversation Analysis: The Study of Talk-in-Interaction*. Thousand Oaks: Sage.

Pugh, Anne. 1990. "My statistics and feminism: A true story." In *Feminist Praxis: Research, Theory and Epistemology in Feminist Sociology*. Edited by Liz Stanley, pp. 103–112. New York: Routledge.

Radford, Jill. 1987. "Policing male violence: Policing women." In *Women, Violence, and Social Control*. Edited by Jalna Hanmer and Mary Maynard, pp. 30–45. Atlantic Highlands, N.J.: Humanities Press International.

Radway, Janice A. 1984. *Reading the Romance: Women, Patriarchy and Popular Literature*. Chapel Hill: University of North Carolina Press.

Ramazanoglu, Caroline. 1989. "Improving on sociology: The problems of taking a feminist standpoint." *Sociology* 23(3):427–442.

Reay, Diane. 1995. "The fallacy of easy access." *Women's Studies International Forum* 18(2):205–213.

Reagon, Bernice Johnson. 1983. "Coalition politics: Turning the century." In *Home Girls: A Black Feminist Anthology*. Edited by Barbara Smith, pp. 356–368. New York: Kitchen Table Press.

Reinharz, Shulamit. 1979. *On Becoming a Social Scientist*. San Francisco: Jossey-Bass.

———. 1983. "Experiential analysis: A contribution to feminist research." In *Theories of Women's Studies*. Edited by Gloria Bowles and Renate Duelli Klein, pp. 162–191. London: Routledge and Kegan Paul.

———. 1984. "Toward a model of female political action: The case of Manya Shohat, founder of the first kibbutz." *Women's Studies International Forum* 7:275–287.

———. 1985. "Feminist distrust: Problems of content and context in sociological research." In *The Self in Sociological Inquiry*. Edited by David Berg and Ken Smith. Beverly Hills: Sage Publications.

———. 1988a. "What's missing in miscarriage?" *Journal of Community Psychology* 16:84–103.

———. 1988b. "Women and intellectual work or the history of women's contributions to American sociology." In *An Inclusive Curriculum: Race, Class and Gender in Sociological Instruction*. Edited by Patricia Hill Collins and Margaret Andersen, pp. 106-116. Washington, D.C.: American Sociological Association.

———. 1989. "Teaching the history of women in sociology: Or Dorothy Swaine Thomas, wasn't she the woman married to William I.?" *American Sociologist* 20:87–94.

——— (with Lynn Davidman). 1992. *Feminist Methods in Social Research*. New York: Oxford University Press.

———. 1993. "Neglected voices and excessive demands in feminist research." *Qualitative Sociology* 16:69–76.

Reinharz, Shulamit, Marti Bombyk, and Janet Wright. 1983. "Methodological issues in feminist research: A bibliography of literature in women's studies, sociology, and psychology. *Women's Studies International Forum* 6:437–454.

Reverby, Susan. 1987. *Ordered to Care: The Dilemma of American Nursing, 1850–1945*. Cambridge: Cambridge University Press.

Rich, Adrienne. 1980. "Compulsory heterosexuality and lesbian existence." *Signs* 5:631–660.

Richardson, Laurel. 1988. "The collective story: Postmodernism and the writing of sociology." *Sociological Focus* 21:199–208.

———. 1990. "Narrative and sociology." *Journal of Contemporary Ethnography* 19:116–135.

———. 1993. "Poetics, dramatics, and transgressive validity: The case of the skipped line." *Sociological Quarterly* 34:695–710.

———. 1994. "Writing: A method of inquiry." In *Handbook of Qualitative Research*. Edited by Norman K. Denzin and Yvonna S. Lincoln, pp. 516–529. Thousand Oaks, Calif.: Sage.

Riessman, Catherine Kohler. 1987. "When gender is not enough: Women interviewing women." *Gender and Society* 1:172–207.

Risman, Barbara J. 1993. "Methodological implications of feminist scholarship." *American Sociologist* 24:15–25.

Risman, Barbara J., Joey Sprague, and Judy Howard. 1993. "Comment on Francesca M. Cancian's 'Feminist Science.'" *Gender and Society* 7(4):608–609.

Roby, Pamela. 1992. "Women and the ASA: Degendering organizational structures and processes, 1964–1974." *American Sociologist* 23(1):18–48.

Rofel, Lisa. 1993. "Where feminism lies: Field encounters in China." *Frontiers* 13(3):33–52.

Rollins, Judith. 1985. *Between Women: Domestics and Their Employers*. Philadelphia: Temple University Press.

Rossiter, Margaret W. 1982. *Women Scientists in America: Struggles and Strategies to 1940*. Baltimore: Johns Hopkins University Press.

———. 1995. *Women Scientists in America: Before Affirmative Action, 1940–1972*. Baltimore: Johns Hopkins University Press.

Rothman, Barbara Katz. 1986. "Reflections: On hard work." *Qualitative Sociology* 9:48–53.

Routh, Jane, and Janet Wolff, eds. 1977. *The Sociology of Literature: Theoretical Approaches*. Keele, U.K.: University of Keele Press.

Rowbotham, Sheila. 1973. *Woman's Consciousness, Man's World*. Harmondsworth: Penguin.

Rubin, Lillian B. 1979. *Women of a Certain Age: The Mid-Life Search for Self.* New York: Harper and Row.

Ruddick, Sara. 1980. "Maternal thinking." *Feminist Studies* 6:342–367.

———. 1989. *Maternal Thinking: Toward a Politics of Peace.* Boston: Beacon Press.

Rupp, Leila J., and Verta A. Taylor. 1987. *Survival in the Doldrums: The American Women's Rights Movement, 1945 to the 1960s.* New York: Oxford University Press.

Rushin, Donna Kate. 1981. "The bridge poem." In *This Bridge Called My Back: Writings by Radical Women of Color.* Edited by Cherríe Moraga and Gloria Anzaldúa, pp. xxi–xxii. Watertown, Mass.: Persephone Press.

Russell, Diana E. H. 1982. *Rape in Marriage.* New York: Macmillan.

Ryan, Jake, and Charles Shackrey. 1984. *Strangers in Paradise: Academics from the Working Class.* Boston: South End Press.

Sandoval, Chela. 1991. "U.S. third world feminism: The theory and method of oppositional consciousness in the postmodern world." *Genders* 10:1–24.

Saraceno, Chiaro. 1984. "Shifts in public and private boundaries: Women as mothers and service workers in Italian daycare." *Feminist Studies* 10:7–29.

Scanlon, Jennifer. 1993. "Challenging the imbalances of power in feminist oral history: Developing a take-and-give methodology." *Women's Studies International Forum* 16(6):639–645.

Schegloff, Emanuel A. 1982. "Discourse as an interactional achievement: Some uses of 'uh huh' and other things that come between sentences." In *Analyzing Discourse: Text and Talk.* Edited by Deborah Tannen, pp. 71–93. Washington, D.C.: Georgetown University Press.

Schenkein, Jim, ed. 1978. *Studies in the Organization of Conversational Interaction.* New York: Academic Press.

Schutz, Alfred. 1962. "On multiple realities." In *Collected Papers,* vol. 1, 207–259. The Hague: Martinus Nijhoff.

Schweikart, Patrocinio P. 1986. "Reading ourselves: Toward a feminist theory of reading." In *Gender and Reading.* Edited by Elizabeth A. Flynn and Patrocinio P. Schweikart, pp. 31–62. Baltimore: Johns Hopkins University Press.

Scott, Joan W. 1991. "The evidence of experience." *Critical Inquiry* 17 (Summer): 773–797.

Scott, Marvin B., and Stanford M. Lyman. 1968. "Accounts." *American Sociological Review* 33:46–62.

Sessar, Klaus. 1990. "The forgotten nonvictim." *International Review of Victimology* 1:113–132.

Shapiro, Laura. 1986. *Perfection Salad: Women and Cooking at the Turn of the Century.* New York: Henry Holt and Company.

Showalter, Elaine. 1977. *A Literature of Their Own: British Women Novelists from Bronte to Lessing.* Princeton: Princeton University Press.

Skeggs, Beverly. 1994. "Situating the production of feminist ethnography." In *Researching Women's Lives from a Feminist Perspective.* Edited by Mary Maynard and June Purvis, pp. 72–92. London: Taylor and Francis.

Smith, Dorothy E. 1977. *Feminism and Marxism: A Place to Begin, A Way to Go.* Vancouver: New Star Books.

———. 1983. "No one commits suicide: Textual analyses of ideological practices." *Human Studies* 6:309–359. Reprinted in Smith 1990a, ch. 6.

———. 1987. *The Everyday World as Problematic: A Feminist Sociology.* Boston: Northeastern University Press.

———. 1989. "Sociological theory: Methods of writing patriarchy." In *Feminism and Sociological Theory.* Edited by Ruth A. Wallace, pp. 34–64. Newbury Park, Calif.: Sage.

———. 1990a. *The Conceptual Practices of Power: A Feminist Sociology of Knowledge.* Boston: Northeastern University Press.

———. 1990b. *Texts, Facts, and Femininity: Exploring the Relations of Ruling.* New York: Routledge.

———. 1992. "Sociology from women's experience: A reaffirmation." *Sociological Theory* 10(1):88–98.

———. 1993. "High noon in textland: A critique of Clough." *Sociological Quarterly* 34(1):183–192.

———. 1994. "A Berkeley education." In *Gender and the Academic Experience: Berkeley Women Sociologists.* Edited by Kathryn P. Meadow Orlans and Ruth A. Wallace, pp. 45–56. Lincoln: University of Nebraska Press.

———. 1996. "The relations of ruling: A feminist inquiry." *Studies in Cultures, Organizations, and Societies* 2:171–190.

———. 1997. "Telling the truth after postmodernism." *Symbolic Interaction* 19(3):171–202.

———. 1998. *Writing the Social: Critique, Theory, and Investigations.* Toronto: University of Toronto Press.

Smith, George W. 1990. "Political activist as ethnographer." *Social Problems* 37:629–648.

Smith, Michael D. 1994. "Enhancing the quality of survey data on violence against women: A feminist approach." *Gender and Society* 8(1):109–127.

Spalter-Roth, Roberta M., and Heidi I. Hartmann. 1991. "Science and politics and the 'dual vision' of feminist policy research: The example of family and medical leave." In *Parental Leave and Child Care: Setting a Research and Policy Agenda.* Edited by Janet Shibley Hyde and Marilyn J. Essex, pp. 41–65. Philadelphia: Temple University Press.

Spector, Malcolm, and John I. Kitsuse. 1987. *Constructing Social Problems.* New York: Aldine de Gruyter.

Spelman, Elizabeth V. 1988. *Inessential Woman: Problems of Exclusion in Feminist Thought.* Boston: Beacon.

Spender, Dale. [1980] 1985. *Man Made Language* (2nd ed. with revised introduction). London: Routledge and Kegan Paul.

———. 1982. *Women of Ideas and What Men Have Done to Them: From Aphra Behn to Adrienne Rich.* London: Routledge and Kegan Paul.

Sprague, Joey, and Mary Zimmerman. 1993. "Overcoming dualisms: A feminist agenda for sociological methodology." In *Theory on Gender/Feminism on Theory.* Edited by Paula England, pp. 255–280. New York: Aldine.

Stacey, Judith. 1988. "Can there be a feminist ethnography?" *Women's Studies International Forum* 11:21–27.

———. 1994. "Imagining feminist ethnography: A response to Elizabeth E. Wheatley." *Women's Studies International Forum* 17(4):417–419.

———. 1995. "Disloyal to the disciplines: A feminist trajectory in the borderlands." In *Feminisms in the Academy.* Edited by Donna C. Stanton and Abigail J. Stewart, pp. 311–329. Ann Arbor: University of Michigan Press.

Stacey, Judith, and Barrie Thorne. 1985. "The missing feminist revolution in sociology." *Social Problems* 32:301–316.

Stack, Carol B. 1974. *All Our Kin: Strategies for Survival in a Black Community.* New York: Harper and Row.

Stanfield, John H., II. 1994. "Ethnic modeling in qualitative research." In *Handbook of Qualitative Research.* Edited by Norman K. Denzin and Yvonna S. Lincoln, pp. 175–188. Thousand Oaks, Calif.: Sage Publications.

Stanko, Elizabeth A. 1985a. *Intimate Intrusions: Women's Experience of Male Violence.* Boston: Routledge and Kegan Paul.

———. 1985b. Presentation at a meeting of the Boston area chapter of Sociologists for Women in Society, November 1985.

———. 1990. *Everyday Violence: How Women and Men Experience Sexual and Physical Danger.* London: Pandora Press.

———. 1994. "Dancing with denial: Researching women and questioning men." In *Researching Women's Lives from a Feminist Perspective.* Edited by Mary Maynard and June Purvis, pp. 93–105. London: Taylor and Francis.

Stanley, Liz, and Sue Wise. 1979. "Feminist research, feminist consciousness, and experiences of sexism." *Women's Studies International Quarterly* 2(3): 359–374.

———. 1983. "'Back into the personal' or our attempt to construct 'feminist research.'" In *Theories of Women's Studies.* Edited by Gloria Bowles and Renate Duelli Klein, pp. 192–209. London: Routledge and Kegan Paul.

———. 1983/93. *Breaking Out: Feminist Consciousness and Feminist Research* and *Breaking Out Again: Feminist Ontology and Epistemology, New Edition.* London and New York: Routledge.

Stanley, Liz, ed. 1990a. *Feminist Praxis: Research, Theory and Epistemology in Feminist Sociology.* New York: Routledge.

———. 1990b. "'A referral was made': Behind the scenes during the creation of a Social Services Department 'elderly' statistic." In *Feminist Praxis: Research, Theory and Epistemology in Feminist Sociology.* Edited by Liz Stanley, pp. 113–122. New York: Routledge.

Strauss, Anselm L. 1987. *Qualitative Analysis for Social Scientists.* Cambridge: Cambridge University Press.

Strobel, Margaret. 1995. "Organizational learning in the Chicago Women's Liberation Union." In *Feminist Organizations: Harvest of the New Women's Movement.* Edited by Myra Marx Ferree and Patricia Yancey Martin, pp. 145–164. Philadelphia: Temple University Press.

Stromberg, Ann Helton. 1988. "Women in female-dominated professions." In *Women Working: Theories and Facts in Perspective* (2nd ed.). Edited by Ann

Helton Stromberg and Shirley Harkness, pp. 206–224. Mountain View, Calif.: Mayfield.

Sylvester, Christine. 1995. "African and Western feminisms: World-traveling the tendencies and possibilities." *Signs* 20(4):941–969.

Taylor, Verta, and Nicole C. Raeburn. 1995. "Identity politics as high-risk activism: Career consequences for lesbian, gay, and bisexual sociologists." *Social Problems* 42:252–273.

Thorne, Barrie. 1994. Review of *Social Science and the Self,* by Susan Krieger. *Gender and Society* 8:138–140.

Thorne, Barrie, and Nancy Henley. 1975. *Language and Sex: Difference and Dominance.* Rowley, Mass.: Newbury House.

Thorne, Barrie, Cheris Kramarae, and Nancy Henley, eds. 1983. *Language, Gender and Society.* Rowley, Mass.: Newbury House.

Thorne, Barrie, and Barbara Laslett. 1997. *Feminist Sociology: Life Histories of a Movement.* New Brunswick, N.J.: Rutgers University Press.

Tobin, Debra S., Johanna Dwyer, and Joan D. Gussow. 1992. "Cooperative relationships between professional societies and the food industry: Opportunities or problems?" *Nutrition Reviews* 50:300–306.

Todd, Alexandra Dundas, and Sue Fisher, eds. 1988. *Gender and Discourse: The Power of Talk.* Norwood, N.J.: Ablex.

Tompkins, Jane P. 1980. *Reader-Response Criticism from Formalism to Post-Structuralism.* Baltimore: Johns Hopkins University Press.

Traustadottir, Rannveig. 1991. "Mothers who care: Gender, disability, and family life." *Journal of Family Issues* 12:211–228.

———. 1992. "Disability Reform and the Role of Women: Community Inclusion and Caring Work." Ph.D. dissertation, Syracuse University.

———. "A mother's work is never done: Constructing a 'normal' family life." In *The Variety of Community Experience: Qualitative Studies of Family and Community Life.* Edited by Steven J. Taylor, Robert Bogdan, and Zana Marie Lutfiyya, pp. 47–65. Baltimore: Paul H. Brookes.

Treichler, Paula A., and Cheris Kramarae. 1983. "Women's talk in the ivory tower." *Communication Quarterly* 31:118–132.

Trinh T. Minh-ha. 1989. *Woman, Native, Other: Writing Postcoloniality and Feminism.* Bloomington: Indiana University Press.

Tuchman, Gaye. 1989. *Edging Women Out: Victorian Novelists, Publishers and Social Change.* New Haven: Yale University.

Tuchman, Gaye, and Nina E. Fortin. 1984. "Fame and misfortune: Edging women out of the great literary tradition." *American Journal of Sociology* 90:72–96.

Van Maanen, John. 1988. *Tales of the Field: On Writing Ethnography.* Chicago: University of Chicago Press.

Volberg, Rachel A. 1984. "Daily work at the zoning counter." Unpublished working paper. San Francisco: Tremont Research Institute.

Waring, Marilyn. 1988. *If Women Counted.* San Francisco: Harper and Row.

Watt, Ian. 1957. *The Rise of the Novel: Studies in Defoe, Richardson and Fielding.* Berkeley: University of California Press.

Wax, Rosalie H. 1971. *Doing Fieldwork: Warnings and Advice.* Chicago: University of Chicago Press.

———. 1979. "Gender and age in fieldwork and fieldwork education: No good thing is done by any man alone." *Social Problems* 26:509–522.

Wellman, David T. 1977. *Portraits of White Racism.* New York: Cambridge University Press.

West, Candace. 1982. "Why can't a woman be more like a man? An interactional note on organizational game-playing for managerial women." *Work and Occupations* 9:5–29.

West, Candace, and Don H. Zimmerman. 1983. "Small insults: A study of interruptions in cross-sex conversations between unacquainted persons." In *Language, Gender and Society.* Edited by Barrie Thorne, Cheris Kramarae, and Nancy Henley, pp. 103–117. Rowley, Mass.: Newbury House.

———. 1987. "Doing gender." *Gender and Society* 1:125–151.

Wheatley, Elizabeth E. 1994a. "How can we engender ethnography with a feminist imagination? A rejoinder to Judith Stacey." *Women's Studies International Forum* 17(4):403–16.

———. 1994b. "Dances with feminists: Truths, dares, and ethnographic stares." *Women's Studies International Forum* 17(4):421–423.

Wilkinson, Doris Y., ed. 1992. Special issue. "Minorities and Women in the Liberation of the ASA, 1964–1974: Reflections on the Dynamics of Organizational Change." *American Sociologist* 23(1).

Windebank, Jan. 1992. "Comparing women's employment patterns across the European Community: Issues of method and interpretation." *Women's Studies International Forum* 15(1):65–76.

Wolf, Diane, ed. 1996. *Feminist Dilemmas in Fieldwork.* Boulder: Westview.

Wolff, Janet. 1977. "The interpretation of literature in society: The hermeneutic approach." In *The Sociology of Literature: Theoretical Approaches.* Edited by Jane Routh and Janet Wolff, pp. 18–31. Keele: University of Keele Press.

———. 1981. *The Social Production of Art.* New York: St. Martin's.

Women on Words and Images. 1972. *Dick and Jane as Victims.* Princeton: Women on Words and Images.

Young, Iris Marion. 1990. *Justice and the Politics of Difference.* Princeton: Princeton University Press.

Zavella, Patricia. 1987. *Women's Work and Chicano Families: Cannery Workers of the Santa Clara Valley.* Ithaca: Cornell University Press.

———. 1993. "Feminist insider dilemmas: Constructing ethnic identity with 'Chicana' informants." *Frontiers* 13(3):53–76.

Zimmerman, Don H. 1974. "Facts as practical accomplishment." In *Ethnomethodology.* Edited by Roy Turner, pp. 128–143. Harmondsworth: Penguin.

Index